Country of
of
Poxes

Country of Poxes

Three Germs and the Taking of Territory

Baijayanta Mukhopadhyay

Fernwood Publishing
Halifax & Winnipeg

Development editing: Tanya Andrusieczko
Editing and text design: Brenda Conroy
Cover design: Evan Marnoch
Printed and bound in Canada

Published by Fernwood Publishing
2970 Oxford Street, Halifax, Nova Scotia, B3L 2W4
and 748 Broadway Avenue, Winnipeg, Manitoba, R3G 0X3
www.fernwoodpublishing.ca

Fernwood Publishing Company Limited gratefully acknowledges the financial support of the Government of Canada, the Canada Council for the Arts, the Manitoba Department of Culture, Heritage and Tourism under the Manitoba Publishers Marketing Assistance Program and the Province of Manitoba, through the Book Publishing Tax Credit, for our publishing program. We are pleased to work in partnership with the Province of Nova Scotia to develop and promote our creative industries for the benefit of all Nova Scotians.

Library and Archives Canada Cataloguing in Publication
Title: Country of poxes: three germs and the taking of territory /
by Baijayanta Mukhopadhyay.
Names: Mukhopadhyay, Baijayanta, author.
Description: Includes bibliographical references and index.
Identifiers: Canadiana (print) 20220273316 | Canadiana (ebook) 20220274878 | ISBN 9781773635545 (softcover) | ISBN 9781773635750 (EPUB) | ISBN 9781773635767 (PDF)
Subjects: LCSH: Indigenous peoples—Diseases—North America—History. | LCSH: Indigenous peoples—Health and hygiene—North America—History. | LCSH: North America—Colonization. | LCSH: North America—Colonization—Health aspects. | LCSH: Communicable diseases—North America—History. | LCSH: Communicable diseases—Social aspects—North America—History. | LCSH: Indigenous peoples— First contact with other peoples—North America. | LCSH: North America—Ethnic relations—History. | LCSH: North America—Race relations—History. | LCSH: Indigenous peoples—North America— Government relations—History.
Classification: LCC E98.D6 M85 2022 | DDC 362.1089/97—dc23

Contents

For Buroma
and all other ancestors who have made the way

Acknowledgements

The romantic vision of writing is that it is a solitary process, an author locked away in isolation furiously scribbling away. Nothing can be further from the truth. Like all offspring, it takes an entire village, a community of labour, to bring it into being.

This book is first and foremost the product of my editor, Tanya Andrusieczko, without whose enduring encouragement and gentle guidance, this book would never have come into being. She deserves many an award for putting up with my temperamental outbursts of frustration and for finding me a way back to focus. It has also been a delight to work with the rest of the team at Fernwood, whose kindness and care in the production aspects of the project made the experience much more tolerable for someone like me who is bemused and irritated by practicalities. Specific and special thanks go to Evan Marnoch for his considered and crisp graphic work on the cover and the maps.

There are too many people who have helped me, sometimes unknowingly, understand both the medicine behind infectious disease and their social implications. I would never be able to list them all. Many thanks to David Mabey at the London School of Tropical Medicine and Hygiene for introducing me to syphilis. Also at LSHTM, the Decolonising Global Health group has been a place for nourishment and ideas that have kept me on my toes, reflecting on the role of colonialism in medicine. My friends in the People's Health Movement across the world are a constant source of insight in undoing the damage of colonialism — particularly the Ecosystems and Health thematic circle. I started seriously on this book after working with the Liberation Health Convergence crew, and I also joined the Collectif Soignons la justice sociale in Montreal in the course of writing I am always learning from all of them, and I am humbled to be able call these committed groups of organizers friends and colleagues.

I owe an immense debt to the communities that have nurtured me as a practitioner of biomedicine for a long time. In particular, thanks to the people of Eeyou Istchee, especially in Waskaganish, who have let me into their lives for so long. They have taught me so much. Darlene Kitty in Chisasibi has been a mentor and a model ever since I was in medical school. I also thank the peoples of Treaties 3 and 9 in northern Ontario, who have shaped me as a professional and a person. In particular I thank Pauline Rickard for humouring my questions about Moose Factory. Yotakahron Jonathan's feedback has been invaluable in improving the text.

Thank you to the staff at the Fischer Library in Toronto, the National Archives in Ottawa, the Sir William Osler Library in Montreal, the Wellcome Library in London, and the Bibliothèque universitaire de l'histoire médicale in Paris for their assistance. My very kind reviewers, whose feedback made the text manyfold better, also have my great appreciation.

I have also benefited from the insights and friendship of Alicja Toton. Anicia and Daniel Makhubu's affection remains one of my life's greatest honours. Ryan Schafbuch deserves particular mention for patiently driving me around Quebec City suburbs when he probably least wanted to do so. Discussions on writing as a process and a craft with Andrew Loewen, Cory Legassic, Elena Johnson, Elizabeth Hunt, and Laura Bisaillon have always been grounding. And even though we rarely discussed writing, without the joy Kit Malo's friendship brings to my life, the rigour of completing a project would never have been possible.

This book is dedicated to the memory of my great-grandmother, who lived for sixty years in the ritual constraints of widowhood after being bereaved by smallpox. I was lucky enough to know her until I was eighteen, and her pragmatic wisdom and sharp wit still guide me. Along with her, I thank all my elders who have brought me thus far. I thank especially my parents: I am not sure I am worthy of their steadfast, uncomplaining support — both moral and practical — in all my meandering efforts in life.

While all these people have been generous with their energy and their time for me, I alone remain responsible for all errors in fact and in judgement in this text.

Foreword

As a Cree family physician working in northern Quebec since 2006, I eagerly share the knowledge in Indigenous health and approach to culturally safe care that I have gained over the years. My clinical practice and work in medical education have facilitated my passion for teaching and supporting the medical trainees and newer physicians who come to learn and work in Eeyou Istchee, our Cree territory.

This is how I came to meet Baijayanta, when he was a medical student, doing his Family Medicine rotation in Chisasibi, the largest of nine Cree communities. I recall that he was very curious and motivated to learn about our health and social issues and how closely these are connected to history, culture, traditions, and the land. We discussed colonization, residential schools, and the social determinants of Indigenous health, which I am certain spawned his enthusiasm to work with Indigenous populations. As a medical student then and now a colleague and friend, Baijayanta continues to explore new knowledge and experiences and reflects on these to satisfy his curiosity and zest for learning and doing more. In fact, a pertussis outbreak in Waskaganish, a Cree community where Baijayanta works, sparked his motivation to write this book.

As physicians, we continually update our clinical knowledge about new treatments and medications for acute and chronic medical conditions, including infections. Usually, what we learn is very scientific and evidence-based. Less is taught about the background leading up to the discovery of diseases and treatments. This book is an exception.

Syphilis, smallpox, and tuberculosis are specifically investigated here, and while some clinical aspects are described, there are additional interesting narratives, from historical facts to modern takes on their science, societal opinions, and fallacies. Biological factors that influence the risk of infection and can cause complications are included so that one can consider how these factors among others may be manipulated to lessen (and sometimes increase) the impact and prevalence of these infections. Baijayanta also explores how society is affected by these infections, from individual experiences to community outbreaks, epidemics, and their political milieu.

The chapter on tuberculosis triggered my interest because of its long history but also due to its ongoing onslaught of Indigenous, migrant, and other vulnerable populations, whose access to treatment is sometimes limited for various reasons. While we still see the occasional case or reactivation in Eeyou Istchee, tuberculosis disproportionately affects the Inuit communities in northern Canada, which shows the need for greater surveillance, case-finding, treatment, and public health campaigns. On a personal note, my mother had tuberculosis as a young woman, and she recovered in a sanatorium down south. It was important to me to learn about the historical context and how it affects Indigenous populations worldwide, which I now appreciate more fully.

Baijayanta adds some personal anecdotes and perspectives, such as his Indian heritage, educational journey, and travels, creating a thoughtful, expressive, and well-researched analysis. He incorporates a racialized lens in looking at the histories behind these three pathogens and how colonization has impacted global health and populations, shaping their outcomes, including relevant antibiotic treatments and vaccinations. You can see the interplay of politics, colonialism, and paternalism in these chapters and how the medical field and public health evolved in the context of syphilis, smallpox, and tuberculosis discovery, diagnoses, and treatments.

Country of Poxes. A fitting name for a book that looks at three infectious culprits that have affected many on a global scale. This makes me think of how pathogens have developed as a result of the interaction between vectors, the environment, and hosts, all of which are changing over time. Here, the historical, social, and political perspectives that have influenced how infections have affected individuals, communities, and the world are woven into each storyline. How timely in the current COVID-19 pandemic, when many crave information and guidance, having become more attuned to infectious diseases and their etiologies.

This book helped me to expand my clinical knowledge of these poxes but also their historical backgrounds and the scientific developments of treatments among the social, cultural, and political contexts over the centuries. At times, the emotions, morals, and values of humanity decry the failures mentioned but also shine in humanity's successes in finding cures and improving health outcomes. For me, this means looking beyond science to broaden our expertise of the microbes that infect us, curing the pathogenics but co-existing with the endemics. This thought-provoking read provides a deeper understanding of these infections on many levels and suggests current and future directions in providing care and support of those sectors of society afflicted.

— Dr. Darlene Kitty

1

Pandemics Past

How Infections Have Defined Humanity

My paternal grandfather was orphaned in early adolescence, a trauma that marked him and his siblings irreparably. His father, given to frivolous extravagance, had died fairly young from complications of diabetes, having run his once middle-class family aground with his general imprudence. My great-grandmother survived her husband by only a year. No doubt the story of her death has been warped by the years that have passed, the unreliable memories, and the deaths of its witnesses. But we do know that as a high-caste widow, especially one of limited means, my great-grandmother was allowed few pleasures in life. The day before her death, she was apparently enjoying one of them — some puffed rice mixed with spice and oil — though perhaps she should have suspected that such hedonism would invite karmic displeasure. As she tossed a handful into her mouth, a fingernail caught and lanced a small boil above her lip. She thought nothing of it until she began to feel quite unwell later that evening. Within twenty-four hours, her face entirely swollen, she was dead.

No one can confirm that a doctor was called, though I wonder what use it would have been had one even been available. Would an accurate diagnosis have been possible with the limited tools at a physician's disposal in an Indian village in the 1930s? And what is the point of naming a condition if there is little to do about it? Eighty years later, I suspect that she died of *Staphylococcus aureus* sepsis, when an otherwise benign species of bacteria that would have usually lived contentedly on her skin, fulminated into the boil and then sneaked through the indulgence-inflicted wound to flood her bloodstream. While she would normally have been able to fend off this disrespect of her boundaries before matters got too out of hand, in this case, for reasons related to both her and the bacteria in those specific circumstances, this assault overwhelmed her immune system, sending it into an inflammatory overdrive. The end result of this response was the shutdown of essential organs.

Had *S. aureus* just waited a few more years before launching its inopportune onslaught on my family's psychological well-being, it is possible that my great-grandmother would not have died, delivering us from the knock-on intergenerational dysfunction her death caused. Penicillin, commercially available as of 1942, might have liberated all her descendants from their emotionally frigid fates, presuming that the drug would have filtered down to a humble village five miles outside of Calcutta early in its commercial history. Beyond potentially rescuing one branch of an obscure Bengali family from decades of pathological behaviours, the advent of antibiotics, more broadly, radically altered the therapeutic relationship between healer and healed in profound ways, changing the expectation of what was feasible within medicine in a way that has haunted the field ever since.

In countries like Canada, we have lived a brief reprieve of eight decades when we have not had to confront this routine part of the human experience. Infectious diseases — whether caused by protozoans or fungi, bacteria or viruses, roundworms or flatworms — have been part of our lot as messy, oozing beings that live as part of this community of all creation. One or two generations in parts of the planet have been able to wander in oblivion of how fundamental our relationship with our invisible neighbours is and how intimately and intensely they shape us, though environmental pressures, including the rise of antimicrobial resistance, now again intrude on our ignorance. Generally, we live in peaceful, entirely unnewsworthy coexistence with many of these creatures and in fact, have learned to glean benefits of cohabitation. In return for our hospitality, certain bacteria in our gut contribute to our bodies' needs for Vitamin K, essential to clotting our blood when we are injured. The vaginal tract is teeming with *Lactobacillus* species, which may sound alarming, but these innocuous guests fiercely defend the territory from advances by pushy yeast infections. Studies have begun to show that appropriate immune responses to airway infections develops after birth once the respiratory tract is colonized by complex communities of bacteria, the balance of which potentially keep pathogenic species from propagating dangerously out of hand.[1]

But on occasion, we all encounter toxic roommates with boundary issues. They get on our nerves with irritating sores; they inconsiderately leave behind crusty gobs of phlegm; they interrupt important events with bouts of frenetic diarrhoea. Indeed, like at the time of my great-grandmother's death, the impact of our tussles with pathogens results in a huge human cost, particularly for those at vulnerable stages of their life — babies, the elderly, the otherwise malnourished or weak. Antimicrobial medications have been a boon in this regard, saving countless lives. In partnership with radical social transformations that have improved sanitation and enforced access to adequate healthcare services, they have given some of us a brief upper hand in our uneasy truce with the wildness among us, such that many people living today remain unaware of how infectious diseases have left indelible traces on our collective psyches.

Our agency as a species determines the way disease is experienced. Some we vanquish, others we endure. In some cases, the germ and we have marched together, in step. Most famously, malaria has been such an intricate part of our ecosystem for so long that vast swathes of the human population have evolved adaptations to its attacks, building strength in genetic diversities (otherwise known as mutations), such as sickle cell trait and thalassaemia, that make it harder for the malaria parasite to infect the red blood cell. For people who are carriers of one copy of these genes, often quite widespread, the relative survival advantage is worth the mild genetic inconvenience. For the minority with two copies of the gene, the resulting illness from having malfunctioning red blood cells can be debilitating. The malaria parasite has found ways to infiltrate our shifting defences too: its rapid development of resistance to waves of antimalarial medication has scuttled many optimistic projections of its eradication over decades.

A similar proposition exists for the predominance of cystic fibrosis in Quebec and in Brittany, from where many of the first European settlers in the St Lawrence Valley arrived. By slowing down the flow of chloride in cells, one copy of the gene involved may have helped their ancestors in Europe survive cholera, which had been endemic there in the past. In that illness, the toxin produced by the cholera bacterium allows chloride to pour out of cells unregulated, resulting in fatal diarrhoea: the mutation is theorized thus to have conferred a survival advantage when present once. Cystic fibrosis emerges when two copies of that gene find themselves in the same person, where it completely blocks the movement of chloride, the controlled transport of which is otherwise necessary for the function of many cells.[2] Speculation continues about diseases that swept through Europe seven centuries ago that may have encouraged the survival of people with the CCR5 delta 32 mutation, which now renders 1 percent of people there resistant to HIV infection (but more susceptible to West Nile virus disease).[3] As another example, my family is from the Bengali-speaking delta of the Ganges, a vast, densely populated area of complex, interconnected waterways, where the river empties the load it carries from the Himalayas into the Bay of Bengal. The region is also known for cholera, endemic potentially over millennia given the high frequency of flooding. People with type O blood seem perhaps to have more serious complications from cholera.[4] Thus, although it is by far the most common blood type worldwide,[5] Bangladesh, which comprises a major part of the delta region, is one of the minority of countries in the world where another type dominates, in this case, group B.[6] My entire immediate family, from the delta's Indian side, carries this type too.

These examples speak to the way our co-existence with infection has moulded the way we live as biological specimens. But humans are not just biology: we are society too. Like imprints on our DNA, infectious diseases leave traces in our togetherness too. Within our own lifetimes, the bug-eat-bug world in which we live has spawned pandemics that have transformed our ways of being. Consider the phrase "safe sex," which anyone aware in the mid-1980s onwards will automatically understand, jolting conceptions of intimacy and desire for at least one generation. An endless litany of organisms — amoeba and leishmania, Epstein-Barr and herpes viruses, *Pseudomonas aeruginosa* and *Clostridium tetani*, *Cryptococcus* and *Blastomyces*, to name just a few — exploit our vulnerabilities. However, our defences not only fail biologically, but as we will see through the examples that follow, socially and politically as well.

We as a species have counterattacked, altering the courses of plagues and pestilences. Communities find resources and strategies to navigate epidemics to minimize their impact and to protect the lives of their members. In places that have been rich through much of the twentieth century into the twenty-first, we have created a somewhat hermetically sealed bubble that has made infections almost disappear from consciousness: we think of them as unusual, rare, once-in-a-lifetime events. Through the indiscriminate use of antibiotics and the fortification of living environments against elements of the wild, we have had the luxury of hubris, to think ourselves separate from a tangled entwinement with the ecosystems around us.

But this separation is only an illusion. Even in Canada, the dynamic tussle for influence between infectious diseases and humans runs through the core of history: epidemics have determined military victories and founded hospitals, just as religious services and trading companies have triggered outbreaks. Continuous confrontation with critters and crawlies has possibly inured healthcare workers to their reality, making it easy for those of us absorbed in the daily machinations of the healthcare system to ignore the residue of past responses and decisions. Reflexes learned through repeated lessons in our structures and processes are now simply part of our jobs. In the summer of 2019, as I started to work on this book, pertussis broke out in one of the remote communities where I work as a physician in the north of what we now call Canada, one of those mystery outbreaks where someone catches an infection seemingly out of nowhere, with no clear chain of transmission. We immediately pursued routine protocols, used only occasionally in our era but not unknown: we isolated the contacts at risk, tested them and treated some prophylactically, asked them to remember who else they saw, ensured their vaccines were up to date, and boosted those who might be eligible for such doses. However, these almost automatic technical procedures in medicine are not the only features of care to become embedded through experience: assumptions, biases, outdated philosophies linger in our healthcare systems as well, through inertia if not outright malice, especially when they go unchallenged. For this reason, on a very tangible level, understanding the history of our healing practices is essential to improving the care we provide as a society.

This book was born in a class on syphilis. Out of the litany of infectious diseases I had studied over the term, this one made me perk up; I was enthralled by the history of an infection so shamed, so maligned. Its biological curiosities are manifold, but what struck me most were its social implications. Not only is it associated with the forbidden, but it is the one disease purported to have come to Europe from the Americas, rather than the other way around. Its emergence through Columbus's returning sailors allegedly seeding the first horrific outbreak in Naples in 1494 compelled me.

As I considered my own life as a healthcare worker in the Americas in this light, I began to wonder how the undertone of this "exchange" may have influenced the structures in which I work, how they might have shaped the way I approach medicine in Indigenous communities in northeastern parts of North America. In addition, it made me reconsider the stories that have so shaped the history of this continent in other ways. Smallpox is famously the disease that was brought to the Americas from the "Old World" — a term with colonial implications of discovery — and I began to ponder how its spread was formative for the health institutions in which I now work too. Then there was tuberculosis, from neither here nor there, but which emerged as a force in the unfolding of our history together.

These contrasts drew me in the more I studied them. Medically, I am fascinated by the evolution of these epidemics, how the teeming germs adapted to the changing social environment which humans provided. Equally important, colonization as a social process disrupted the biological environment too: how colonizer and colonized fuelled or stymied outbreaks as a function of their position in the newly forming order is a critical part of Canada's taking of territory.

I have no particular training in history, much less in the specificities of the Americas five hundred years ago. I have never treated smallpox and only intermittently deal with syphilis and tuberculosis. It seems strange that this doctor, born in the heat of the desert sun and now working in the icebound villages of the boreal forest, should be so engrossed in the stories of these particular diseases. But their historical arc puts into perspective the trajectory of epidemics I see now. They also help me understand my place in the world in significant ways.

As a physician, knowing this history of the places where I work seems crucial, and as someone who became unwittingly engaged in the project of Canada through immigration in adolescence, I think it my duty to undo my ignorance by critically examining the institutions in which I now participate. Far from simply being epitomes of a functional democracy, the structures in which we live are borne of our past, including — or especially? — of its most sordid episodes. In this era of reckoning with Canada's role as a colonizing state, we need to remember that every time we step into a courthouse, a police station, a school, a library, a museum, a theatre, a legislature, a studio — we step into a system that has come from stealing land. The same principle applies every time we walk into a healthcare setting. For me, this remembering cannot come down to a brief land acknowledgement at the beginning of each meeting. It comes through an exploration of my place within this process, of learning and of unpacking that history, and working to repair the damages it has wrought.

There has already been plenty of work that eloquently confronts this reality. Samir Shaheen-Hussain's exemplary 2020 book, *Fighting for a Hand to Hold*, captures both broadly and deeply how medical institutions in Canada promote and profit from the colonial mission.[7] James Daschuk's account in *Clearing the Plains* is excruciating in the detail it provides on how disease shaped the reach of the colonial state into the prairies.[8] Mary-Ellen Kelm showed the way tuberculosis policy entrenched the

grasp of Canadian authorities over Indigenous Nations.[9] Gary
Geddes' more recent volume is a searing, highly personalized
journey into the tales of Canada's colonial "care" — in residential "schools" (a euphemism if ever there was one), tuberculosis
sanatoria, and general hospitals.[10] His stories highlight the strategies and tactics Indigenous people used to survive the intent of
these institutions.

In this book's exploration of infection as a defining concern of
Canadian politics, I focus on three pathogens, telling the stories
through historical material and my own experience. Each narrative reveals something particular about the unfolding of colonization in the Americas, which I interpret through my lenses as
a racialized settler and as a healthcare worker. These diseases
demonstrate clearly how the web of relationships we have with
other creatures gets entangled within the web of relationships we
have with ourselves, with some of us getting caught in the knots
more than others. Ecological connections that were obliterated
in the founding of Canada were replaced by new ones, as North
America's landscape was altered to serve economic interests from
afar. Syphilis, smallpox, and tuberculosis were initially only symptoms of colonization's impact on human relationships with each
other and with host environments. But as they became established,
the diseases in turn became powerful enough in themselves to have
a reciprocal transformative effect on the process of colonization
too.

One of the most radical classes I took at university was a course
in precolonial African history. It gave my young mind a name for
the disservice traditional education had done for me. As a child,
I had attended a school that followed a British curriculum. Our
history lessons in secondary school included a long chapter on
the Spanish conquest of the Aztec Empire.[11] I remember being assigned an elaborate project on the sophistication of Tenochtitlan.
I recall too studying Peter Shaffer's play *The Royal Hunt of the
Sun* in English class, recounting the death of Atahualpa of the Inca
Empire at the hands of the conquistadors.[12] Yet I learned very little
about the British conquest of anything — except for the English

victory over the Spanish Armada. Once, I was assigned the peculiar exercise of identifying whether the French or the British had strategically "won" the colonization of Africa. I tried to argue to my very English history teacher that the French had — and being told that the answer was incorrect, in what was termed "an unusual piece of work from you." Perhaps the caprices of memory cloud this recollection of my past, but the mystification I carried for years about that response resolved only when more conscious as an adult of how colonizing societies grapple with their contested legacies today and how a solitary history teacher in the wilds of the former colonies might handle that tension. The library at my school was filled to the brim with epic romances, invariably between a handsome English soldier and an Indian princess, set in the opulent courts of the Raj against a background of vague skirmishes and political intrigues that never became threatening enough to derail the affair completely. I read them all — the only formal source of my education on British colonial history. Professor Green's class at university many years later, on Axum and Mali and Zimbabwe, filled in many blanks, if not in specificities, then in my understanding that there was much I had not been taught and that there was beauty and wealth in all I had been told to dismiss, even within my own history.

By the time I was studying syphilis in London in late 2017, I thought myself well-versed in the implications of centuries of consolidation of Euro-American power on the world and how it had robbed so many of so much. Perhaps naively, I considered medicine as a tool to address those inequities in concrete and tangible ways. That autumn, I attended an event of literary readings at the Canadian High Commission to commemorate 150 years of Canada. Canada House has been at Trafalgar Square since the 1920s, the consolidation of Canada's presence in the British capital, bordering the National Gallery and sitting across from South Africa House. Admiral Nelson's statue still stands in Trafalgar Square, marking the battle where he was killed but where the fleet under his command definitively vanquished Napoleon. I have always wondered whether this British victory over France, as parallel to Canada's confirmation on the Plains of Abraham as part of the Empire, was in the mind of Peter Charles Larkin, the Canadian

High Commissioner in London from 1922 to 1930, when he decided this place was appropriate to centralize Canada's presence in the imperial metropole.

I did not know then that Canada House partly sits on a site that was the long-time home of the Royal College of Physicians. The old professional establishment was refurbished to make way for the diplomatic mission, and there are probably few residues of that past left. Established in London in 1518, the College was one of the first bodies in the British Isles to regulate the profession of medicine formally, after colleges of surgeons were established in Dublin and Edinburgh shortly beforehand, in an attempt to gate-keep who was considered a genuine practitioner.[13] Interestingly, in 1869 this same College established the "Nomenclature of Disease," which became an international model for diagnostic categories before the World Health Organization's system took over in the mid-twentieth century.[14]

As I attended that literary event, I was unaware that I stood on ground that shaped forevermore how disease was understood as physiological phenomena. Just as the College was being founded, syphilis was raging through Europe as clusters of the first small-pox outbreaks were roiling through the Iberian colonies in the Americas. The same earth below that now represented the might of imperial militarism in the North American colonies also bore the traces of those who tried to classify and to comprehend the way disease worked — on their terms. The two ventures are not unlinked.

My first exposure to the health aspects of colonization in the Americas came through a class I took at university over fifteen years earlier. I was the only undergraduate of four people in the seminar on Indigenous history and the only one who was not Indigenous. It did not occur to me then, as it might now, that I might have been intruding on a space: I was young and oblivious and intently focused on my own intellectual journey, unaware then my presence may have been at the expense of others. One of the books we read that left a lasting impact on me was Anastasia Shkilnyk's 1985 work *A Poison Stronger than Love*, discussing the mercury poisoning of Grassy Narrows.[15] The community continues to fight to address the aftereffects that persist to this day.[16] At the same time, in another class, I was looking at the role of British colonization in the contemporary health experience of women in India. The inchoate, incoherent links in my head were slowly beginning to crystallize. Looking back on Shkilnyk's work, there is much to be said about how it sits uneasily as a product of its time, but one fixed memory is the review at the back of the book which said how the community's struggles occurred despite "no one intending any harm." I was reading these works about five or six years before I ever even contemplated medical school. Troubled by that observation then, it has taken me a long time to make sense of it: that people working within a system whose fundamental precept is to extinguish Indigenous title can be as good-hearted and well-meaning as they want, but they are nonetheless facilitating a system designed to extinguish Indigenous title. The brute reality is that I feature among them.

Those of us who work in healthcare may not be able to comprehend how our modes of operation are deeply tainted by this history. We tend to absolve our tools and our skills of any political baggage, considering them technical assets that are designed to help people. And indeed, the context in which they emerge into the world may not make much difference to how clinical instruments and practices live useful lives in a mundane, daily setting. But we do need to know their stories, to understand that the weight of their meaning may vary depending on who measures it and that little in our basket of tricks comes from a fount of magnanimous universality. The advancement of Euro-American science that is foundational to modern medicine occurred because colonialism enabled it, with the extraction of materials to support its infrastructure, the appropriation of knowledge that could be commodified, and the reliance on undervalued labour to sustain this work. Many significant developments in Euro-American medicine occurred, either directly or indirectly as we shall see in the cases of syphilis and smallpox, because of the violence of the colonial encounter, coming at a cost. This evolution is often obscured by our glib belief in the progress of science, but we can trace interactions within healthcare going back to the earliest days of Portuguese expansionism, demonstrating how medicine slowly transformed through the contact zones of colonialism in evident precursors to practice today.[17]

To lift health outcomes globally, there is little dispute that in its capacity to cure, to decrease suffering, and to prolong lifespans, contemporary medicine, for all of its past, often proves efficient and effective. But European medicine five hundred years ago had no further claims to efficacy than other traditions — perhaps even less. Its rise is not because Europeans suddenly were endowed with intellectual superiority by divine bounty but by processes that allowed the accumulation of healing wisdoms, skills, and resources in the hands of a few. Antimicrobials and vaccines do not have to be automatically associated with contemporary Euro-American medicine alone, as variations have been used in healing traditions elsewhere — and we do not have access to a parallel universe where those knowledge systems might have developed further had it not been for the decimation caused by imperial might.

It has been a process for me to recognize that the tools I have learned in medicine are themselves the product of this past. To this day, we can easily remain oblivious to the innumerable ways centuries of European expansionism still have discernible impacts on people's lives in ways we might not immediately comprehend: the simplest tool we use for the measurement of oxygen levels in a person's blood may not work as well for people with darker complexions;[18] people of African descent are denied definitive kidney therapy simply because their bodies are assumed to be inherently different from others;[19] we do not teach how to diagnose skin conditions on darker skin — I have only seen pictures of measles on light skin, though most of the outbreaks in the world currently affect places where people tend to have more melanin present in the organ.[20]

This pattern ripples out into macrocosmic scales too. Areas that were subjected to coercive colonial French medical campaigns against African trypanosomiasis (sleeping sickness) are reportedly more likely to resist vaccinations and blood tests for many health concerns to this day.[21] Paul Farmer's volume on the 2014–2016

West African Ebola epidemic shows how structures, both historical and contemporary, shaped the devastating outbreak.[22] The regulatory framework of healthcare professions in India that began under British rule continues to result in a maldistribution of healthcare workers in the country.[23] For Canadians who might pride themselves on being "good" global citizens, it is perhaps easiest to consider the impact of these injustices worldwide, rather than looking uncomfortably inwards at home. But with time, with the guidance of many, many teachers, I have seen how Canadian medicine, as an institution and in my daily practice, has both shaped and been shaped by the colonization process here. For instance, the conflation of morality and medicine, as has happened many times in healthcare in relation to infectious disease, to substance use, to reproductive choices, cannot be seen in isolation from how syphilis profoundly scarred the European imagination, where sexuality became associated with the grotesque and the insane. I have a clearer understanding of how the rollout of the smallpox vaccination, initially determined by the logic of empire and commerce, demonstrates that medicine is not medicine alone but an expression of its political context — and that people will react to it as such. The institutionalization enforced on people by tuberculosis outbreaks has repercussions that reach us to this day.

I have explored before what it means to be a migrant doctor on stolen lands, working as I have as a physician almost exclusively on Indigenous territories.[24] In a recent exchange on global health where people were tackling the thorny role of the outsider intervening in other contexts, I offered that I did not think that simplistic binary approaches of outsider/insider were a productive way to understand complex power relations. As a queer person, I have been an outsider even in communities where I was otherwise considered an insider — and my role as a queer care provider from the outside is often helpful to people who are stifled by alienation within their own communities. I think we need to be clear and conscious of the multiple skeins that weave us into relation with each other, some warp, some weft. As an immigrant to Canada, I have only relatively recently come to understand my role in the state's strategy to extend its control over the lands of others. I am also aware of all the multiple ways colonization and disease have had an impact on my family's life in other colonized spaces too, even though India's context is quite different than the settler colonialism experienced in North America. There is no easy romantic solidarity between those who have been displaced from here and those who have been displaced to here. But the stories of smallpox, syphilis, and tuberculosis show how our own disparate experiences are the local tentacles of a grasping global system.

How have I learned of these connections? Although much of my formal education growing up came from the British, other influences instilled in me a wariness of what I was taught. My own family has a legacy of fighting British rule in India, and perhaps I knew from a fairly young age that some stories were not to be trusted, a realization that possibly did not truly concretize until I started to relate to my family elders as adults, as individuals with histories and perspectives independent of their roles in my life. The lessons they shared with me, coupled with the political education I received through social movements in Canada, helped me approach the records of medical history I consulted in preparing this work with some scepticism. Set in the context of my decade of doctoring in northern Canada, where communities with whom I work have taught me so much, my experience in witnessing the clinical consequences of colonialism also makes me apt to question what is written and by whom. Although detailed archival research was interrupted by global events in 2020, I nonetheless had the opportunity to consult documents in the Fischer Library in Toronto, the National Archives in Ottawa, the Sir William Osler Library in Montreal, the Wellcome Library in London, and the Bibliothèque universitaire de l'histoire médicale in Paris. While the written material I encountered may be true, I learned to ask incessantly why this person would say this thing at this time. Those questions apply even when reading of the allegedly objective progress of medicine in the Americas over the last few centuries. Histories of healthcare systems in archives predominantly developed by colonial authorities are distorted by the same power relations that record, for instance, military victories.

Not everyone's experience has equal likelihood in being preserved for posterity, but colonial bias in the record is not the only struggle in looking back. The information which we can access is determined by the languages we use. Contemporary English may not translate concepts people used to describe their experiences, which we will encounter later as we describe some of the murkiness in the process of diagnosis itself — what gets named and why? The frameworks in which we understand the world, the paradigms of analysis we use now — often determined by linguistics — may obscure details that people found important when understanding the universe through a different way of knowing, which is why Indigenous scholars speak of the importance of "two-eyed seeing."[25] Also, conclusions depend on who is telling the story, and how — in what light they choose to cast the context, what elements they emphasise, what they let slide.

In picking through the history of these diseases, perhaps I am not unlike those who study bones for signs of syphilis centuries ago: I find markings in texts and in buildings that seem to commemorate the story I want to tell. There may be vast canons of knowledge, outside of the medical world, beyond the voices I have heard, that tell an entirely different understanding of the way these diseases have shaped the way we heal and cure in Canada today. Many Indigenous scholars and activists continue, patiently, to guide our attention to all that has been ignored, but I think there is a particular need for settlers to read settler accounts and to expose them for what they are: part of an evolving mythology of who we are. And while myths serve as compelling stories and reveal much, they are often aspirational alone and not to be taken as truth. For me, the writing of this book has served that purpose of unpacking the stories we tell about ourselves.

The act of writing itself is not neutral. As much as I would like to relate the stories of syphilis, smallpox, and tuberculosis simply as interesting tales, narratives told enough times contribute to mythologies too. I worry that in my obsession with telling their histories yet again, there will be unintended consequences — that in some way, I will end up harming the goals of true, liberated health that so many have been trying to build for so long. If so, I hope the communities of which I am a part will hold me to account. For writing is not solitary either. In no way will I be able to thank all the communities, the caregivers, the scholars, both living and not, both known and not, who have permitted me to participate in this learning and this labour.

I have sat at the bedside of many a patient who has inadvertently found themselves drawn into a battle not of their choosing with an invisible enemy, a pathogen that uses their body as a battle-field in the war of survival. Whether it be diphtheria in the throat, Escherichia coli in the blood, HIV in the lymph nodes, malaria in the brain, or tetanus toxoid in the muscles, the messy relations we have with our fellow creatures sometimes erupt into the violence of illness. The suffering can be monumental. But the frontlines are not only drawn between us and them; they are also drawn among us for it is not only these single-celled organisms that choose who will suffer, how, and for how long. We choose too. Human agency can determine the response to infectious diseases, but human agency influences the assault too. All of us who engage in clinical work need to live with this deep discomfort: that we alone may not be the cure. In reflecting on these experiences in the past, perhaps those of us who believe in a more just, a more healed, a more rec-onciled future, even from the limited vantage point of our work, can learn to contribute in some way to cobbling together a truer liberation.

Syphilis

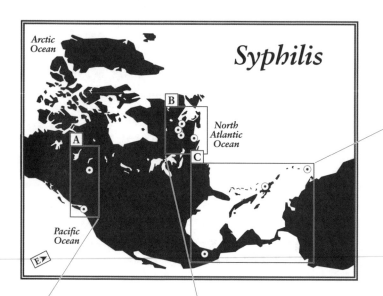

Syphilis

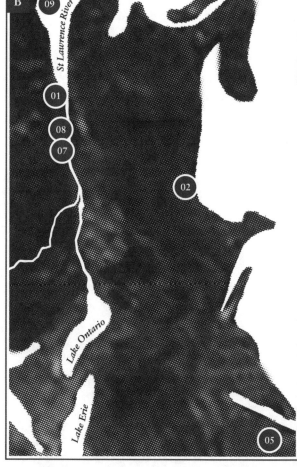

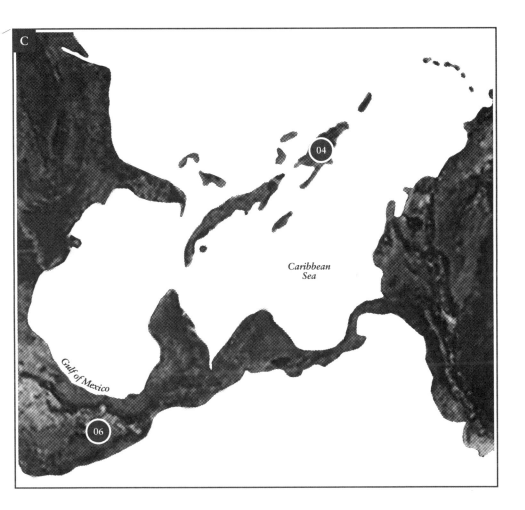

Locations

2

Syphilis

Conventional wisdom dictates that syphilis, considered the American revenge, came to Europe from across the Atlantic. The debate over its origins has continued for five hundred years, but it is not whether syphilis was originally an American disease that matters to this story. The controversy itself, dominated by scholars of European descent, frames how we understand the health and well-being of Indigenous peoples in the Americas today. Well into the twenty-first century, argument rages about how syphilis emerged, some calling its history "one of the most contentious issues in science."[1] While some articles state that syphilis came from the Americas as though uncontested, others claim that traditional healers in many parts of the world offered treatments for syphilis, suggesting longstanding knowledge. The amount of ink spilled over five hundred years that wrestles back and forth whether syphilis is American or not says more about the politics of colonialism than about the biology of syphilis. Unravelling that debate is key to understanding the role of medicine in the conquest of the Americas.

The debate over syphilis's origins came to my attention whilst I was pursuing a diploma in tropical medicine at the London School of Hygiene and Tropical Medicine. There is nothing particularly tropical about syphilis, its reach worldwide, but poor access to care has meant that it has significant implications in parts of the world where the global economy since the colonial era has undermined healthcare systems, which happen often to be tropical areas. Syphilis's burden on neonatal and maternal health, as well as on fragile healthcare resources in these regions, requires attention, and so we studied the disease closely.

During this time, I also struggled with my historically strained relationship to London. As part of a dislocated Commonwealth elite on the global scale, I have innumerable connections to the city, know it deeply without really having lived there: I have passed through many times, friends and family live scattered through it, and references to the city litter my cultural repertoire. Even though it has always been a place of friendship, beauty, and learning for me, I still balked when there; London's wealth was so blatantly from empire, all its glories stolen from elsewhere and fuelled by exploited labour. Sitting in a classroom in a school that only existed because of the colonial enterprise, a repository of global knowledge extracted from the rest of the world, infuriated me.

And yet, the medicine I knew best came from this very venture, this particular place. And I practise it still, aware that the regions where I work most, in northern Canada, grapple concretely, on a daily basis, with the legacy of European expansionism. In the plethora of diseases I studied that term, it is syphilis, with the role it played in the so-called "Columbian exchange" that resonated, echoing off my discomfort with medicine at large. In the realm of healthcare, this "exchange" balanced the brutal decimation of ecosystems and livelihoods in the Americas against a sexually transmitted infection in Europe that was perhaps new. On occasion, the potential health consequences of Columbus bringing tobacco back to Iberia is included in this transatlantic transaction.[2] Even with this addition, this medical "exchange" is unequal at best. But nonetheless, the idea has a long lineage. Cotton Mather of Boston, whom we will meet later, wrote in the early eighteenth century that the syphilis given to Europe by the Indigenous peoples of the Americas was in recompense for the smallpox brought over by the colonizers.[3] This enduring motif made me wonder if the belief that the Americas were the source of this sexual shame had an impact on European perceptions of the colonies, influencing how we talk about illness and healing to this day. Though people have tried to trace the story of syphilis to the Americas for centuries, the disease increasingly seemed to me to be a European tale, not an American one, disputes about its history more about the colonial enterprise than the infection itself. Its meaning may be more shaped by colonialism than even malaria, which dogged European imperial plans worldwide even after its endemicity receded in their home countries, as the tale of syphilis has been entirely constructed as the result of contact between Indigenous and colonizer.

If the bacterium that causes syphilis were not already troublesome enough, it has also proven difficult to pin down. Belonging to a family of curious spiral-shaped cells called treponemes, the species is difficult to grow in laboratory settings, and so study has been complicated. It was considered for many years to be identical to the bacterium that also causes diseases like bejel, yaws, and pinta, common in tropical climates across the world. All four diseases cause damage to skin, and if untreated, all except pinta can progress to causing deformities of bony structures, though syphilis's disfiguring tendencies are most commonly known. Syphilis was also long considered the only one of the four that could eventually infect major organs such as the heart and brain, though we no longer believe that to be the case. It is the only one that is transmitted sexually.

Significant parts of the obsession with syphilis come from its association with sex and madness, which is how I think my own knowledge of the disease emerged in youth, an adolescent imagination enthralled by furtive innuendo regarding European royals gone mad. Louis XIV in France is famously supposed to have struggled with the consequences of syphilis, including bringing wigs into fashion to mask the hair loss associated with the disease. Wikipedia lists Lenin, Hitler and Al Capone as suspected of having syphilis. It is possible that many cases of "insanity" for centuries were related to undiagnosed syphilis, as the disease became endemic among humans.

The other syphilitic diseases have caused less social ruckus because they have less stigma associated with them. Pinta, described by Europeans in the 1500s among Indigenous peoples in the Caribbean and Mesoamerica, was almost certainly present prior to the arrival of Columbus. The mildest in the family of diseases, sporadic cases in the medical literature suggest that pinta, albeit poorly tracked, continues to circulate in the tropical Americas today, particularly in areas with limited access to formal healthcare

services.[4] It affects only the skin, creating plaques which shift colour over the illness's trajectory, eventually leading to a mottled
appearance that may last a lifetime. As no one has ever collected
an appropriate sample, we are to this day unable to tell if the bacterium is identical to any of those causing the other diseases in the
syphilis family on a genetic level, but its causative agent is at the
very least so closely related to the others as to be indistinguishable
under the microscope visually. Pinta is transmitted through direct
contact, usually in childhood, when skin is most exposed.

Bejel and yaws both spread in a fashion similar to pinta, though
the former tends to occur in dry climates, the latter in more humid.
They were known to be present outside the Americas before colonization but caused less illness than syphilis and were not morally
suspect. Climate has been bandied about as a factor in their distribution, with no clear evidence of these syndromes in places like
Japan and Northern Europe, but some to suggest that these treponemal diseases existed in the Pacific islands before the arrival of
the Europeans. The illnesses were well-known to many across the
African continent. As with pinta, bejel and yaws are transmitted
largely (but not exclusively) by childhood skin contact. But when
these infections linger, they can infect the skeleton, causing disruptions in somewhat characteristic ways, with a predilection for
certain parts of the body. This possibility was not always known,
causing some confusion in differentiating syphilis from the other
diseases. They can cause serious disability, but they do not cause
death, generally leaving vital organs intact — but again, not always.

In syphilis, the primary site of infection develops the well-known
chancre, which sometimes goes unnoticed, a painless ulcerating lesion at the site of sexual contact, which will heal in about a month.
It becomes a systemic infection in that everyone will show signs
of exposure in a blood test after this point, but only about one-
quarter of infected people will proceed to have the symptoms of
secondary syphilis: fever, a characteristic rash that extends onto
the palm and soles, patchy hair loss, aching bones and joints, and
sometimes eye inflammation. Often this phase also resolves on its
own even without treatment.

The final phase of syphilis happens in about a third of untreated people, whether or not they are even aware of the first two phases. In the infection's contemporary form, it can take three decades for this stage to emerge. In this case, the bacteria have retreated into hidden corners of the body, but continue to work slowly away at distorting bone, brain, and/or blood vessels. This stage results in symptoms as varied as heart failure with swelling legs and breathing issues or a progressive dementia with movement disorders. The diversity of syndromes caused by syphilis is why it has been given the moniker the "great imitator," as it disguises itself as many other potential diseases. The clinical findings can be numerous, but a few are said to be highly suggestive. Years later, I still remember the line offered by our otherwise staid neuroanatomy professor in my first year of medical school describing the classic Argyll-Robertson pupils of neurosyphilis. For a long time, they were called the "prostitute's pupil," for "they accommodate, but do not react," describing the damage to the iris muscles whereby the pupil does not shrink as expected in reaction to bright light but does retain the ability to constrict when focusing on close objects (known in medical language as accommodation). While this dubious reference might have served medical students well, it says a lot about where this knowledge was extracted. The other legend of clinical medicine I remember learning about syphilis is the so-called sailors' handshake; while shaking with the right hand, maritime workers would apparently grab the elbow of a potential sexual partner with the left in a semblance of warmth, but in actual fact checking for swollen lymph nodes at the elbow, which can happen with secondary syphilis.

One of the most critical aspects of syphilis that has been used to distinguish it from its non-sexually transmitted counterparts is its ability to infect a foetus. Congenital syphilis has profound repercussions for the health of a child, leading to neurological and ocular damage if untreated, and this aspect of the disease was claimed as a visible marker for its presence within a population — with considerable consequence on concepts of racial purity and eugenics in the Western world.[5] But some scientists claim that the other forms of treponemal disease may on occasion cause congenital disease.[6] If so, they probably do so with less frequency than syphilis, given that they are caught mainly in childhood, and the levels of bacteria in the body would be quite small, and thus improbable to transmit, by the time pregnancy would occur.

Prior to the antibiotic era, syphilis and its family of diseases went largely untreated and simply progressed. There were attempts at cure, such as with sarsaparilla and guaiacum, which were derived from plants found in the Americas and whose trade played a key role in Spanish colonization. Mercury also became a prominent therapeutic agent. At that point, it becomes difficult to know whether the symptoms described in texts were due to the disease itself or the side effects of its treatment. It is presumed there was some efficacy to the mercury treatment in killing the bacteria, although unfortunately sometimes through killing the patient themselves. It remains uncertain (and unlikely) that the other products had any real effect on the syphilis bacterium, though some physicians in Europe swore by them well into the nineteenth century.[7]

For many years, the bacteria at the root of these infections were considered indistinguishable as they appear the same under a microscope and in the chemicals that show up in the blood upon infection. Genetic analysis now suggests that there might be some difference, although whether the differences are clearly separate lineages, flukes of where the few samples available have been collected, adaptations to the particular environments in which these strains flourish, or simply "genetic drift" in evolution remains unclear. Are we talking about variants of the same species causing slightly different types of disease, dependent on context? Or instead, are they truly distinct creatures doing different things to the human body?

These classifications are human and mean nothing to the bacteria themselves. Given that the strains have over 99.8 percent identical DNA, they would seem to meet a biological definition of being the same species.[8] But the global reach of syphilis renders it the ultimate expression of this family of pathogens in the human body. It is not skin contact that transmits it but contact with the wet, warm parts of our bodies — mucous membranes present in the genitalia. Although it appears to have been particularly aggressive when it was first identified five hundred years ago, it has since developed a more indolent course like the others, but it can much more easily progress to deep invasion of the body. The characterizations are not perfect as some overlap between the syndromes exists: body fluids from patients with syphilis have been known to infect non-genital areas of another person. Bejel and yaws may sometimes progress to causing neurological or cardiac complications, but not as systematically as untreated syphilis might. Each of these complications is part of the relationship the bacteria develop with their individual host: the immune response of the infected person, the number of bacteria that takes up residence, the site of infection. We know today it is not inconceivable for one pathogen to cause a range of illness in humans, from asymptomatic to fatal, so the difference in symptoms alone is not enough to claim distinct species.

These variations in the expression of disease by this germ are not relegated to the tropics alone. Today, Baie-Saint-Paul is known for its art galleries nestled among the hills in the picturesque Charlevoix region in Quebec, marked by the surprising tides of the broadening St Lawrence River as it approaches its estuary. Established in 1678 as part of New France, it was relatively isolated given its geography, at the mouth of a tributary to the St Lawrence among steep cliffs. But in 1775, it was the site of one of the most famous outbreaks of what is sometimes referred to as syphilis. We now understand the epidemic as probably an asexually transmitted version of syphilis — therefore, similar to other treponematoses, such as yaws or bejel.

La maladie de Baie St Paul was not unlike Scottish sibbens, another form of treponematosis which caused much debate in Britain three hundred years ago. Assumed to be either a version of yaws brought from the West Indies or, in this post-Columbian era, a form of syphilis adapted to rural life that spread by contact alone through familial clusters, another rumour claimed that sibbens was brought to Scotland by the invasion of Oliver Cromwell. Its ulcerating lesions of the face pushed doctors to classify it with other treponemal conditions, although of course at that point in history, the organism causing it was never identified. Sibbens haunted Scotland during the 1600s onwards, emerging and then lingering in communities or sometimes passing quickly through villages. It seemed clinically distinct from syphilis, which circulated in Scotland at the same time, though the treatments offered were not that different. Sibbens was clearly connected to social class, with poorer people most affected. Although descriptions were horrifying through the 1700s, the disease seemed to become milder through the nineteenth century, perhaps due to improved living conditions in Scotland, with better housing limiting person-to-person transmission. The last case was reported in 1851 before mention of it simply vanished.[9]

Comparatively, in 1780, *la maladie de Baie-Saint-Paul* had been around for a few years and was considered to be such a threat that it was believed it might bring about the extinction of the "Canadian" people (which at that time meant specifically the French colonists of Quebec) should it escape Charlevoix. In the wake of the British conquest of Quebec, this potential trigger of demographic decline held particular resonance. That year, when a British surgeon went to study the disease in the region, he noted that about 5 percent of people had undergone mercury treatment as either a case or a household contact of a suspected case, showing a sophistication in public health measures that resemble optimal practice even today — although hopefully these days we would abstain from the liberal prescription of mercury.[10] The symptoms were described in some detail in pamphlets distributed in French and English in the region as part of awareness campaigns. Again, as treponemes would not be identified until over a century later, it is impossible to know which germ exactly caused the disease, and it left no traces for us to identify. By the 1790s, references to *la maladie de Baie-Saint-Paul* seem to have almost completely disappeared. Whatever the cause, its contagiousness was legendary, with even contact with fomites such as bedsheets and pipes were noted to transmit the disease, causing erosive, purulent ulcers on the moist surfaces of the face and genitals and progressing to the characteristic erosion of the nasal bones — the collapse of the midface we might associate today with syphilitic stigma.[11]

Recent genetic evidence endorses the possibility that there have been other strains of this bacterial lineage causing disease now gone extinct, outcompeted by more successful strains.[12] These bewildering uncertainties with diagnostic classification demonstrate some of the nuance with which to approach accounts of the history of syphilis. In the context of dynamic biology, the history of syphilis is much like the history of malaria: our relationship with the pathogen is likely one of a close dance, with one partner sometimes leading and then the other responding, though over a more compressed timeframe than malaria. While the syphilis bacterium knew little of the context in which it first started to spread, as we shall see, humans experienced it both as a consequence of a changing world but also a catalyst for further transformation, its sexual spread critical to the way it was understood. So, in tracing the story of syphilis, we are rarely telling the story of the organism in and of itself given its mutable nature, but we are relating how perceptions of the pathogen played into power structures, prejudices, and political agendas.

Some of the diagnostic confusion is illustrated in a fascinating paper that describes the difficulties in distinguishing between the diseases in Fiji.[13] Syphilis became a particular issue in the late nineteenth century in the Pacific islands, four centuries after it was first recognized to sweep through Europe. The psychiatric symptoms associated with neurosyphilis (late-stage syphilis infecting the brain) were widely feared in Europe, with psychosis and dementia sounding alarming death knells for people watching their loved ones' personalities alter dramatically during the final phase of the illness. The link to syphilis had become abundantly clear even before the technology allowed for identification of the pathogen, as crude laboratory investigations such as the Wasserman test began to be helpful in identifying the cause of such symptoms.

What puzzled doctors in early twentieth-century Fiji were the signs of neurosyphilis in Indigenous Fijians, since they were all assumed to have been inoculated against syphilis in childhood through being infected by yaws, endemic in the islands, considered essentially the same disease with a different manifestation. At that time, invasive infection was still thought to be definitively related only to syphilis and impossible with "milder" infections like yaws and bejel. But if Indigenous Fijians were not getting syphilis, how were they getting the signs of a brain infection associated with the syphilis manifestation and not yaws?

Questions of race and morality were an intrinsic part of this debate. The possibility that yaws could cause neurological manifestations was routinely dismissed by experts of colonial medicine in London — partly because yaws was not associated with sex. To suggest that the Indigenous peoples of Fiji were going mad without being involved in tawdry sexual liaisons confused the question. The longstanding puritanical belief that madness was the karma of illicit sex made colonial dogma impervious to the possibility that simple childhood play might be at cause and that yaws could indeed have invasive consequences. The fact that signs very similar to neurosyphilis existed prior to the confirmed arrival of syphilis in Fiji and that doctors in the colonies could provide evidence that yaws could progress to deep internal infections were ignored. We remain unsure about the immunological and clinical relationship between yaws and syphilis, but it is clear from this scenario that science could easily be subjugated to the demands of supremacy.

In early March 2020, I sat in a dark reading room in the bowels of an impressive old Parisian building which housed the historical collections of the medical faculty's library. Newspaper headlines at the time made sedate, mildly worried remarks about outbreaks of an enigmatic disease arriving from Italy in eastern France, but life in Paris continued relatively normally, although my friends would fret about forgetting that they were not meant to shake hands, and *la bise* was no longer *de mise*.

I only peripherally paid attention to the news filtering in from outside Paris on new pathogens because I was in that creaking, dusty room to try to understand another outbreak that had shaken France seemingly from Italy about five hundred years prior. Texts in old French that hurt my brain to decipher with their peculiar spellings argued about the arrival of syphilis in Europe. The debates at the time, based on considerably less information than we have now, were clearly vociferous, dry though the academic texts may have been.

Waves of writing grappled with the origins of syphilis — first in the 1490s, in the aftermath of the first recognized outbreak, in Naples, that seemed notable for its virulence by the standards of the profoundly damaging but less dramatic disease we know today.

But why syphilis should suddenly storm onto the scene at that time was hotly debated. Was it a new disease brought from elsewhere? Had it always been present but unrecognized? Did it emerge from the particular context of the day? By the late sixteenth century, the great pox, as syphilis was known *(la grande variole)* to differentiate it from that other disease of pustules and disfigurement smallpox *(la petite variole)*, had infiltrated art and culture in Europe as an entity of its own. Girolamo Fracastoro, who famously wrote a treatise in poetry on the infection in the 1530s, the disease becoming the namesake of the protagonist suffering from it in his work, spoke of it in astrological terms, its cause being due to an unfortunate conjunction of Mars and Saturn, the planets traditionally designated to be the bearers of bad news. Fracastoro was born just as the scourge came into Europe's consciousness, and in his writing, he rejected the idea that the malady could have come from abroad since it seemed to occur with the same frequency in Iberia, much more exposed to the Americas at that point where he conceded it appeared more, as anywhere else in Europe. He found it somewhat incredulous that the disease should have emerged in so many different places at the same time, popping up in disparate places with no clear deference to the logic prevalent at the time that disease was a product of place.[14] But urbanizing Europe was a ripe breeding ground for syphilis, and at least part of its spread was a reaction to the changing demographics and the resultant impact on sexual relations.[15] Commercial maritime traffic across the region was considerable as Europe developed its shipping capacities and the blockades of the Ottoman Empire dissipated. Pathogens and parasites took advantage of this expansion of human contact, their methods inscrutable to the naked eye.

The linguistic argument some thinkers provided for syphilis predating the arrival of Europeans in the Americas is that some Indigenous peoples had a word for the disease. But this claim is troubled by the perils of translation, as well as the reality that the diagnostic terminology used by Europeans was often inexact. Mapping from one conception of disease in a worldview onto another is not a straightforward task. Indeed, all diagnoses are in some sense created by their cultural context: famous studies demonstrated the ambiguity of menopausal "hot flushes" as a symptom in Japan — for which many people there undergoing menopause did not automatically have a word in the 1980s, a shocking finding to North Americans.[16] Diagnosis is a social process, not detached from environment, technology, and power dynamics. In contemporary times we name infections by the different microbes we can now see. In other times, with the tools available, it would have been simpler to amalgamate all illnesses caused by sexual contact into one category, when it seemed evident that the source of what we call the herpes ulcer or the gonorrhoea discharge was the same. Differentiating between them is only useful to healers if they have different interventions to offer for each. If not, it makes little sense to parse them out. So, to be certain syphilis existed because a word for it possibly existed before Europeans arrived in the Americas is dependent even on whether the definition Europeans were using for syphilis was an appropriate label — were they talking about sexually transmitted diseases in general, skin lesions in general, a disease linking the two? Despite the manifold attempts to identify the diseases definitively, our evolving knowledge of treponematoses makes it highly improbable to determine what variant might have existed at the time of European contact in the Caribbean region and which syndrome associated with the bacteria people in the Americas experienced — bejel, yaws, syphilis, pinta, sibbens, or something else entirely?

Textual mentions of the "American" hypothesis occurred with regularity about a generation after the epidemic broke open in Italy in 1494. By then it was established to be a disease transmitted sexually. It was only on his third voyage in 1498, six years after the initial one, that Columbus noted that many of the European settlers of Hispaniola were suffering from syphilis. Nothing had been mentioned on previous voyages, suggesting recognition of the disease — or spread? — contemporaneous with Europe.[17] The simplest answer is that they contracted it in the Caribbean. But what if syphilis had surreptitiously been among the Spaniards at the outset, only brought to the island by the first or second wave of sailors, symptoms finally erupting at the same time as their compatriots at home? Settlers were the main source of subsequent syphilis outbreaks among Indigenous communities across the Americas, so this pattern would not be unusual.

A cluster of writers in Spain in the 1520s and 1530s began to propound that the disease had been apparent in the 1490s among sailors who had been to the Americas — Gonzalo Fernandez de Oviedo y Valdez mentioned it in 1526, followed by Bartolomé de las Casas in 1530. Ruy Diaz de la Isla in 1539 said as a physician he had treated it decades before in Barcelona.[18] Why this theory should gain traction thirty years later is unclear, but by then a presumed treatment found in the South American colonies — guaiac wood — became a key commodity in Spanish trans-Atlantic trade, infrastructure for its importation driving contact and control of American resources.[19] Some offer that de Oviedo y Valdez in particular, a powerful member of the aristocracy who bewailed the alien sexual mores in the Americas, had interests in this trade and was keen to profit from the growing commercialization of this commodity. Europe clamoured for a cure, and Iberian merchants may have exploited the mediaeval Christian belief that God placed the antidote to every poison nearby: if syphilis came from America, then so did this handy, lucrative treatment.[20]

Trade in this ingredient, which the Indigenous peoples in the region knew well, became a draw for the imperial Spanish state, missions sent to try to access the trees grown in Andean regions. Indeed, it played a serious role in the politics and economy of the continent. Ulrich von Hutten, the famed German reformer who followed Martin Luther, was the subject for the first known portrait of a syphilitic patient in 1523, the year of his death, his face famously depicting lesions considered to be related to advanced syphilis.[21] He wrote a book on guaiac in 1519 as he believed he had cured himself of syphilis (although he probably just fell into a latent period of infection, where the disease retreated into hidden corners of the body) with a treatment from a "barbarian" land with no doctors.[22]

The question of the origin of syphilis thus became more prominent as it began to serve a political purpose. In his blazing satire *Candide*, Voltaire refers to syphilis as the "first fruit" of the conquest of the

Americas, the price Europe must pay, he notes, for chocolate and cochineal.[23] The debate about the origins of syphilis was already present through the medical texts of mediaeval Europe, but as time wore on, as in any space of competing explanations, it was not necessarily objective truth that won. The politics of where the disease might have emerged became rife with multiple agendas to control the narrative, perhaps seeking expediency over accuracy.

From the 1500s on into the late 1600s, European expansionism became institutionalized, and the continent entered the throes of rapid transformation. Competing nations were beginning to flex the muscle of global mercantilism as technology allowed the quest for resources to venture farther afield. Relations to land and labour were also undergoing changes as Europe's population grew steadily after the demographic losses of the plague-ridden 1300s. Internal colonization in Europe had reached its geographic limits: an expanding urban bourgeoisie eager for continued accrual and domination had to look elsewhere. The Catholic monarchy in Spain was fresh in the thrall of evicting the Muslim and Jewish populations of the Iberian Peninsula, and fear of the "other" haunted their neurotic insecurities about power for a considerable time thereafter.[24]

The apparent apparition of this new disease fit into that tumultuous context. As Europe warred with itself, what became known as syphilis, with its seemingly unforgiving nature and grotesque culminations, was part of this heaving world. Accounts early on, from the 1490s into the sixteenth century, struggled to make sense of it, and in the public sphere, it was convenient to apportion blame to the closest enemy. The Italians called syphilis the "French disease," associating it with the invasion of French forces at the time, but to the French it was the "Neapolitan disease." The Dutch named it the Spanish disease, and the Russians the Polish one. In India, when syphilis arrived centuries later, it became known as the white person's sickness, and the Ottomans associated it with the Christians of Western Europe. Of note, no one in Europe initially called it the American disease. After Spanish doctors began to write from 1526 onwards that the disease was associated with Columbus's voyages to the Americas, the concept gradually became entrenched in European thought as the continent transformed through the sixteenth century.[25] By the eighteenth century, the American origins of venereal syphilis were part of European lore, for reasons probably more political than scientific.

Linguistically and culturally, syphilis was probably unknown to many people in the form it takes today, as even Chinese and Indian traditions of medicine, with their centuries of accumulated knowledge and empiricism, appear not to have described a similar syndrome. For all the obsession of Western scholars on whether Indigenous peoples "gave" Europe syphilis, they spend much less time on the fact that Europeans almost definitely later gave it to Africa and Asia. But because sixteenth-century science could not provide definitive alternative hypotheses, its rough contemporaneity with the first voyages to the Americas fit well with a discourse that increasingly justified the subjugation of Americans. Sexually transmitted disease being the result of lax moral behaviours of Indigenous peoples was a convenient trope. Writers from Spain hurled outlandish accusations of "terrible" behaviours: not only that of sodomy, but unfathomably to the Iberians, not having private property.[26] It helped build the argument for Catholic missions in this "New World" to bring salvation to the savage tribes of the colonies.

Even in the late 1690s, doctors were arguing about the appearance of syphilis two centuries prior. Ucay, a physician in Toulouse, wrote vehemently that people should not accept the established narrative that French soldiers brought the disease back from Naples. Ucay argued that even though syphilis was mentioned neither in the scriptures nor by Hippocrates — whom he apologetically excused as not able to get everything right — there were descriptions of chancres on penises in texts from great European physicians such as Guillaume of Saliceto, in 1270, a monk who as professor of medicine in Bologna married Hippocratic medicine to surgery. Bernard de Gordon, at the medical faculty in Montpellier in 1305 also spoke of curing penile chancres, which Ucay perhaps unwisely took to mean syphilis.[27] There is no clear way to confirm that the diseases described by the Italian monk and the French physician were indeed syphilis. On my cursory reading, it could also be herpes, as the ulcerating vesicle we would describe in that condition today might conceivably have been described as a "chancre," and there was no indication of the consequences of the untreated disease on the bones and the heart. Another option might be an illness like chancroid, a sexually transmitted infection not related to syphilis which is common today globally in people surviving in unhygienic, unhealthy living conditions, perhaps reflective of social circumstances in mediaeval Europe. Ucay was convinced however that most ancient doctors were unable to tell leprosy — a disease of close, but not sexual, transmission — apart from syphilis, thus obscuring the latter from the historical record in Europe.[28] This view had already been present in European thought a hundred years earlier, expressed for example by Dodoens, a famous professor of medicine in Leiden in the 1500s.[29] Ucay is somewhat forgiving of the conflation as he notes it would have been difficult to distinguish between the two because without adequate treatments, according to him, everyone ended up dying anyway. With our knowledge now, we might express bemusement at this confusion, as syphilis in its contemporary form is not known for its rapid progression from chancre to deformation of bones: there is a latency period of no symptoms, while leprosy slowly eats away at the body, a constant gnawing if untreated. The progression of syphilis from chancre to rash to bony changes with potential neuropsychiatric symptoms would be absent in leprosy too. It is of course possible that the disease itself has changed, rather than just our understanding of it.

Writing in 1717, the English physician Daniel Turner said he was agnostic about early writers' assertions about the emergence of the disease from the Americas, pointing out that some argued that syphilis had spread from the African west coast, where it was known as yaws, and transformed into the terrible plague of syphilis as divine retribution for the sin of the slave trade. This early connection between the two treponemal diseases despite having no access to microscopic diagnosis, shows that clinicians were beginning to formulate theories we might find plausible today just through accumulated clinical reasoning. Turner also notes that syphilis as it was known in his time was evidently a much gentler disease than when it had first emerged, with many signs and symptoms no longer seen over two centuries after it was initially recognized.[30] This transformation suggests that the bacterium had reached some sort of truce with the human species by the 1700s, which would concord with a contemporary assumption that germs evolve to keep their hosts alive longer to prolong the period of possible transmission. This belief in actual fact does not hold universally true. While the HIV strains predominant in North America and Europe in the early twenty-first century might be presumed less aggressive than ones prevalent in the initial epidemic phase in the 1980s, evidence shows that more aggressive variants of HIV have co-evolved in pockets at the same time.[31]

These explorations of the origins of syphilis are somewhat undermined by the fact that they might have conflated many sexually transmitted infections. The distinction between syphilis and gonorrhoea may not have been explicitly made until 1837, when Ricord in France definitively differentiated the two diseases.[32] This fact would throw some doubt on the preceding three centuries of discussion around a single sexual plague that ran rampant through Europe. As a physician, I am a strong proponent of the classical medical school teaching that the physical examination and patient interview are the most important diagnostic tools: the bells and whistles of tests should be ancillary as most people's bodies will tell you the story of what is happening if you pay close enough attention. We have become much worse at that skill of observation in contemporary medicine as we rely more on numbers on a computer than what we hear and observe. I thus have a deep respect for the physicians of the past who were much more astute and in tune with the subtleties of diagnosis through the clinical examination.

But I do not want to over-romanticize the past: without tests to differentiate between them, physicians might have very easily collapsed all venereal symptoms such as genital discharge and lesions into one disease, especially if discriminating between them did not much change what they would do with the limited treatments at their disposal. Ucay, for example, as late as the turn of the eighteenth century said only the degree of systemic infection differentiated invasive syphilis from any superficial symptoms in sexual organs such as penile discharge (*chaudepisses*) or chancre

— although we would suggest nowadays that syphilis would not cause the former and gonorrhoea not the latter.[33]

Turner, who seemed as learned as one could be about these matters in the early eighteenth century, demonstrated this slippage with gonorrhoea in an unwittingly comic interlude in his serious treatise on the origins of syphilis by narrating the story of a dog that lived in the same house as him. This mongrel would often return home after a week's absence, activities during this period revealed by a certain yellowish discharge from its penis — not unlike, Turner reported solemnly, that of gonorrhoea. After several similar episodes, this dog also developed mange. Turner leaves us hanging to draw our own conclusions about this observation, but I think his argument is presumed to be self-evident, based on the debate at the time about whether other species also suffered from syphilitic diseases. Given the incapacity to differentiate between sexually transmitted infections, Turner supposes that someone who had any such illness would eventually have the chronic stigmata associated with syphilis: in humans, bony deformities; in dogs, mange.[34] We now know that mange is due to a mite infestation in dogs, and they transmit other pathogens sexually but not gonorrhoea. But the possibility of co-infection with two pathogens in the dog — and in humans! — does not seem to have been explored at the time. The maxim that the simplest explanation of a phenomenon is the most accurate, while often helpful, does not always hold true. The eliding of categories we now consider distinct obscures some of the detail that might otherwise have proven helpful in establishing the history of syphilis.

Even to this day it is highly likely that the first confirmed reports of a disease only occur much after circulation has already been established. The first few cases are often misdiagnosed, or even undiagnosed, physicians not recognizing that they are confronting a new clinical phenomenon that only begins to make sense once anecdotal evidence accrues across a large enough number of cases through time and space, with patterns beginning to emerge. The rapidity of progression of syphilis initially seems to have been explained by the early virulence of an outbreak of any new disease with limited innate immunity in a community. But it could also be that the disease arrived much earlier than Columbus and the most significant signs of advanced disease in the mid-1490s were the result of an outbreak that had taken shape much earlier. Given that nowadays only a minority of untreated syphilis infections progress to clinically evident corruptions, such as ataxia (imbalance in movement and muscle coordination), aneurysms, gummae (bony outgrowths), and dementia, if we extrapolate from the disease's current characteristics to five hundred years ago, it is possible there would had to have been widespread latent syphilitic infections beyond the ones that were recorded as obvious cases in Europe in 1490s. Many Europeans might have died, with the shorter life expectancy at the time, of other causes before being diagnosed with syphilis. And even for those who did survive to show signs of the disease, there might have been considerable social pressure to find less shameful, less blatantly sexual explanations. So perhaps the disease was already well established before it began to be named.

But these ideas are speculative, and in light of the protean nature of syphilitic syndromes, it might be unwise to compare characteristics of today's syphilis with that first wave. It is plausible that Diaz de Isla's retrospective account of Barcelona's epidemic of syphilis was real: he might not have understood the cases he saw as an identifiable illness then, and only when it had become spread out across the continent as a recognizable entity was he able to frame his patients from thirty years prior into that diagnostic category. But even though Spanish physicians later associated the initial cases of syphilis with Columbian sailors, no account of the months-long voyage returning from the Americas made any mention of a plague setting upon the men of the ship. One possibility endorsing the American origin story is that syphilis spread as the result of Indigenous people trafficked into sexual labour in Europe by Columbus. There are varying accounts on whether Indigenous people whom Europeans encountered on subsequent voyages knew syphilis as a syndrome, though the lack of clarity among Europeans about the diagnosis and the interaction across languages, varying medical traditions, and the diversity of possible syndromes in the family of diseases makes drawing conclusions a challenge.

We could perhaps forgive European physicians at the time their obsession with origin. In the theory of medicine then, the environment in which an illness was experienced was key to understanding it — logic at which I would not scoff even now. European thought was also influenced by the biblical belief that the cure for a disease could be found where it had emerged. But nonetheless, it is sometimes easier to manage anxieties around an unknown disease by equating it to an enemy we do understand, stoking age-old fears about foreign contagion. The disease marked the European consciousness, becoming ingrained in the developing imperial economy and politics, particularly in Iberia. The works of Nicolas Monardes detailing the botanical pharmacopeia of the Americas, complete with his editorial preference for one sarsaparilla variant over another, egged on Iberian exploration.[35] Eventually, syphilis would also have significant implications for imperial endeavours for the British and French. Equating syphilis with the Americas set the stage for much that followed. Understanding how this medical "product of contact" shaped Europe makes sense for understanding how medicine in colonial North America evolved thereafter.

By the time the French established a settlement in the St Lawrence Valley over a century after Columbus's voyages, the trade in purportedly anti-syphilitic plants was fully established between South America and the Iberian Peninsula. The Catholic quest for conversion had also begun in earnest, and competition in the imperial enterprise was entrenched in Europe. Though Marie Madeleine de Vignerot du Pont de Courlay, otherwise known as the Duchess of Aiguillon, never left France, this swirling world around her made her dream big, the grass of salvation greener across the blue. Widowed early, she retained influence in the French aristocracy and devoted herself to work as a patron of the arts and charitable institutions. With the help of sixteenth-century priest Vincent de Paul, who later became the patron saint of all works of charity, she was instrumental in founding in Paris the Bicêtre Hospital, which was initially an orphanage and eventually served several other purposes, famously detaining the Marquis de Sade and being critiqued by Michel Foucault for its practices during its stint as an asylum. The Duchess was also involved in reforming the Hôtel-Dieu in

Paris, considered today to be the oldest still-functioning hospital in the world. In the midst of this frenetic activity never far from her comfortable home, her influence on what would become Canadian medicine far across the Atlantic was indelible.

In her letter to Paul Le Jeune, the superior of the newly established Jesuit missionary in New France, the Duchess spoke explicitly of her desire to respond to the call in his annual account of the colony in 1634:

> God having given me the desire to work for the salvation of these poor savages, after having read the missive you wrote, it seemed to me that what you believe could most help their conversion is the establishment of a hospital nun's order in New France: to the point where I have resolved to send this year six workers to work the terrain and make a shelter for these good women. I beg you to please take care of this establishment ... If I could contribute something else for the salvation of these poor people, for whom you take so much pains, I would consider myself very happy. (My own translation.)[36]

Not far from the Jesuit mission at the foot of the escarpment west of Quebec City, the Hospitalières nuns thus founded Hôtel-Dieu de Québec at Sillery, which had become the site of an Algonquin settlement for converts. There are few markers left in Quebec City, the site swallowed up by suburban houses with dramatic views of the wide St Lawrence, though a side street has been named in the nuns' honour. Two hundred Indigenous people were given shelter for a day or two at the hospital, and over a hundred were cared for longer in the first nine months of the sisters' ministrations from August 1639. Twenty-four of the latter died — the implication being that it was of a "pox," a generic term used at the time to describe illnesses that resulted in skin eruptions and ulcerations. We use the same term now for specific viruses that can cause certain rashes. The nuns were most pressed to record that the twenty-four deceased were baptised before their deaths, as were about twenty of those who passed through.[37]

We can only speculate how and why people accepted baptism at a much greater proportion in the face of death than the 10 percent who did so whilst merely sheltering with the nuns. Perhaps it was the search for certainty in confronting mortality. Or perhaps it was surrendering to endless pestering when weak, agreeing to whatever apparently well-meaning people tending to them were suggesting. Confusion and incomprehension very probably played a role. There were no doubt also genuine conversions. The Jesuits did note that of all their institutions around Quebec City, Indigenous people seemed to appreciate the hospital the most. They were also aware that it was where the local Algonquin were most influenced by their proselytizing.[38] An account a century later also notes a surge in dysentery in 1638 that felled colonist and colonized alike, which reassured the French because it apparently demonstrated to the patients that the nuns were not witches casting spells on the Algonquin alone as it was apparently otherwise believed. This later French historian also claimed that although the Huron-Wendat people were able to treat "wounds and fractures," they were not skilled in curing "internal illnesses," and so the ministrations of European medicine, to which they turned as the colonists recovered more quickly, taught them "patience and docility," with the attentions of the missionaries winning over hostile hearts.[39]

The eventual shift of the hospital to Quebec City was caused by Iroquois attacks on the Sillery installation. The establishment of hospital care in Canada spread, following the steps of the settlers. From Mexico to Quebec, Catholic hospitals were built as a site for both physical healing (with the assumption that mediaeval European medicine was more effective than Indigenous traditions) but also as a place of tending souls. The hospital as site of conversion was a key feature in their development.

The first records of healthcare services founded by Canadian settlers do not explicitly mention syphilis, or sexually transmitted infections in general, focused as they were on smallpox and a range of other new diseases that struck communities at the time of contact. Questions abound on whether leptospirosis was imported into the Americas through colonization.[40] Yellow fever's presence in Canada is uncertain aside from an apparent outbreak among sailors in Quebec City in 1710,[41] and an epidemic attributed to it occurred as far north as Philadelphia in the eighteenth century.[42] The absence of reference to treponemal infections upon arrival in the St Lawrence Valley is perhaps not surprising given that most suggestions of the spectrum of syphilitic disease in the Americas point to its prevalence in warm, humid environments closer to the Caribbean region, not unlike its preponderance in Africa and Asia.

Did the concretizing arguments in Europe regarding syphilis as American feed into perceptions of a moral abyss in which Indigenous peoples wandered? Clashes English, French, and Spanish colonizers had over gender and sexuality in the Americas have nuanced differences, but sexual violence occurred consistently as part of conquest, perhaps more so with initial Spanish contact than with the others. Claims about the ubiquity of homosexuality in Indigenous peoples, in particular vociferous from early sixteenth-century Spanish physician Gonzalo Fernandez de Oviedo y Valdez, lamented the varied gender presentations in the Americas. These protestations shaped discourse around moral standing across the Atlantic.[43] Considerations of such behaviour played into the work of some missionaries, such as the Moravians, who in at least one instance avoided establishing a mission near a settlement of Two-Spirit people (whom Europeans termed "berdache") for fear of the proximity of "wanton women."[44] The reformed conquistador Bartolomé de las Casas, who also wrote of the arrival of syphilis in Europe from the Americas but who eventually became dedicated to stopping the dispossession of Indigenous peoples by Spanish settlers and government, assured the world of the Americans' moral innocence, noting with no little paternalistic condescension that the people of Hispaniola are "void of and averse to all manner of Craft, Subtlety and Malice."[45]

Columbus himself had talked of the Taino peoples as trusting and strikingly generous, projecting ideas of the innocence of paradise onto them. But these allusions to the uncorrupted stoked other fantasies. The erotic promises of far-off lands, both monstrous and enticing, ran through the adventurous imaginations of the largely free-roving men who set out on the boats.[46] As rules governing relationship and gender expression clashed with European mores, colonizers saw behaviours through the lenses of their own moral baggage, the relative sexual freedom they encountered simultaneously abhorrent and fascinating. In the effort to counter the belief that Indigenous women were unsuited to the vow of chastity required to set up a convent at Corpus Christi, Jesuit priests in Mexico in 1724 published a translated 1717 account regarding Catherine Tekakwitha of Quebec, to disprove the idea of Indigenous women as inherently given to sexual promiscuity, incapable of Catholic moral rigours, with a preface harkening back to the tradition of virgin maidens serving the gods in the Aztec Empire.[47]

Sexual sin and shame may have made it tempting to see syphilis as something belonging to a distant, foreign, more immoral world. And the thread of this concern continued throughout North America well into modern-day society. Colonial sources initially associated Indigenous syphilis in what is now the southeastern United States with their purported proclivity for practices such as sodomy and cannibalism. But though considered a disease of the Americas, when syphilis ravaged Jamestown in Virginia over a century after Columbus, it could have just as easily been stoked by settlement from Europe (where syphilis had by then become endemic) as by an outbreak of local disease.[48] The town provided the first archaeological evidence of syphilis in the Americas as the study of bones began, where the remains of person presumed to be African had signs of tertiary syphilis. Conjecture about the origin of this person's infection seems pointless — Africa, Europe, or the Americas. Similarly, Boston, founded in 1630, started to have outbreaks of what was reportedly syphilis in the mid-1600s.[49] But there is no easy way to tell what seeded these epidemics in a port city.

Peter C. Newman served as popular chronicler of the Canadian establishment in the twentieth century, more of a myth-maker for a nation than a historian. In his telling, the first traders of the Hudson's Bay Company in the late 1700s in James Bay had frequent complaints about the incidence of sexually transmitted infection (not necessarily only syphilis) in Indigenous people. This irritation is telling as in the cementing of trading ties, Company men developed sexual relationships — both paid and unpaid — with Indigenous women, built on the tradition of the initial French traders. This new economy likely greatly contributed to the spread of infection. Unlike the French though, English employees of the Company returned to Britain when the contract was done, and the relationships were generally not pursued further, their utility gone. On paper, the Hudson's Bay Company disapproved of such transactional connections, and officially, sex between Company traders and Indigenous women did not exist.[50] However, Company representatives such as Alexander Henry (the younger) wrote exasperatedly of the outbreaks of sexually transmitted illnesses among employees on the west coast during the nineteenth century, worried that the rampant infections in the "women of this quarter" would have an impact on trade. He did note though that venereal disease had been brought to the peoples of the Columbia River basin by white traders.[51] This picture undermines a notion of an American continent riddled with syphilis prior to contact.

There was certainly syphilis present among both settler and Indigenous populations by the eighteenth century in North America. Advertisements for syphilis cures increased after the 1760s, following the influx of soldiers from Europe during the French and Indian Wars.[52] It seems not to have been an issue on the Pacific coast until the arrival of Spanish-speaking settlers in California in the late 1700s.[53] As syphilis became endemic in the nations in the west by the 1800s, it resulted in many miscarriages and morbidity in young children as it was transmitted across the placenta to a new generation.Other diseases were probably more important in the demographic decimation of Indigenous nations, but syphilis may have contributed to it.

Similarly, syphilis had become endemic in Quebec — a French doctor reported 5800 cases in 1801 among French Canadians — and the fur trade is presumed to have been the conduit for its spread westwards through the interior too.[54] During the Lewis and Clark expedition of 1804–1806, Lewis was aware that the disease had spread to Indigenous populations, likely through close contact with the *coureurs de bois*. Lewis thus carried medications specifically for syphilis and included a syringe to inject medication directly up the urethra to treat the penile discharge typical of gonorrhoea.[55] And not unlike the smallpox blankets, but somehow receiving less notoriety, the Governor of Louisiana in 1724 suggested that a number of "useless women," infected with syphilis and responsible for ruining men, should be sent to the interior to live with Indigenous peoples — presumably to spread the disease among them. No evidence exists that this proposal was carried out.[56] But its expression suggests once more that even in the steamy South, syphilis was not necessarily rampant among Indigenous nations. Surges of infection coincided with influxes of Europeans, whether troops or traders. It is possible that the increase in contacts in times of societal upheaval associated with the arriving colonists resulted in an exponential growth in cases of an endemic disease that was already slowly transmitting in the background in a population with some immunity. But even if so, European settlers would then have been a source of reintroduction of cases for many regions, especially if the "original" syphilis was only to be found in the periphery of the Caribbean.

Concerns about miscegenation and the puritanical disapproval of the norms governing sexuality in many Indigenous nations often infiltrated accounts of relationships between settlers and Indigenous peoples. Examples of the resultant colonial obsessions with sexuality in the Americas abound. As a symbol of how the colonial imagination of conquest became conflated with sexuality, Emile Petitot's writings of his sojourn as missionary among the Dene in the Northwest into the late nineteenth century were influenced by his tortured obsessions with the sexuality of Indigenous boys, the tensions leading him to have psychiatric crises.[57] Indigenous women's supposedly corrupting sexuality was the excuse to relocate a reserve in Unama'ki (Cape Breton Island) in the late nineteenth century.[58] The fear of the sexuality of the Indigenous woman was actually the fear of the sexuality of the settler man because Anglo-American imperialism saw racial hybridity as undermining the project of dispossession and settlement.[59] Knowing now about the ubiquitous abuse in residential schools, one of the core institutions of the colonial endeavour in Canada, the obsession with Indigenous sexuality as opposed to settler sexuality was misplaced.

The gold rush heightened settler anxieties about sexual frenzies at hubs of resource extraction that were part of the colonial proj-

ect: routine handwringing about the transmission of venereal disease from Indigenous sex workers to settler men was amply demonstrated in Victoria, whose population exploded in the 1850s,
and Indigenous women were made essentially the sole target in a
frenetic policing of prostitution.[60] Who is decided to be the trans-
mitter to whom is always a question determined by politics. To
this day, the concentration of male labour in the extractive projects
that the Canadian state continues to use to extend its sovereignty
over Indigenous lands comes with an explosion of cases of sexually
transmitted infections, including syphilis. In 2010, the highest rates
of syphilis in Alberta were in Fort McMurray, the centre of the
oil industry. Out of all demographics province-wide, Indigenous
women bore the brunt of the highest rates.[61]

Collective neuroses about Indigenous sexuality persisted into
twentieth-century Canada. As late as 1921, a bill by Conservative
Minister of Justice Doherty proposed to make it illegal for "any
white man to have illicit connection with an Indian woman."[62] A
social worker's master's degree thesis from 1950, despite language
that may seem difficult to get past today, still offers people seemingly sympathetic support under a public health regime in British
Columbia that legally compelled people to have their syphilis treated, in the wake of wartime panic about the moral and physical fibre of the population. The thesis does note that Indigenous women
were disproportionately likely to have repeat sexually transmitted
infections compared to Indigenous men. The writer ascribes this
trend to the economic necessity of survival in the city with few
options to sell their labour outside of sex work.[63] Even in May
1976, when the *Globe and Mail* printed sensationalist coverage of
a gonorrhoea outbreak at an Indigenous-run education institution,
an Indigenous leader wrote a letter to the editor lambasting the
newspaper for focusing on this problem rather than other challenges facing Indigenous communities, such as mercury poisoning,
loss of land and livelihood, and overcrowded housing.[64] A sympathetic settler wrote in the week following, asking why the reporter
had thought the graduation ceremony he attended was not more
worthy a story than the confidential health records of students.[65] A
collection of short stories written by Jake MacDonald about small-
town life in northern Ontario in the mid-1980s includes one where

an American on a fishing trip with his ribald, obnoxious co-workers has a sexual encounter with a young Indigenous woman. His colleagues play a joke on him by insinuating that she has a sexually transmitted infection, sparking worry in the married protagonist that he might carry and transmit "an exotic Canadian strain — Galloping Indian Jungle-Rot." When the situation is resolved, the only people to have suffered actual violence following this episode of perceived sexual impropriety are the two main Indigenous characters: the woman in question, Diana, and the fishing guide aspiring to be her boyfriend, Sonny.[66]

Black women's sexuality was scrutinized too in North America, twisted by white men's entitlement and power, but ripples of this colonial policing of desire extended far beyond the Americas, with variations in local nuance. Nineteenth-century Australian settler rhetoric considered syphilis to be more damaging than tuberculosis, cancer, and leprosy.[67] Fretting by British colonial authority about whether syphilis in tropical countries was more virulent, or that Europeans — skin light and allegedly more delicate — showed the signs of infection more, accentuated syphilis as a disease of the colonial imagination: a threat to Europe from the Americas becoming a threat to Europe in Asia. Sexually transmitted infections in the military confirmed a menace to British concepts of racial purity, but governments knew they would lose control of empire if they tried to impose too many restrictions on soldiers' sexuality. The resulting enthusiasm with which the British state instead policed sex workers in their colonies— notably in India, where examination for venereal disease became mandatory — reveals the lineage of European colonial public health logic: the source of disease is them, not us. Lock hospitals, which the British used as institutions for the treatment of sexually transmitted infections, were associated with the military across the empire and were first established in India in the late eighteenth century, specifically targeting women sex workers.[68] A letter from a military doctor in 1886 in the medical journal *Lancet* pilloried the decision to close four lock hospitals in towns with important military bases, the statistics demonstrating a sharp rise in cases thereafter. He noted that it was much cheaper to treat Indian women than British soldiers, and as Britain had to "hold India by the sword," the inefficiencies in having soldiers away on treatment were "simply suicidal."[69] Many sex workers in the Indian subcontinent resisted the intrusion of British military health policy on their bodies and did not show up for their examinations when they were no longer compulsory.[70]

All of this effort placed much pressure on clinicians working in the colonies. Training around sexually transmitted infections was minimal in England, and ascribing a diagnosis is a complex cognitive process, rendered more difficult if only a few cases are seen in formative years. Even well into the height of imperial science's might in the nineteenth century, distinction between gonorrhoea and syphilis continued to be difficult, but both played on the same apprehensions in the metropoles, proof that rampant exchanges that went unregulated by empire seethed and roiled underneath the veneer of rule. In India, tackling syphilis became more important than providing sanitation in rural parts of the country. But colonial officers of health on the ground were sceptical of directives from above on controlling syphilis: the disease, far removed from the outbreaks dramatically recorded in Europe three centuries earlier, did not kill in vast numbers, and there were more pressing health issues. But syphilis represented more than just illness: it was a question of imperial prestige, which drove the agenda for imperial medicine's care.

In nineteenth-century Hawai'i, the link between Indigenous sex workers and syphilis also continued tropes around Indigenous sexuality that suffused Euro-American perspectives. When Europeans first arrived on the islands in 1778, Captain Cook worried about his syphilitic sailors' interactions with Hawai'ian women. As colonizers settled on the islands and took over its resources, local communities navigated the rapidly changing contact economy, which eroded their access to livelihoods. Sex work was one of the options available to ensure survival. But this survival strategy was viewed by colonizers as proof that naive, innocent women were easily corrupted, confused by "civilization." While syphilis is considered to have contributed to Hawai'ian depopulation (presumably through congenital infection), the disease became a convenient way to deflect attention from the transformations Hawai'ians had to navigate as they were drawn into imperial economies.[71]

In eastern Asia, British doctors became convinced that 10 percent of Chinese people were afflicted by syphilis, a belief boosted by their faith in imperfect blood tests for syphilis — which could not distinguish between other treponemal syndromes — and sampling that was highly biased by social convention, representativity already dubious in a port city like Shanghai.[72] Imperial medical arrogance did not end there. Patrick Manson, the Scottish parasitologist who confirmed the role of mosquitoes in malaria transmission, founded the London School of Hygiene and Tropical Medicine. He worked for many years with the British colonial offices in Asia, where he was disparaging in 1887 about the capacity of Chinese medical professionals to treat their patients, accusing them of operating out of ignorance and greed.[73] The astounding lack of self-awareness encompassed within this sneering dismissal of other healing traditions obscures that not much else could be said of the profession elsewhere, as he himself became wealthy through his work in Taiwan and Hong Kong. Of note, as not quite an aside, almost 150 years later, an independent review found that the history of the School, where this book's journey started for me, twinned as it was to Britain's colonial mission, was still having deleterious impacts on the experience of racialized staff and students well into the twenty-first century.[74]

It was not only the British who obsessed about syphilis in others. France fixated on the disease's meaning, one anthropologist writing gravely about the intrinsic link between opioid addiction, homosexuality, and inherent ethnic faults in the outbreak of syphilis in its Asian colonies, though the infection had very probably been introduced to the region by Europeans themselves. There was considerable debate about whether these sins were intrinsic to the decaying Asian civilizational order of Vietnam, the result of navigating the colonial economy through sex work, or the perversion of Oriental innocence by European influence, the concern with the latter being that it would diminish Vietnamese perception of their rulers. Some also offered that if indeed a bad influence, Europeans were not really guilty as they were simply victims of an unforgiving climate disrupting their moral compass.[75]

Syphilis was also greatly studied in the Maghrebian colonies into the twentieth century as healthcare services were set up in Algeria, Tunisia, and eventually Morocco. Algiers even hosted the Clinique des maladies des pays chauds et des maladies syphilitiques et cutanées (Clinic for Diseases of Hot Countries and Syphilitic and Skin Diseases). French scholars discussed how the Arab or Muslim body and way of life led to a particular North African experience of syphilis. But one influential study of "Arab syphilis" published in the early twentieth century was actually likely about bejel, and not sexually transmitted syphilis, though it argued colonization and industrialization made the latter (and its long-term sequelae on the brain) more prominent in North African populations as they became more "civilized."[76] The French empire's imagination named what we might now consider one manifestation along a spectrum of illness as the product inherent to an ethnic or racial group instead.

This repeated pattern of considering people in the colonies as simple, stupid, and sexual — and thus syphilitic — continued to be laid out late into the nineteenth century, four hundred years after Europeans began to associate syphilis with the American "other." Politically useful to view the infection as part of the inherent flaws of distant peoples, this association was revived when expedient across time and context. Policing sexuality may have been framed in moral terms, but reshaping communities within units of kinship recognized in Europe also allowed for better control by European powers as part of the expansion of "civilizing" programs through church, school, business, and government. As a colonial import, healthcare actively assisted in this task as well.

From a contemporary healthcare worker standpoint, we should examine how this history reverberates through our practices. Screening the pregnant for syphilis is part of standard prenatal care in Canada, unless a patient, such as a migrant with precarious status, happens not to be covered by "universal" healthcare. From a public health perspective, this opportunistic screening is essential: prenatal care is one of the most reliable methods to accomplish population health goals as most people strive to meet their care providers during pregnancy. But just because a practice is universal and is offered to everyone does not mean that it will be received by everyone in the same way. With the background of history, it may be easier to understand why so many worldwide might balk at being unquestioningly tested for sexually transmitted infections. Even if patients are not aware of the minutiae of history that shape the institutions in which they must seek care, past events echo, even faintly. No one with whom I have worked has ever questioned routine blood tests they undergo in pregnancy, trusting them as for the best for their future child. We may consider now that there is little shame in living with the risks associated with being a sexual species, but perhaps syphilis screening in pregnancy, for instance, may need to be explained differently in communities once sullied through associations with it. In my own practice, I have only historically explicitly asked if the person is interested in screening for Trisomy 21, but otherwise, most places I work have an automatic battery of tests which pregnancy prompts, including syphilis, which I have never described in detail to the patient. The collective health value of screening for syphilis in pregnancy is unquestionable, but in now knowing its place, I might make more of an effort to name it, to lay out the logic of testing, to describe its benefits and its risks, and to elicit my patient's feelings about it, particularly in racialized and Indigenous communities.

Pharmacological dynamics in the body mean that oral or even intravenous doses of penicillin do not last long enough to give the slow burn required to destroy treponemes in recesses of the body where they hide from the immune system in a syphilis infection. When I prescribe the trusty injections of the antibiotic deep into muscle that we still use over seventy years later as the most reliable cure, I do not spend much, if any, time considering the infection's evolutionary history. Where the disease emerged and when makes no difference to how we treat it in our daily clinical practices. The drive to identify its source has in fact little to do with medicine.

The insistence on the question of where syphilis came from has served agendas from outside the field.

The nascent publishing industry may have fed off the frenzy during the initial syphilis panic in sixteenth-century Europe, with works such as Fracastoro's poem.[77] But as Europe began to externalize its neuroses, the arguments took on a life of their own, despite their profound irrelevance to managing the impact of the disease on people's lives around the world. No disease is born in the absence of political context, and this truth is no less so in syphilis. As medicine developed, the classification of the disease went through a variety of logical models, shaped by the worldviews of the physicians constructing them. Tropical medicine grew as a field in the process of Europeans discovering diseases that affected their endeavours in the colonies. The emphasis on the origins of syphilis in the Americas began in earnest in the 1600s, perhaps not coincidentally at the time the empire was expanding. Tools such as bioarchaeology, a branch of anthropological study that Euro-Americans used to understand distant peoples by scrutinizing their remains, used the development of the microscope to take this colonial concern into the study of the stigmata of disease. Eventually genetics could be recruited into this concern as well. New technologies fuelled the question on even further, devoting resources to confirm syphilis as foreign to European civilization.

In the early periods of colonialism, the idea that disease reflected the environment in which it was found was an important thread of medical thought — in line with the belief that the place where a disease emerged also had its cure. We may be returning today to a more nuanced conception of disease as a product of a person's context, but the initial European syphilis outbreak in the late fifteenth century disrupted the understanding that diseases belonged to a place, and it may have been why it initially did not register as directly connected to the American adventure. This philosophy of disease also rendered Europeans oblivious to any impact they might have had on the initial demographic disaster Indigenous peoples faced in the Americas: it was more likely to be an "Indian" disease that killed people, rather than disease that could have been carried from one place to the next. Infectious disease — the principle of contagion — had not yet filtered through to the European world, the idea not firmly taking root in the Americas until the 1720s. Even when transport of disease was recognized as a possibility, Europeans thought themselves as superior stock naturally more resistant to illness.[78] In the early 1800s in India, the assumption that sickness was due to climate was also prevalent among the British, a logic common in Europe at the time. Dr Desruelles, who studied syphilis at a military hospital in Paris, suggested in 1819 that outbreaks of syphilis were the result of Europeans arriving in hot tropical climates, with an excess of sexual contact in places "where they are not yet acclimated." He added that what was more important was the circumstance from which the disease emerged, that the food, climate, and numbers and types of people in an area were key to understanding the development of disease.[79] But the idea that biology could be determined by an ecology underpinned racial anxiety that people born in different places would immediately undermine the Europeanness of settlers.[80]

Early in the colonial era, clear ideologies of hierarchical racial structures had not quite been established in scientific practice, only beginning as political domination over resources became increasingly important and the hubris of conquest settled into consciousness. Initially, when the political imperative to subjugate Americans in sixteenth-century Spain became more prominent, the idea that the sexually transmitted disease was the result of the lax moral behaviours of Indigenous peoples in the Americas was a useful trope. It helped build the argument for Catholic missions in the New World to bring salvation and medicine to the savage tribes of the colonies. But the debate around syphilis became more urgent in the late nineteenth and twentieth centuries as the confluence of racial theories being used to hold on to colonial power, concerns about strategic military advantages in imperialism, and the rise of scientific tools that could be harnessed to buttress these theories became more evident. This period also coincided with increasing control of sexuality to project an image of civilized European modernity, with upright mores and unimpeachable standards, central to a sense of racial superiority in contrast with savages in the colonies.[81] The Reformation's earlier drive to regulate sexuality had greatly influenced European thought and had an impact on how people perceived syphilis and where it came from, in particular cementing the role of women as harbingers of disease and depravity. Women became the "other" that was the cause of disease in medical work that was rapidly being appropriated and monopolized by men, fitting into patriarchy's demand to subjugate women.[82]

The role of women as childbearers also contributed to racialized complexes about syphilis as the great enfeebler of subsequent generations of a race through uterine transmission in congenital syphilis. Reproduction became a flashpoint in settlers' struggles of racial dominance and a key part of the need to suppress syphilis in the colonies, including Canada. As cities in Europe urbanized while the elite tried to establish empire, the malnourished, stunted masses that were to be fed into mighty imperial armies led to much embarrassed, nationalist handwringing.[83] How could anyone rule the world relying on lust-ridden workforces with germ-eaten brains? Syphilis was a convenient framework to latch onto as an explanation, lax sexual scruples blamed rather than economic structures that kept much of Europe poor. Even in the early twentieth century, just as the capacity to trace syphilis to an Indigenous race considered "degenerate" was emerging through archaeology, American elites, who felt immigration from the Mediterranean and Eastern Europe threatened established conceptions of whiteness in the United States and Canada, also expressed concern about the decline of a settler stock already threatened through syphilis. The pressures of smaller families and later marriages were exacerbating tense racial anxiety.[84] Eradicating syphilis — and associating it as something not of white origin — was very important.

This desire to ensure that syphilis was something external to white America became integrated into immigration laws. By 1891, the US Immigration Act asked for the examination of all immigrants for obvious signs of sexually transmitted infection. Considering this law passed before there were reliable diagnostics (which we still sometimes struggle with today when it comes to syphilis!), suspicious critics said that the low rates identified in people coming from elsewhere must be due to improper, incomplete examinations, unwilling to let go of the perceived threat that the outsider held to the racial purity of the United States: immigrants often provided the bulk of sex workers in American cities even at this juncture in history. The panic syphilis instilled in the American psyche infiltrated all the way into healthcare: from 1822 to 1851, no person deemed to be suffering from venereal disease was allowed admittance to the Massachusetts General Hospital. From 1851 to 1881, they were admitted only with the permission of the trustees but had to pay double, and after that they were excluded from admission again. With the advent of better treatment, the MGH showed records of treating venereal disease from 1905 onwards and of actively recruiting patients by 1913. Cynically, one considers the remuneration that came with this reversal.[85]

In Canada in 1919, the second interim report on venereal diseases produced for the Royal Commission on the the Care and Control of the Mentally Defective and Feeble-Minded in Ontario (and the Prevalence of Venereal Disease), discusses extensively the role of the federal government to prevent the entry of "undesirables" into Canada as a means to control syphilis, noting as an aside in the context of the Great War that no immigrant of "Teutonic origin" would presumably be permitted to enter Canada. Of note given its current relevance, the report also has an extensive discussion on how patents were limiting production of the arsenic-based compound that was proving to be a potential treatment of syphilis, complicated slightly by the fact that the company owning them was German.[86]

Black Americans with syphilis were also accused of being improper and slovenly with loose sexual morals — with suggestions that education would not be sufficient to overcome the base impulses of the "race."[87] Racial overtones in the discussions around syphilis were influenced by eugenic discourses, with such examples as Dr Morrow, well-known in the United States for his interest in preserving traditional family life, who discussed implications of the spread of congenital syphilis for white Americans. Similarly, the understanding that gonorrhoea could lead to infertility if untreated in women also aroused similar racial neuroses, as stated by Dr Burr of Chicago, who, comparing it to the dangers of abortion, said that "the ban placed by venereal disease on foetal life outrivals the criminal interference with the products of conception as a cause of race suicide."[88] That particular sexually transmitted infection is often unpleasantly obvious when infecting a penis but can be less symptomatic in the vagina. For a long time, gonorrhoea was thus considered simply to be inherent to women — she the blithe corruptor, the dangerous one. These ideas of sexuality both emerged from social prejudices and also reinforced them.

Male sexuality would eventually fall under the purview of public health to preserve the continuity of racial supremacy: it simply would not do to have any infectious corruption taking hold of the man before marriage and causing the birth of a syphilitic child, thus leading to generational decline. Syphilis's associations with the violation of a moral code became entrenched. Though some medical professionals in the early twentieth century critiqued the sensationalist fears that syphilis and gonorrhoea were about to take over the world, the main thrust of discourse emphasized that the foundation of the American family was at threat, suggesting that up to one-fifth of the US army was infected, sick leave taking a toll on military supremacy. At the time of World War I, American physicians were not far from equating catching syphilis as aiding and abetting the enemy Germans in an act of national betrayal, with sex work simultaneously demonized.[89] While all Allied governments struggled with sexually transmitted infections among their troops in the wake of the war, the fact that Canadian troops had some of the highest reported rates was a cause for intense official embarrassment.[90] In 1917, Canada passed a regulation under the Defence of Canada Order criminalizing any woman with a sexually transmitted infection who had intercourse with a soldier, Britain following in similar suit a few months later.[91] While few made the explicit connection to the tale of the disease's origins, it is not hard to see why a convenient story about syphilis's birth might become so embedded within the Euro-American psyche — a disease sent to them by Indigenous peoples, now causing a threat to the very foundations of the society they had built upon those lands: the army and the household.

The unreliability of narrative accounts, with their diagnostic uncertainty, both at the time of the first European outbreaks and those that came later, proved to be unsatisfactory. European science thus began to turn to more "objective" measures of history, such as those left in physical, tangible records, as a more appropriate means to determine the threads of storytelling around syphilis that filtered through over the centuries. The possibility that it was a disease indigenous to the Americas caught the imperial imagination. Physicality is in no way more "real" than oral history and is also vulnerable to interpretative fallacies. But renewed scrutiny on the origins of syphilis in the Americas came in the nineteenth century, quite distant from the initial Italian epidemic, with the advent of technological tools for the tangible. Idle curiosity may have been sufficient reason to return to this question four hundred years after the fact, but we can nonetheless note that this resurgent quest for the origin of syphilis coincided with the racialized moral panic about the disease that stretched across the American, British and French empires, as well as their satellite states.

This obsession found an answer in the arrival of archaeology as an established field of study. Although ancient peoples around the world had always demonstrated an interest in their own pasts, global archaeology that uncovered the buildings — and the bodies — of other peoples' societies was only established in the nineteenth century in the heyday of European imperialism. The term firmly took on its contemporary meaning in the 1830s though excavation seems to have been practised worldwide before this. Large-scale digs in Italy around Roman ruins, including Pompeii, began in the mid-1700s. Napoleon's foray into Egypt at the advent of the nineteenth century was the first time known that Europeans engaged in organized archaeological excavations outside the continent in an effort to consolidate knowledge of the newly acquired territory.[92] I now realize that a formative literary encounter I had as a child, Agatha Christie's *Murder in Mesopotamia*, recounts a peculiar collective experience set in the early twentieth century when a bunch of British and American people went to gawk at the ruins of a country far away — *just because they could*.[93] It was theirs for the taking. Amateur archaeology developed as a tradition through the middle of the 1800s, a chance for the wealthy to discover the riches of empire, to win trophies that were "their birthright."

In 1856, the first bones of a Neanderthal man were uncovered, which began the practice of studying the remains of people who had been buried by their loved ones. Identifying skeletal lesions in people from elsewhere in their graves was part of the development of anthropology, as white European thought began to try to systematize and classify "others." This process of generating and organizing knowledge served political aims. A crude, disruptive practice to begin with, bioarchaeology was also initially beset by many technical problems, including the lack of a consistent method of study, often falling into the interpretations of colonial imaginations as the most reliable frameworks available, though some of these concerns may be addressed in today's work. But still, the fact that initial recovery or conservation methods were not perfect limits the amount of accurate information that is available in older "collections" of bones — or more appropriately, in the remains of ancestors.[94] As time progressed, innovations in scientific method were also employed to bolster conclusions. Carbon dating, initially used to determine the age of bones, was unreliable, though refinement and triangulation with other methods have improved the technique considerably. In more recent times, trying to track down DNA in ancient bone lesions for genetic tracing of treponemes has proven not to be viable because it is unclear whether enough bacteria exist in the residual scars in skeletons. Furthermore, bacterial DNA is less stable than human DNA so is less likely to survive in the acidic environment of decomposition.[95]

For a long time in the expansion of archaeology, the Americas were a sideshow in the race to discover the origins of humans — perhaps because of the beliefs that a continent that was so thoroughly settled by Europeans would have less to offer in the study of bones than elsewhere, or that there would be little of interest to find in an allegedly unurbanized history. But with settler expansion, curiosities such as mounds in the Mississippi Valley became sites of various forms of study from the 1700s onwards, accompanied by an attempt to erase Indigenous agency in their history, preferring to ascribe other origins to the engineering marvels.[96] Even at the level of the macroscopic, study was greatly influenced by colonialism's intent to belittle and demean, so there is little hope that microscopic study was any less objective. Physical anthropological techniques — looking at the physiognomy of the bodies of the colonized — became part of the ambit of archaeological study, the racialization of bodies becoming more pronounced in the 1800s. The Bureau of Ethnology was established in the United States in 1879 as a means to document Indigenous nations that were at that point considered to be threatened with or close to extinction.

Archaeological studies of treponematoses, unwittingly or not, play into this discourse of colonial might. In North America, these studies are concentrated in the southeastern United States, although there are signs that some form of the syphilitic range of diseases probably existed in other parts of the continent too. The convergence may be either the result of actual distribution of disease or simply where people sought for its signs the most. Studies outside of the Americas have failed to find reliable signs of syphilis in human remains, although research in Asia and sub-Saharan Africa has been limited. Much of the argumentation in academic papers is quite technical, focusing on the propensity of which syphilitic syndrome to infect which bones. The first studies of pre-Columbian syphilis in North America looked at remains that were appropriated in Tennessee in the late 1860s, using criteria for non-microscopic findings that are similar to what would be done today. This paper did mention the possibility of non-sexually transmitted treponematosis, not necessarily syphilis, being the cause. Since that time however, the bones that Jones, the author in this study, used to suggest treponemal infection was quite common in the region, have been dispersed and are difficult to trace, and so a re-study of its conclusions are difficult, let alone honouring the remains with dignity.[97]

Uncovering skeletons is quite rare, and so many conclusions have been proposed from limited research. The language in many of the archaeological studies is cautious, though the political imperative to use these findings as certain truths may have trumped scientific circumspection. Adelaide Bullen, who studied the bodies of buried ancestors for decades in the mid-twentieth century and then withdrew out of sympathy for growing Indigenous objections to the practice, examined syphilitic lesions particularly in skeletons that later reviewers thought might have been suggestive of non-sexually transmitted forms such as bejel. Most early archaeological studies of syphilis did not take into account the possibility that the syphilis we see now is not the same syphilis that might have existed when the people died. Temporal shifts suggested by contemporary dating methods hint at a change in the bacterium's relationship to humans in the few centuries prior to European contact in the Americas that increased its rate and means of spread, including perhaps through sexual contact.[98] We do not know which variant of treponemal infection existed in the region, extant or extinct, nor does this tentative conclusion provide a definitive source for syphilis being transferred to Europe from the Americas.

There have been persuasive arguments that the early study of bio-archaeology should not be held to our current moral or political standards. Even within the structures where people worked, individuals were often trying their best and making claims for progressive policy. Categorizing by race was not considered inherently morally repugnant at the time, but it was the use of these studies to enhance racist policy that became the issue, not the field of study in and of itself.[99] Scholars would not necessarily be able to look into the future to know how their theories would be used. The tradition of perceived academic neutrality in reporting "only the science" continues. I certainly have some sympathy for that argument in the sense that I too work within institutions that come with power to dispossess and oppress both individuals and communities at large, the tools at my disposal used to discredit and demoralize susceptible populations. Does this reality mean all my colleagues within medicine, as individuals, are suspect? Hindsight refines medical practice to this day, and the full effects of our current approaches may not be completely understood until decades later, when unintended, unimagined consequences of the interventions undertaken now are uncovered and we learn from them.

Should we not hold the fields of anthropology and archaeology with the same forgiving tenderness? While this terrain is contested — and should continue to be — the stark lack of self-reflection in early texts of bioarchaeology of how they might be playing into contemporary political projects can be striking. Critically, the concern of scholars today to absolve individual scientists in the past of accusations of racism falls into the trap of believing that it is individuals who make or break racism, rather than evolving structures and institutions. Either way, dissident countercurrents existed even at the time, coalescing into anti-imperialist associations and leagues within the UK and the US by the 1890s. So not everyone "of that time" believed categorization by race was a useful measure. But whether or not a scientist actually believed in depriving a group due to their alleged inferiority is a distraction from the fact that social structures — independent of the will of any one individual — can lead to outcomes where such oppression occurs regardless. What matters is the end result, not the intention behind it.

There were indeed people with unabashed racist ideologies involved in bioarcheaology, such as Arthur Keith, knighted by George V in 1921, who even in 1932 believed that "the spread of English-speaking peoples [was] the greatest attempt to rationalise the peoples of the world that has ever been made."[100] But the field was not devoid of political implications even when done by people without such openly abhorrent views, narratives of physiological inferiority and demographic extinction feeding into policies that enabled the dispossession of land.[101] Archaeology in and of itself did not become a source of new information on syphilis until the colonizing gaze established itself and people looking for confirmation of the American source of this scourge perhaps began to will it into existence. While many people might say that research on the origins of syphilis is in its essence apolitical, simply uncovering knowledge for its curiosity, the determination of what makes it onto research agendas is rarely devoid of politics. The scientific process is by its nature acquisitive, avaricious: it seeks to understand processes in order to control them. If there is no profit — not always financial in nature — to be gained, perfectly valid research questions can be shoved aside. That the birth of the great pox has been considered so worthy of such scrutiny is telling. Even a seemingly dispassionate, technical field would no doubt have been influenced by the mores of its time: telltale signs of past or primitive promiscuity were easy to see in etches and scratches from centuries ago, certainly if doing so bolstered images of self or society as more virtuous and civilized.

The profound sense of entitlement Euro-American science felt for the bodies of others even in death was for its own advancement, overriding all other concerns that people might have had for their loved ones. Even to this day, the use of the bodies of racialized peoples, without the consent of families or communities, continues in respected institutions of learning. The use of remains of Black children killed in a police bombing in Philadelphia in 1985 in an anthropology course in 2021 without the consent of their surviving relatives made headlines.[102] Increasing mobilization among Indigenous communities to protect ancestors and to own the retelling of their own histories has made progress. Examples are beginning to abound of Indigenous peoples using tools they find useful in order to interpret and retell their histories.[103] In Alberta, the first institute to practise archaeology scholarship formally in line with Indigenous principles was founded in April 2021.[104] Elsewhere, the Gkuthaarn and Kukatj people in Oceania allowed for the publication of data on eight individuals whose remains had been stolen in the 1890s by settlers for scientific sampling once they were repatriated, and the communities participated in analyzing and sharing the data.[105] The narration of their stories is a helpful reminder of how the alleged confirmation of syphilis as a disease of the Americas also came about: not by a process of dispassionate science but as part of a plunder of graves by the power of empire.

Contraception was one area of Indigenous sexual health practice that did not initially fall under the surveillance of the government or church, perhaps influenced by the belief of the "dying race."[106] When Indigenous identity became more of a threat with the rise of more public resistance to the reach of colonial government, birth control as late as the 1970s in the north of Canada for Indigenous women was subject to increased social, medical, and political scrutiny.[107] Ideas of racial purity continued to dictate policy as governments engaged in the forced sterilization of Indigenous women during the twentieth century. Alberta, which oversaw the longest-running eugenics board in North America, from 1929 to 1972, added people with syphilis to be monitored in 1942, although the individuals in question were to provide consent prior to sterilization, unlike many other people who were compelled into giving up their reproductive capacity. The overarching framework of the board was to weed out "feeble-mindedness." This understanding includes congenital syphilis in its scope, but it also had significa-tion creep as it became code for morally suspect people, such as those who might get syphilis anyway. This link was often made through the concept of *pauperism,* or being wilfully poor, which, even if a parent did not pass syphilis on to their offspring, a eu-genics paper argued in 1877, was a dubious enough characteristic to warrant intervention and was considered to be most definitely transmitted.[108] Women were overrepresented in the sterilizations that took place in Alberta, and Indigenous people were particu-larly targeted by the eugenics board, their weight in those records exceeding theirs in the general population by a factor of two. They were overwhelmingly classified as "mentally defective" when com-pared to white subjects, whether of older or more recent immigrant origins and thus were far less likely to have required consent before proceeding to sterilization.[109]

Patterns of thought that conflated sexual health with racial politics extended well into the twentieth century. The belief that Indigenous women were a threat to white domination of the Americas tracks back to their wanton, monstrous sexualization, of which the debate around the origin of syphilis has been a logical dénouement. What does it mean to undo the impact of the tales we have told about syphilis in how we provide sexual and reproductive healthcare services today in communities that resist colonialism? Certainly, advances in sexual liberation in general have had a net positive impact in my clinical work. Hypersensitive to this aspect of my practice given my own experiences as a queer patient, I have noted how the sex positivity emerging out of feminist and queer move-ments has transformed the way we understand sexuality and how healthcare professionals approach such questions. I witness much less moralizing about people's decisions around sex in today's med-icine, although some does remain.

But after the triumphalism associated with the discovery of anti-biotics, today much of the Western world is seeing a resurgence of syphilis. Infectious diseases go through cycles shaped by multiple factors, including waning collective immunity and less preventative action as people become less wary in times of low spread. In Canada, most provinces began to see a rise in syphilis as sexual practices relaxed at the turn of the twenty-first century, an era more liberated from fear of HIV, the outbreaks initially considered to be largely confined to men who have sex with men. But as HIV prevention in North America turns towards pre-exposure prophylaxis (PrEP), more and more men who have sex with men get routine testing for other infections, including syphilis, as part of this public health intervention that requires more frequent contact with healthcare professionals than, say, condom use. Syphilis through heterosexual contact is now a major driver of outbreaks in Canada: the rates of women contracting it have climbed quickly, with the proportion of female cases over 50 percent in some jurisdictions and this shift confirmed with the return of congenital syphilis. Indigenous peoples are seeing particularly high rates: the barriers to care that decades of colonial antipathy and underinvestment have resulted in a syndemic of syphilis, where multiple illnesses synergistically worsen outcomes for a population.[110] Another vulnerable group in Canada is migrants with precarious status, who may not have access to routine prenatal care due to provincial policies restricting access to "universal" health insurance. In Alberta, the first case of transmission in pregnancy in over ten years was reported in 2002, with a cluster of cases in the mid-2000s apparent in children born predominantly to Indigenous sex workers, many of whom who had not been able to access prenatal care.[111] Physicians in Quebec were put on alert after the province, which saw a total of five congenital syphilis cases from 2001 to 2015, saw seven in 2016–2017 alone.[112] British Columbia saw no cases of congenital syphilis from 2014 to 2018, and then saw two in the first half of 2019, prompting changes in screening frequency.[113] Manitoba reported record numbers of congenital cases in 2020.[114] That year did see a slight decrease in cases of syphilis overall in Canada, both infectious and congenital, but this blip might reflect reduced contact between people and disrupted access to testing and so not reflective of a sustained trend.[115]

For a disease that was allegedly born among them, Indigenous peoples are now facing disproportionate suffering from the infection all these centuries later, not unlike the burden the infection places in other parts of the world that have confronted European colonialism. Between 2016 and 2020, rates of syphilis more than doubled in Canada, the highest increases noted across the prairies. In the Northwest Territories and Yukon, rates were essentially zero in 2016, but had started to rise by 2020.[116] In Alberta, the most rapid increase of syphilis in 2018 was seen around places like Fort McMurray, the centre of contemporary Canada's extractive boom.[117] Syphilis rates for two Indigenous communities studied in Arizona in 2007–2009 were significantly higher than the American average, and the gender prevalence was more equal, suggesting an outbreak related to heterosexual sex.[118] In the 1980s, misclassification of racial identity in the United States in the context of American race politics — with stigma associated with Indigenous identity — may have affected reported rates of infection in certain Indigenous populations, with the potential complication that rates have always been high and are only now being properly identified.[119] A study in Peru in 2008 showed the expansion of HIV in remote Indigenous communities accompanied by high rates of syphilis, possibly associated with high rates of travel outside of the community.[120] If syphilis had been known to Indigenous communities in the tropical Americas before, one might have expected it to be more endemic, with less association with contact with external populations as a risk factor, but the mapping of transmission pathways in this particular context remains unclear.

Diagnosing and treating syphilis have not necessarily become easier in the march of medical progress either. I routinely confront the issue of a positive syphilis test in people who have had only intermittent access to healthcare. It is difficult to tell from one test alone whether the infection is new, advanced, or previously treated. Among transient, unhoused communities where I occasionally work, it is perhaps safest for good outcomes to presume an advanced infection, which however requires a series of three penicillin injections, each a week apart — a requirement to return which is not often possible for people. But even this proactive approach to treat aggressively does not address the possibility of syphilis having infiltrated the brain, which requires a special test of spinal fluid, difficult to do in cramped mobile clinics, and a separate protocol of intensive treatment to ensure cure.

Kent Monkman's depictions of sexuality in his staggering works of art pervert the relationship between colonizer and colonized. Often using aesthetics of classical Euro-American art that celebrates tropes of the wild magnificence of the Americas, his paintings trouble established colonial dynamics. Monkman's work teases the almost erotic transcendence in settler imagination of being dominated by the Americas. Even though they sought control, in many ways, the colonists surrendered to the perceived wildness of the "other."

Studying the colonizer, instead of the colonized, is now an established means to rebalance some of the injustices entrenched in the world since the height of Euro-American imperial influence. What drove so many Europeans to participate in a project that clearly hurt, harmed, and oppressed others? How does mass delusion of supremacy take hold? Why does it become so intensely important to pinpoint the origins of a disease like syphilis? This twist matters today too: Indigenous health researchers ask why we spend so much time studying why Indigenous people are sick, for instance, rather than studying why Canada makes Indigenous people sick.[121]

Many argue that contact with Europe at its most expansionist need not always have been necessarily bad. Approaching the zenith of imperial might, medicine was still quite primitive. Leech use for medical purposes to encourage bleeding peaked in France in 1832, with 55 million leeches employed (considerably more than the 33 million people estimated to be living in France at the time).[122] But with the introduction of smallpox vaccination and quinine, incorporated through the knowledge of colonized peoples, Western medicine too began to transform. Coupled with the burgeoning industrial manufacture of synthetic opiates and the introduction of anaesthesia, technical interventions were helpful in building medicine into the practice we know it today, right up to the introduction of antibiotics at the "end" of the colonial era in the 1940s.

But the most important advances in medicine were changes in society, with improving housing and adequate sanitation in cities as they grew quickly, which might lead some to suggest that colonization — in and of itself — had little impact on the evolution of medicine. However, the ameliorating health conditions in Europe were probably due to the impoverishment of the colonies, as wealth accrued in European capitals. There is no way to know that the rest of the world would not have developed effective medical tools on its own anyway if it had not been colonized. After all, China and Japan had independently adopted medicine based not only on empiricism but with rigorous experimentation too.[123]

There is nothing inherently bad about contact with others, but relationships of domination and exploitation are not merely contact. While it is difficult to disentangle the causes and consequences that led to the overarching trajectory of European colonialism, it seems improbable to me that Western medicine would have reached the heights of efficacy and accomplishment it has now if it had not had the entire colonial system supporting it in its extraction of knowledge, labour, and material resources. There are in fact strong arguments that the tools of epidemiology, for instance, only emerged because the illness to which colonialism contributed allowed the methods of counting and predicting disease to develop to a high degree.[124]

But as medicine derived benefit from colonialism, the need for it also grew as the direct consequence of poor health to this day that has occurred as a result of colonialism. Just as we must address how Euro-American institutions such as courts and schools have been complicit with the processes of colonialism, we must do the same for medicine.

In healthcare, we have to be wary of the moralizing nature of Canada's healthcare history, entrenched in the missionary tradition of policing behaviour into what we as a society might collectively decide is good. Liberating our approach to sexual health could be an integral part of decolonizing our futures, especially as sexually transmitted infections come back to affect Indigenous communities disproportionately. The declaration that Indigenous nations with seemingly transgressive sexuality were the source of a venereal plague gripping Europe might still echo through Euro-American medicine's practice of care to this day. Syphilis has had its meaning constructed through otherness: as white supremacy took hold of the globe through the expansion of colonial empire, it became associated with the sexual practices and the morality of savage or simple "others." Its actual evolutionary trajectory unknown, stories that conveniently fit preconceived narratives of Indigenous backwardness justified the place they would serve in the imperial endeavour. We can see the residual impact of such foundational beliefs in institutions through the twentieth century, when syphilis was deliberately left untreated in Alabama and in Guatemala. The investigators, publicly funded by the United States government, were no doubt aware in the late 1940s that the experiments were unethical but found it easier to inflict them on Black and Indigenous bodies than on white ones.[125]

Training healthcare workers in a structural analysis of infectious disease, with moralizing arguments weeded out, is central to a transformation of practice. May the Duchess of Aiguillon forgive me, but healthcare work is not about trying to better the lives of others by pitying them for making poor choices out of ignorance or trying to show them the light. That ethos in medicine, which unfortunately I have seen at work in Africa, Asia, and the Americas, emerges out of the myth of the naive colonial subject in need of guidance. That guidance first came from the redemption of European faith and then eventually from the primacy of European rationality.

In colonial condescension, that model of assumed rationality still warps medical practice. We have the tendency to blame addiction or diabetes on individual lifestyles rather than recognizing that people have to make choices out of a palette of options that their position in global hierarchies limits. It is easy to disparage people's sexual choices, for example, rather than taking the time to understand the options available to people to limit their exposure to infectious hazards. Instead of accompanying it with the habitual grimace of embarrassment, treating sexuality in clinical contexts as a joyous sharing of our bodies with others makes it easier to discuss its concomitant risk of inadvertently sharing with other creatures as well. Few people willingly seek out infection but are more likely exposed through lack of knowledge, lack of resources to protect themselves, or lack of power to avoid it.

To associate alcohol abuse with moral failing is facile without looking into the drug's role in consolidating commercial and political aims in North America.[126] Other substances have been used elsewhere for similar purposes — such as the opium trade in nineteenth-century India and China.[127] Sanctimonious approaches to illness are hopefully happening less in today's medicine, although they are being replaced with an equally shorthand medical model, focused on the biochemical and neuroanatomical. Supporting a structural analysis among workers in our healthcare systems addresses some of the legacy of blame associated with infectious disease. Our role as practitioners of healthcare is to expand the choices available for people's well-being, which they can often identify for themselves, and not to harangue them for making what we consider mistakes.

Another concrete step medical educators need to take is to confront the attribution of racial characteristics to disease that persists routinely in curricula to this day. Medical assumptions about racialized peoples encourage lazy cognitive shortcuts that have an impact on people's health outcomes. Differential distributions of disease across race may of course exist, but the unqualified assumption that there is a biological basis for inequities needs to be contested: very often, disparities may be due to factors of social and political structures that have had impacts on communities through racism's long historical reach, rather than biology. We have to ensure that we are no longer making spurious connections or imposing stories we want to believe onto the way the world works. When we say that racialized people are susceptible to diabetes, we need to think beyond genetics and wonder why nutritional systems for so many people worldwide have been so compromised as to cause pathology.

As a healthcare worker myself, the debates around the origin of syphilis seem to me both unimportant and critical. Unimportant because the actual answer to the question is profoundly irrelevant to anything I do in my day-to-day professional life. Critical because the fact that the debate exists tells us so much about how we use science to tell stories of our past for our own convenience and our own comfort. Science does not work in a vacuum: it has political import, and it shapes how we understand the world. The scientific process produces truths, but the truths that get pursued are determined by many other things than science alone. The argument around the origin of syphilis reveals to us the nature of the evolution of medicine, how what we chose to pursue as knowledge influences our understanding today. The studies on syphilis often reflect not the importance of the disease to Indigenous Americans, but they instead centre the experience of colonial Europeans themselves, and their place in the world. The actual birth of syphilis does not alter the way I work with patients, but the fact that the discussion has even happened shapes the terms by which we interact.

We might never have a neat, comfortable answer for the beginnings of the great pox — the further removed we are from its origins, the more obscured the details. Perhaps we can simply chalk it up as a child of the colonial encounter, awareness of its existence — grotesque and insidious — a mirror for the time it came to people's consciousness. There is poetic delight in a disease that deforms and deranges as being the revenge of the Americas, but in reality, we will never know. The Americas too have suffered its consequences after all, firstly enabling colonial commercial interests. And then, when it became expedient, the illness revived the ogre of the corrupt sexual savage, apt to cause much damage to the world if left unchecked by civilizing forces. And even later, Indigenous peoples in the Americas began to bear the brunt of the bacterium's burden into the twenty-first century. To me, after the question around syphilis first emerged as a curiosity in a classroom in London, as a doctor studying diseases "discovered" and named by colonialism, delving deeper into this history has highlighted how we have folded the concept of the "diseased other," the tainted foreigner, into our practice: the colonial encounter continues to shape how we work in medicine today. In this time of reckoning with reconciliation, just as in law and art, education and botany, religion and gender studies, so too, in Canadian medicine, we must trouble the stories we have been told. And the story of syphilis, that great pox, is that original sin, the one that may have begun it all.

In 2008, researchers announced finding a strong candidate for the missing link between treponemes in the Americas and syphilis. Yaws had not been reported in the Western hemisphere for decades. But when a doctor found unusual treponemal-like lesions in children in Guyana in isolated communities, uncertain what else to do, he treated it as yaws. Genetic samples from two children showed that it was a form of treponemal infection very close to syphilis. It is impossible to make this determination on the sample of two alone, but one tentative hypothesis is that this particular syphilitic syndrome might be a branch of the treponemal family tree bridging yaws to syphilis.[128] This link would fall in line with current archaeological arguments that treponemal disease did exist in the Americas prior to European settlement or African displacement — just as it did elsewhere — but there is no incontrovertible proof that there was a specifically sexual syndrome that emerged in the Western hemisphere first.[129] We could speculate that in a warm, moist environment, the variant might have simply spread from skin-to-skin contact, but when Europeans arrived in the central region of the Americas, the variant would have jumped to adapt to the warm, moist environments in the human body to allow for transmission in Europe's cold climate, where the strain had enormous success in a population with limited immunity. This transition may not have happened with documented earlier contact between Americans and Europeans — for instance, Inuit and Beothuk interactions with Vikings — because of the apparent predisposition of the spectrum of treponemal syndromes such as bejel and yaws for warm climates.

But additionally, perhaps there was something unique about the intensity and violence of contact at the time of Columbus that would spawn deceptive, distorting diseases. If this hypothesis does hold true, then in this way, it is not the Americas that gave the world syphilis but the very basis of colonial contact that did. The ecological jolt of colonialism allowed the transport from the Caribbean to the Mediterranean of an otherwise unremarkable everyday treponematosis that mutated and exploded with a vengeance across the world. That understanding of it may shape the way we approach the story we tell about it, may revise our thinking of the history of sex and sexuality and how we care for people today. What actually occurred in the evolution of syphilis is secondary to the way it has been perceived and interpreted — because social meaning is what determines all that follows. But in contrast to several centuries of

vociferous scholarly arguments, contemporary writers are beginning to focus on treponemal infections on their own terms and
trajectories, as they should be, "rather than focusing solely on the
perennial question of who is to blame for the purported surge in
sexually-acquired syphilis in 16th-century Europe."[130] The choice
of words "purported surge" throws into ambiguity what was recorded at the time. Phenomena that are less understood might be
more feared and thus recorded much more dramatically than actually experienced. Was there really an outbreak of a new disease, or
did the wave of an infection that had already existed simply crest?
And was that surge an actual blip in the data, or were people just
paying more attention? Was the disease itself new, or was people's
understanding of it new? Had it been introduced, or was it an old
disease that had suddenly found a foothold in increasingly crowd-
ed cities where options for sexual interaction were more available?
Or that, in the new environment, one small slip in the bacteria's
genetic material allowed for spread, no longer limited by needing skin-to-skin contact, which may not have been possible in the
chilly cities of Europe among adults, instead relying on something
that most adults could be counted on doing at some point in their
lives as a means of transmission instead?

In all probability, like many pathogens that have coexisted with
humans from time immemorial, treponemes adapt to changes in
our interactions in ways that benefit their survival. Often the shift
is gradual, but a species may take advantage of a radically new
environment to make an abrupt leap. Waves of different types of
syphilitic syndromes — although we remain uncertain about the
exact microbiological cause, whether distinct species or closely
related variants — appear to have occurred with some regularity through history in specific ecological contexts. Sometimes they
arrive, then fade, like sibbens and *la maladie de Baie-Saint-Paul*.
Sometimes they stay with us for a long time. Perhaps no simple explanation exists why syphilis appeared at the time it did in Europe,
other than that the transforming circumstances of the region either
enabled its spread or enabled focused attention on it. And as those
who hail from places colonized by Europe have always known,
perhaps Europe's incessant questioning about its rise is more revealing than the answer itself.

Smallpox

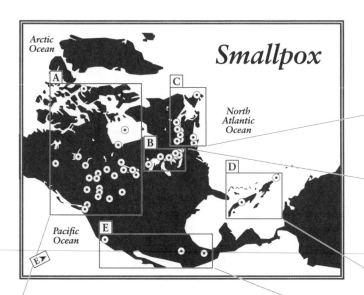

Smallpox

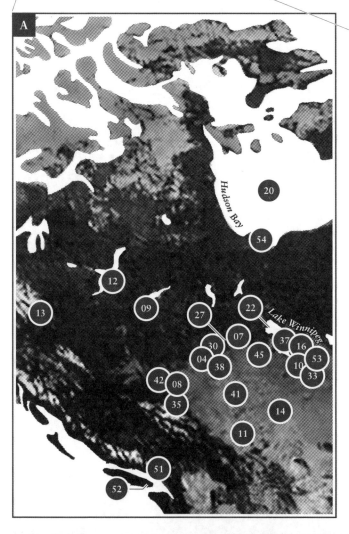

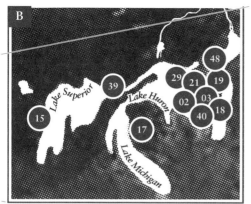

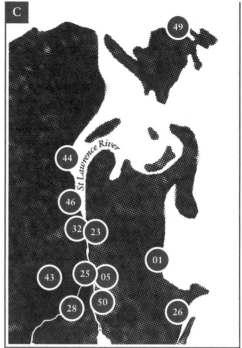

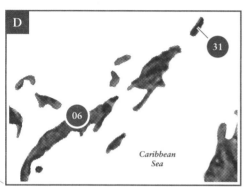

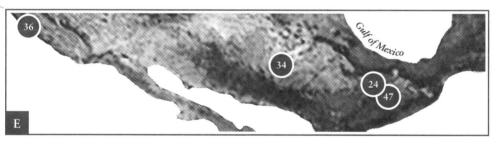

Locations

01 Boston	15 Fort William (Thunder Bay)	29 Palmerston	42 St Albert (Alberta)
02 Brantford	16 Gimli	30 Prince Albert	43 St Francis (Quebec)
03 Caledonia	17 Great Lakes	31 Puerto Rico	44 St Lawrence River
04 Carlton House	18 Hagersville	32 Quebec City	45 Swan River
05 Chambly	19 Hamilton	33 Red River Settlement (Winnipeg)	46 Tadoussac
06 Cuba	20 Hudson Bay	34 Rio Grande	47 Tenochtitlan
07 Cumberland House	21 Kitchener-Waterloo	35 Rocky Mountain House	48 Toronto
08 Edmonton	22 Lake Winnipeg	36 San Francisco	49 Trinity (Newfoundland)
09 Fort Chipewyan	23 Lévis	37 Sandy Bar (Manitoba)	50 Trout River (Quebec)
10 Fort Garry (Winnipeg)	24 Mexico City	38 Saskatoon	51 Vancouver
11 Fort McKenzie (Montana)	25 Montreal	39 Sault Ste Marie	52 Victoria
12 Fort Resolution	26 New London	40 Six Nations	53 Winnipeg
13 Fort Simpson	27 North Saskatchewan River	41 South Saskatchewan River	54 York Factory
14 Fort Union (North Dakota)	28 Ottawa		

3

Smallpox

In 1799, the British defeated Tipu Sultan, the ruler of the Kingdom of Mysore in what is now South India. It was a battle that effectively sealed their domination over the subcontinent. That same year in England, doctors learned of the possibility of vaccination against smallpox, and the first dose was delivered to India in 1802. A rapid dissemination for its time, the alacrity with which this technology arrived was without a doubt an attempt to consolidate empire by demonstrating the glories of British rule. Evidently, it was also met with considerable popular resistance for a plethora of reasons in India, where elaborate rituals already surrounded the management of a disease that had been known since time immemorial.[1] It is possible that the Wadiyars, the once-sidelined royal family that the British reinstated in the new protectorate of Mysore as a puppet government, were among those recruited to receive the injection as a demonstration of the benefits of vaccination — and of British magnanimity.[2] But even with a compulsory vaccination law passed by British authorities in 1892, by some estimates only 80 percent of Indian districts were covered by 1938, and even then, perhaps only on paper.[3]

That coverage has peculiar, poignant resonance in my life. In 1934 or 1935, my great-grandfather worked for the Indian railway system and was stationed in Lucknow, about a thousand kilometres from our home in a village five miles north of the city limits of Calcutta, once the second city of the empire after London. Away from his family for long stretches, he travelled for his work with an attendant in his own small carriage attached to trains plying the busy tracks between Calcutta and the more recent capital Delhi, on which Lucknow — once a royal city itself — lay. He arrived home at one point that year and asked for the municipality to send its vaccinators, instructing them to immunize everyone in

80

the family against smallpox, including my seven-year-old paternal grandmother. When my great-grandmother turned to him and asked, "But what about you?" he smiled softly, shook his head, and made preparations to return to Lucknow. Halfway there, he developed a high fever. His attendant quickly turned the carriage around to find a train back, but by the time they arrived, it was clear that my great-grandfather had smallpox. For fear of contagion, the attendant fled, leaving my ailing ancestor, swollen and delirious, on the station platform in our village. A neighbour saw him there and had to coax a reluctant taxi driver to take him home. My great-grandfather died two days later, forever changing the course of my family's history in ways perhaps fit for another book. None of the rest of the household, now vaccinated, contracted the disease.

Our loss was not unique, of course. Before its eradication, the ravages of smallpox had been known worldwide for centuries. Accounts conflict regarding where it first emerged, the beginnings of the disease lost to the details of early human history. The first characteristic descriptions of it may have appeared in western China about 1500 years before the English were using the vaccine for geopolitical gain.[4] Archaeologists dispute whether an Egyptian pharaoh may have died of the disease in a localized outbreak even 1500 years earlier.[5] As syphilis has shown us, there are perils in identifying diseases in hindsight. Medical historians seem to agree that it was probably unknown to ancient Greeks, despite their expansionism, and Roman references to epidemics may have been smallpox, though definitive diagnostic details are lacking.[6] The disease ostensibly did not reach Europe until much later, after the Arab conquest of Spain, or perhaps the Crusades, its arrival perceived as a contamination from the Orient.[7]

Smallpox emerged from a family of viruses that cause fluid-filled eruptions of the skin in a variety of mammals. A relatively large virus, its origins remain unclear though one common theory is that it leapt to humans from a rodent around the time of agricultural settlements. Once this leap was made, the virus evolved to fit comfortably into its niche, and only humans suffered from smallpox, which is what made its eradication from the planet possible, as there was no hidden reservoir of the virus from which it could come back to haunt us. Monkeypox, in the same family, continues to circulate in the wild to this day, particularly in regions of the African continent, and can infect humans, with a prolonged outbreak in Nigeria starting in 2017.[8] Though milder, one strain can cause death in up to 10 percent of patients, particularly because few are vaccinated against smallpox anymore, which can provide some cross-immunity.[9] Cowpox (otherwise known as vaccinia), in the same cluster of viruses, is a relatively rare infection in bovines, though cats seem to get it too. It causes mild illness in humans, which became historically significant as we see later on. Chickenpox, confusingly, though its features may resemble mild smallpox, comes from a completely different virus family and is actually not known to infect chickens: the reference is believed to come from its general propensity to be a common illness of childhood. It was sometimes difficult for this illness to be differentiated conclusively from smallpox until modern virological techniques emerged.[10]

Smallpox, however, could be lethal and is one of the most contagious viruses known to humans thus far. The major variant could kill up to half of unvaccinated people it infected. Spread primarily through respiratory droplets, its dramatic course struck fear into the heart of many communities; it was marked by a high fever before its telltale lesions erupted in spectacular fashion first in the mouth and throat and then on the skin, sometimes growing together into one vast bubbling horror. Some people succumbed to a haemorrhagic version of the illness, with uncontrolled bleeding setting in. If they survived, many bore scars of the illness throughout their lives, though infection conferred lifelong immunity. The violence of the illness rendered most people incapable of doing much, thereby minimizing social contact during the symptomatic, transmissible phase, and thus could have contributed to limited spread despite the ease of its contagion. One estimate suggests that even among the unvaccinated, just two-thirds of household contacts would become ill. The rate would drop to 4 percent once vaccination became widespread — and would explain why my great-grandfather's illness had no impact on the rest of his family.[11] In the virus's favour, however, was the prolonged incubation period of around two weeks, so that people could be unaware of their infection for quite some time before falling ill, triggering a new cluster of cases after an apparent quiescent period.

It is unclear when smallpox became recognized as a distinct clinical entity in Europe as the symptoms and prognoses of many diseases overlapped. Given there were few interventions that could have helped anyway at the time, telling illnesses apart did not always serve any real medical purpose. There have been suggestions that health records did not separate out smallpox from measles in London until 1652.[12] This conflation shows how difficult it is to trace the history of illness — not only do diseases themselves evolve over time but so do the medical paradigms that identify a syndrome as a distinct diagnosis. London's death records in the seventeenth century name conditions such as "flox," "flux," and "bloody flux," whose corresponding contemporary diagnoses are a matter of debate.[13] Nonetheless, Queen Elizabeth I was one case of smallpox to be documented in Britain in 1562, and she was notoriously scarred for life by a mild case of the illness. Certainly, when smallpox struck the Nahua people in 1521 and 1527 with the arrival of the Spanish conquistadors in Mexico, observers from both Europe and the Americas identified the disease with some consistency, suggesting familiarity with the condition despite the possibility of multiple simultaneous new epidemics with similar trajectories clouding the diagnoses.[14]

One possible confounding factor in charting the course of small-pox in the Americas is the mutation of the virus itself. Historical accounts suggest that infection resurged in Europe with unusual virulence in the 1600s.[15] The changing landscape of human relationship to the environment as expansionist capitalism extended its grip out of Europe could explain the emergence of new mutations in infective agents — an idea of some importance in many other diseases, ranging from coronaviruses to treponemes. By the time it was eradicated, smallpox was recognized to have two strains in circulation: a devastating major one and a milder minor one. A more recent genetic study suggests that these smallpox variants that dominated in the 1970s all came from one common ancestor in the 1700s, other lineages having faded into extinction.[16]

Regardless of its origins, smallpox was one of the most transmissible agents to infect humans, with each case infecting four to six nonimmune others if no preventative measures were taken, although there was no asymptomatic contagion. This feature also made its eradication possible since infectious people were very obviously ill and could be isolated. It spread throughout Eurasia and Africa, following patterns of migration and trade. It remained unknown in the Americas until settlement by Europeans. At some point, it is presumed to have traversed Southeast Asia, but there is no clear evidence of its presence in Australia until the eighteenth century, with the Sydney outbreak of 1789. Cities were crucial for the disease to become endemic — that is, constantly circulating at a low rate, with intermittent major outbreaks. Because smallpox infection conferred lifelong protection, urban settlements provided a rotating pool of uninfected children and new migrants to keep the disease in an endless chain of transmission among the nonimmune. In small communities, outbreaks only happened once a generation or so, after enough previously unexposed people were born to fuel an epidemic. This feature would become crucial in the disease's history in North America, as it was in isolated parts of Europe where people's exposure to the virus would wane, such as on the Scottish island of Foula in 1720, when 90 percent of the people died in an outbreak.[17] More robust immunity to smallpox from previous exposure is sometimes cited as one of the reasons why Europeans opted to enslave Africans, especially in the Caribbean, over Indigenous peoples.[18]

The lack of consistent contact with the disease, either because of widespread immunity or because of isolation from outbreaks, may have made it difficult for some communities to gather medical knowledge in how to respond to the illness. I myself am often flummoxed now when trying to identify measles or chickenpox, no longer certain despite countless pictures in textbooks, because I rarely see them in daily practice. But in general, well before its arrival in North America, smallpox was a disease whose ravages in some form or another were well known for at least a millennium, especially in societies with a high degree of urbanization. Steeped in medical lore, elaborate clinical rituals developed in these contexts to manage its consequences. One of the most important of these practices was variolation, which likely emerged in China but was practised across the Indian subcontinent, Arabia, and into Africa. Although smallpox usually spread through respiratory droplets, it could also be contracted through contact of a moist, wet body surface with the scab or fluid from the pox lesions. Variolation took advantage of this route of transmission, which often led to more localized symptoms than the systemic illness habitual through respiratory infection. The most common method was to introduce some infected material into a small nick in the skin, this less serious encounter nonetheless immunizing the person against future, more serious systemic infection. In parts of India, this process was done under the auspices of the goddess Sitala, the deity of smallpox, whose demands had to be appeased to fend off the disease and whose worship was an inherent part of variolation.[19] The rituals surrounding it may now seem esoteric, but they included practical considerations: for instance, the patient was placed under strict isolation. Given that active viral matter was used in the inoculation, practitioners of "folk" medicine knew that isolation was fundamental to prevent setting off a chain of transmission.

Three doors down from my great-grandmother's home is a temple to Sitala, whose divine blessings my parents had to seek as part of their marriage rites in 1973. Smallpox was still an active consideration in those times. Eight years prior, the famous Bollywood actor Geeta Bali died of the disease in her mid-thirties while shooting a film in a rural area in the north of India. A year after my parents' marriage, 15,000 people, mainly residing in the eastern part of the country, died of smallpox in one of the worst epidemics of the twentieth century, forcing the federal government to launch a concerted program to eliminate it.

The last smallpox case identified in India may have been in 1975, but Sitala still exists, as does the shrine my parents visited during their wedding. On a trip to India in late 2019, when calling on an aunt, I ran down the street to peer into the temple, tended to by a local family. The gate was closed, and even though my aunt encouraged me to enter the low building whose insides were dark even in the bright light of day, I hesitated, somehow embarrassed and not entirely sure what I wanted — of the family or of the goddess. Smallpox had been eradicated from the planet when I was less than a month old. What did it mean for us in the twenty-first century for this member of the pantheon to still be here, this goddess now of generic epidemics and fevers? I turned away from the shrine, deciding, perhaps out of naiveté, that I had nothing left to ask.

In 1773, ten years after the Treaty of Paris surrendered Quebec to the British, Dr R Huntley in Montreal wrote to a friend, complaining of his own ill health, but noting with satisfaction that three patients of his with smallpox had recovered in Quebec City.[20] Even the firm grip of imperial rule did not protect settlers in eastern North America from smallpox. But its course among colonists serves as a counterpoint to the experience of smallpox in Indigenous communities: political power and social structure could alter epidemics the same virus launched.

Over a century later, in 1890, a publisher in Montreal printed a book by Mrs Daniel MacPherson on how to care for people struck by smallpox, in which she tells the story how her son was infected in Quebec City. He had been out on the Esplanade, the fields right on the walls of the old town in front of the provincial legislature, when he noticed a young girl in a neighbouring group who was covered in smallpox. He left quickly, but inevitably fell ill along with his brother. As they lived across the St Lawrence in Lévis, MacPherson struggled to find a way to get to the hospital in Quebec City without spreading infection to others. The Lévis doctor suggested the risks of transfer were too great and so taught her how to treat smallpox at home without leaving any scars, apparently her most pressing concern.[21]

MacPherson was obviously someone of means — an anglophone living in nineteenth-century Quebec with enough contacts to publish her experiments in nursing, which no doubt were not all that original. As might be expected of those descended from the English conquerors of the colony, she states without pretension that she lived in a "very large double-house." She had hired help to do the washing for her too. Clearly, MacPherson was not too badly off, and neither of her children bore "the slightest mark of ever having had the disease."[22] But her story demonstrates how smallpox ran rampant through settler North America. Montreal was badly hit in 1885, and MacPherson's sons were caught in its wake.

Even before germ theory was formally confirmed, the settler colonies in North America had developed mechanisms to manage infectious disease outbreaks. Quarantine was used in colonial North America for a long time: the Spanish instituted it for ships early in their conquests and eventually developed an infrastructure to prevent disease from reaching Mexico City. The French imposed quarantine to prevent the spread of plague from Marseilles to Quebec in 1721–1724 and against smallpox from British North America in 1731 — although the disease infiltrated into New France anyway.[23] In the 1840s, Nova Scotia became so taxed by the costs of shipwrecked sailors, smallpox, and otherwise sick migrants that the legislature passed a law requiring boards of health to send vouchers of costs incurred for managing illness on sailing vessels before any payment would be made from the coffers of the colony.[24] Despite such measures, by the nineteenth century, smallpox was as endemic in North American cities as it was in Europe.

In 1855, as scientists in England began to grapple with the possibility that cholera might be an infectious disease, Dr George Gibb insisted that disturbing burial grounds was a source of contagion of both cholera and smallpox, stating from his experience that municipal works in the odd topography of Quebec City near the famous Cimetière des picotés was the cause of the smallpox outbreak in late 1854.[25] There are references to the fact that Indigenous people who died in the first outbreaks of smallpox around 1650 were buried in the vicinity, but the "smallpox cemetery" right by the Hôtel-Dieu hospital was officially inaugurated in 1702 after an influenza outbreak in 1700–1701 almost filled the three other cemeteries in Quebec City. Immediately thereafter, in 1702–1703, approximately three hundred people died in a smallpox outbreak, thereby giving the new cemetery its nickname. Epidemics of cholera, diphtheria, and typhoid fever all contributed to the graveyard as it grew in the close press of the city, a high wall cutting the buried off from their living neighbours. Gibb was not impressed with the lack of administrative concern for this history by the public works department 150 years later. Nonetheless in 1855, a law was passed regulating interments in accordance with public health. The cemetery was closed in 1857, all bodies exhumed and transferred by 1861, with contemporary downtown bustling over it. Today, some of Quebec City's most expensive condominiums rise over the grounds in the narrow streets around Hôtel-Dieu, with little to mark their historical significance. Gibb's theory of spread from the dead did not find traction. No evidence suggests smallpox survives in buried remains, though ominous (but as yet unfounded) references to infested bodies thawing in the permafrost are made to this day as we confront climate change.[26]

The potential threat from the dead aside, the very real struggle against smallpox among the living continued. In 1875, Henri Julien, Montreal's famed satirical cartoonist, drew a caustic image of the city's "night mayor" — the grim reaper, trawling through the city surrounded by clouds of smallpox, cholera and what is presumably malaria (endemic in the region until around 1900).[27] In 1885, within twenty years of Confederation, the worst outbreak of smallpox in settler Canada gripped Montreal, killing 3000 people — almost 2 percent of the city's population — disproportionately francophone Catholics, especially children, relegated as they were to the poorest quarters of the city since the British conquest a century prior. That year, Robert Harris painted a sketch published in *Harper's Weekly* in New York of Montrealers resisting police as they quarantined children affected by smallpox — men trying to hit officers with sticks as the police lifted young ones into a van, women calling from behind constables cordoning them away.[28] These images exemplify scenes where the state intervenes in family life, separating children from their parents, highlighting the troubling question of public health as a coercive arm of the expanding state. We might assume that Mrs MacPherson would not have had to confront the brute force of government-sanctioned kidnap, protected by the socioeconomic status that many anglophones in Quebec inherited and from which they benefited.

The general assumption in English Montreal was that dirt was the disparity: the Québécois were considered to be unaware of hygiene. In reality, access to vaccination determined death rates, compounded by cramped living conditions. Linguistic resentments in nineteenth-century Montreal were in essence translated class tensions. Considered a disposable workforce to British colonial capital, many francophone Quebecers, living in deep poverty, eyed public health with suspicion. When factory owners (anglophone, almost assuredly) demanded compulsory vaccination, many francophone workers resisted, associating it with British medicine. On principle, they also balked at an employer demanding an intervention on their bodies in order to exploit their labour more securely. This 1885 smallpox outbreak also coincided with the year of Louis Riel's trial and execution — which soured most Quebecers, sympathetic to the North-West Resistance against the federal government, on any pronouncements from (English) authorities. Thus, repercussions from events completely unrelated to the outbreak influenced its course.[29]

Even versions of the story on the start of the outbreak are tainted by French–English frictions. The first patient arrived in Montreal on a train from Chicago, an employee of the railway company, falling ill as he travelled. Formally diagnosed with the disease at the English Montreal General Hospital, he was refused admission on policy to limit contagion. The doctor nonetheless provided him a referral letter to the French Hôtel-Dieu, where the critical information of the diagnosis seemed to be lost in transfer. The nuns there, aware that he had no place to go since rejected from his "home" hospital, admitted him on the basis of the referral, without isolation. The mildness of his symptoms confused further diagnosis, but even if it had been clear, Montreal's smallpox isolation hospital had been closed for four years for want of cases.[30] Though "patient zero" recovered, a laundry worker caught smallpox from washing his sheets and died in April but not before infecting her sister. As the outbreak grew within the hospital, the institution rapidly discharged asymptomatic patients into the community. But with smallpox's long quiescent incubation period, this move launched the epidemic that raged for over six months. As late as 1991, an anglophone writer notes with shock that the doctors at a "Roman Catholic hospital" admitted the first case to the institution knowing how infectious the disease was, offering only that hospital doctors there should have somehow quarantined him back on the train.[31]

Canada's then-largest city became known worldwide that year as plague-infested, to be avoided at all costs. Sir Francis Hincks, who had been prime minister in the 1850s of the united Province of Canada prior to Confederation, before going on to other colonial posts in Barbados and Guyana, died in Montreal in the outbreak and was hastily buried.[32] Statistics show that the death rates from smallpox in one week in September 1885 among francophone Montrealers was ten times the rate for the English, with lack of vaccine access the main determinant of death. But there was some evidence that affluent, educated francophones were more likely to have vaccinated children than poorer ones. Just a few streets over from wealthy francophones on tony St Denis and St Hubert Streets, with no smallpox deaths for six weeks studied in 1885, Wolfe and Montcalm Streets — though gentrified in contemporary Montreal, very poor then — each saw more than sixty smallpox fatalities in that same period. There was also a passing recognition that people who were racialized were "peculiarly susceptible to the contagion of smallpox, and the mortality ... much greater than among whites."[33] We could speculate what explanations were provided for this observation back then and what might have actually been the causes of the discrepancy. Complicating the story was that public health officials in the city had earlier cancelled vaccinations for three months after a bad batch allegedly made people ill, fuelling scepticism.[34] On September 28 of that year, as the city's board of health moved to make smallpox vaccination compulsory, crowds of angry people, largely francophone, ransacked the board's East End office, shouting anti-English slogans, in what became known worldwide as the Montreal vaccine riot of 1885.[35]

This view of settler outbreaks of smallpox provides two telling themes that have relevance when understanding how Indigenous communities confronted outbreaks of what was to them an entirely novel infectious agent. First, explanations of the disease's impact based on biology alone — who had immunity and who had not — are not sufficient to understand how epidemics unfolded since who has access to immunity was profoundly shaped by sociopolitical contexts. Second, public health as an extending arm of the state is an important factor in how people react to health interventions in everyday life, shaped by predetermined relationships with authority.

Smallpox continued to circulate in Canada until 1946 before it was considered eliminated. Saskatchewan had 598 cases in 1913 and 961 cases in 1921, with death rates of about 1 percent. Ottawa had 1352 cases in 1920–1921, with two deaths. The worst outbreak in the twentieth century in Canada was in Windsor in 1924, where sixty-seven cases were reported. The thirty-two deaths occurred among the forty-five patients who were unvaccinated, suggesting a case fatality ratio of 70 percent in the nonimmune well into the 1900s. In 1927, the year my grandmother was born oceans away to the household of my railway employee great-grandfather, Canada reported 3300 cases, which was the highest for the country in the twentieth century. Numbers thereafter began a gradual decline, with the last death from smallpox in Canada occurring in 1938, about three years after my great-grandfather's in India. Nova Scotia had a suspected case in 1949 with a visitor from the United States, but a rigid quarantine did not let it spread if it indeed was smallpox. The last reported case in Canada was in 1962, when the teenage son of Canadian missionary came back from Brazil symptomatic from a mild case. As he had travelled by train through the eastern United States, both the US and Canada undertook mass vaccination campaigns to prevent spread.[36] Within a few years, the Ontario-based Connaught Laboratories would become the reference centre for smallpox vaccines in the World Health Organization's program for eradication in the Americas. Of note, Ali Maow Maalin, the last person to contract smallpox naturally in the world, in 1977 in Somalia — with a mild, nonlethal variant — died of that other infectious killer, malaria, thirty-six years later.[37]

The first recorded outbreak of smallpox in the Americas occurred in 1507 in the Caribbean, ferried to the continent with the stream of arrivals from Spain in the years following the voyages of Columbus. Although other diseases no doubt played a role, the known high transmissibility of smallpox makes it a likely candidate for decimating populations in Hispaniola, Puerto Rico, and Cuba, dropping the census by about a third by 1519 according to missionary reports. Smallpox was identified as the contributor to the 1521 collapse of Tenochtitlan, the Aztec capital, and then spread south across the burgeoning Spanish empire, taking advantage of the teeming, flourishing urban life in Mesoamerica.[38] Although enslavement and transport of Indigenous peoples worsened the spread, unwitting messengers and traders between Indigenous communities that had not had direct contact with Europeans also propagated smallpox onwards, its silent (but non-infectious) incubation period of around ten days allowing forward movement of the epidemic to continue unabated. Smallpox eventually arrived in the Rio de la Plata region in contemporary Argentina before spreading northwest into Inca territory by 1524, killing that empire's leadership.[39]

Smallpox's characteristic lesions, with its sometimes-aggressive clinical course, was striking as a disease, but concurrent epidemics often made sorting out what disease caused which death difficult. In the Nahuatl language, dominant in the Aztec Empire, *totomonalliztli* was translated to make reference to pustules, but the Nahuatl words *cocoliztli* and *huey zahuatl* were also used to describe great plagues, with the latter possibly indicating ulcers.[40] But the apparent haemorrhagic complications that the former caused, although possible in smallpox, suggest that concurrent outbreaks involving another infectious agent might have been occurring. Potential culprits could be either an untraced viral haemorrhagic fever akin to Ebola or a simpler bacterial infection that could become critical in poor living conditions engendered by a possible drought and the forced relocations, with disrupted subsistence patterns imposed by Spanish conquest.[41]

It is unclear whether smallpox also travelled north beyond what would become known as the Rio Grande from this first Spanish incursion, as we know happened in later outbreaks of the disease. From the vantage point of history recorded by settlers, the first confirmed outbreaks of smallpox among Indigenous communities in what is currently known as Canada are presumed to have happened around Tadoussac in 1616 as the French settled in the region.[42] But the disappearance of both Stadacona and Hochelaga — the Iroquoian villages Jacques Cartier encountered in 1534–1535, which became the sites of Quebec City and Montreal respectively — has been attributed to many possible factors: the cycle of agricultural land exhaustion for seminomadic peoples, warfare with neighbouring nations, or the spread of epidemic diseases, which started to have an impact once the Europeans arrived, particularly in Stadacona.[43] There, popular accounts note how the Iroquoian community assisted Jacques Cartier and his crew to overcome scurvy, which was devastating the Europeans, by making a brew of pine bark but reportedly began to succumb themselves to another disease not entirely recognizable in accounts. Given the range of other infectious disease produced by contact, ascertaining diagnosis is a challenge, although smallpox seems a likely offender.

Smallpox appeared farther south on North America's east coast as the English arrived. In Massachusetts, the link between colonization and smallpox was famously made explicit by Governor John Winthrop in 1634: "For the natives, they are all near dead of the smallpox, so the Lord hath cleared our title to what we possess" — the relative immunity of settlers fuelling the doctrine of divine providence facilitating a right to land. The belief that otherworldly will slayed Indigenous people, convenient for English settlers, persisted in repetition over decades, for instance in 1677 by Increase Mather and in 1705 by a missionary named Moor (although the latter concedes that Providence's hand may have been aided by "some new Distempers we have brought among them.")[44] On occasion, colonists used smallpox outbreaks as tools to further destroy Indigenous towns, such as the 1637 raid on the Pequot, who were vastly weakened by an outbreak around what would then become New London, Connecticut.[45]

These examples of direct exploitation of disease capture the imagination in the retelling of colonization but are perhaps more the exception in the historical record than the rule — and to me, underline how much more sinister colonial power actually is in extending control. Some have argued that by the time the English arrived, the introduction of disease by the Portuguese, Spanish, and French to the American landmass meant populations were already

struggling with epidemics, rendering physical resistance to settlement impossible. However, this version of the past seems unduly
simplistic in understanding both epidemiology and history and
perhaps dampens the reality of the way English colonization proceeded. To suggest that all the complex societies scattered across
the vast geographical diversity of the Americas faced equal impact
from disease over the course of some decades is untenable and also
erases the way Indigenous nations may have responded and adapted in varying fashions.[46] Waves of disease are well-documented to
have broken out in nations scattered across lands stolen by English
colonists at different points over the decades, with no single uni-
form context.[47]

The epidemic rolled from the coast towards the Great Lakes,
with a particularly bad outbreak in that region from 1634 to 1636.
Some evidence points to the assistance early European settlers
provided to Indigenous people afflicted by smallpox, expressing
wonder that they themselves were not affected. But as colonial arrogance grew, the tables did slowly turn, such as in a 1662 municipal ordinance in East Hampton, Long Island, which forbade
the appearance of any Indigenous person in the street of the town
until free from smallpox for fear of a fine or a whipping, with the
same punishment meted to any "English or Indian servant (who)
shall go to their wigwams."[48] French missionaries were more likely
than the English settlers and the Dutch traders who carried the
disease inwards towards the Great Lakes to make an effort to care
for those who were stricken by smallpox — likely out of religious
conviction, which came with its own particular currency.

Jesuit missionaries were particularly active in Huron-Wendat communities struggling with the outbreak, with one missionary noting
that were it not for the deaths from the epidemic, including almost
five hundred children in one mission in 1640, there would have
been few other baptised souls to "harvest."[49] Under pressure in
France from competing ideologies, the Jesuits used their mission in
New France as a way to score points at home.[50] In a classic case of
shifting the goalposts, the missionaries note that having been unable to recruit bodies for the church here on earth (church militant),

they were nonetheless pleased that, with "diseases as labourers," they were able to recruit souls for the church in heaven (church triumphant) through rapid deathbed baptisms.[51] Incredibly, 250 years later, 2500 kilometres away in Alberta, missionaries were using the same arguments when they watched over the tuberculosis death of a hastily baptised child at their residential school, their "Christian deathbed … a source of much pleasure."[52]

Relations between Indigenous communities and the missionaries were clearly strained, the French friars affronted by the observation that even converts would sometimes seek the assistance of traditional healers. Indigenous people thought only of life in the now rather than the hereafter, the religious Europeans lamented, with "no other God than the belly."[53] The insinuation by one of their Huron friends that people may have converted for access to tobacco disappointed them profoundly.[54] The preferred theory for missionaries was that Huron travels to Quebec, where they carelessly mixed with Algonquians, brought smallpox to the communities, and missionary reports were self-righteously outraged that the Huron dared to accuse them of being the conduits of disease, even beginning to shut their doors to them. With no theory of contagion, one missionary observed that the more they were welcomed into communities, the more disease there seemed to be. In the joyous oblivion of ideologues, he attributed the resulting more souls to harvest to the mysterious practices of divine will.[55] The connection the Huron formulated between colonial interlopers and disease may not have been universal among Indigenous peoples: in the south, the Cherokee for instance may have viewed their relationships with Europeans as distinct from the relationships with the spirit world that unleashed disease upon them. Yet early on, the Cherokee seem to have adapted to outbreaks by instituting measures of isolation and even incorporated a smallpox spirit into their cosmology to account for the disease.[56] In the accounts of the missionaries, the Huron-Wendat, despite making the link between smallpox and the French, did not adopt quarantine as an intervention for control.[57]

I am surprised, when first reading the volume of their correspondence, to feel a twinge of sympathy for the Jesuit missionaries and their evident hurt at the rejection they confronted in the face of disease. Queer immigrant that I am, I suspect I am highly sensitive to the age-old association of the outsider as the bearer of disease, and this emotional resonance I feel with colonists troubles me. The contexts of course are very different — I carry scars the Jesuits did not have. As colonial states became established in North America, their history has been marked by repeated scapegoating of migration, especially racialized migration, as a public health threat.[58] Canada has been no different than the United States.[59] It may have all started when the Spanish, as they settled in the Americas, offloaded responsibility for smallpox by pinpointing one particular enslaved person as bringing the disease from Cuba to the Mexican mainland, not wanting to be seen as instigators of illness themselves. Additionally, the HIV epidemic made it clear that the borders people transgress need not be physically marked in order to be painted by the brush of peril.[60] Cementing a narrative is certainly politically useful, whether it be centred on pox-ridden Africans, promiscuous gay flight attendants, or covert Chinese warfare. So the closing of doors in people's faces because of a fear of illness makes me uneasy, both as a person and a professional in the work of care, despite the fact that I feel no sympathy for the role the missionaries played in stealing land and in destroying livelihoods. How do I navigate this tension?

Part of this discomfiture comes from the glib connection many of us that study the history of medicine make with the introduction of new infectious diseases to the Americas. When the Europeans arrived, we say, with a dismissive wave of the hand. But arrival in and of itself is not the original sin. Infectious diseases circulate all the time: humans trade, migrate, mate beyond and across all sorts of borders, and have done so even since times deemed prehistorical. Living in fellowship with us, infectious organisms thrive on our inherent sociability and curiosity. But biological determinants alone do not shape the course of an epidemic. The sociopolitical context within which it is experienced and the response to it influence outcomes too, a fact to which even the Jesuit missionaries alluded: in 1650, as more than a decade of disease roiled on, famine struck the Huron-Wendat, due to poor weather and warfare with the Iroquois. The missionaries noted that it was those who had no protection against famine who succumbed most to the disease.[61]

So even then, the Jesuits understood that social context mattered in the experience of disease on a relatively microcosmic scale. But they did not engage explicitly, at least publicly in their writings, on how it might have appeared at a macrocosmic level. The missionaries did not address how the wars that added to the stressors upon the Huron-Wendat were an extension of their presence, fuelled by feuding European powers wanting control of the trade along the St Lawrence waterways. As a thought experiment, it seems entirely feasible to contain and treat a smallpox outbreak without inevitably resorting to pillage and plunder. Had I arrived in Canada like a French missionary with a mysterious transmissible illness, I would like to think that I would have managed to refrain from taking over. Smallpox outbreaks shaped the colonization of the Americas, yes, but European agendas determined their course too. The virus itself is an insufficient explanation for all that followed.

The British attempt in 1690 to invade New France was foiled by a smallpox outbreak among the soldiers. When emissaries, still obviously ill, came to their Iroquois allies for assistance, the Iroquois were appalled — for good reason, as about three hundred of them died thereafter and the remainder refused to join the campaign.[62] The outbreak of smallpox from 1755–1757 had huge implications for the way Indigenous history played out during this time of intensifying European rivalries. Smallpox afflicted missions and French forts in the St Lawrence Valley, and a British ship arrived in Philadelphia in 1756 with many soldiers sick. If there were any control measures such as quarantine instituted, there were perhaps inevitable leaks, and predictably, the region became engulfed in disease. As hostilities between the English and French grew, drawing in Indigenous nations in complicated alliances and axes, the smallpox epidemic accelerated. Some nations balked at going to war at military installations where there was known smallpox, and when outbreaks occurred, recriminations and negotiations for compensation sometimes took place. Indigenous nations made strategic decisions on how to engage in diplomacy and in militancy depending on their circumstances, with epidemic disease one of several factors determining their response.[63] Even for communities aware of the need for isolation, the insecurity of the times made the possibility of undertaking it unlikely.

Clear in North American collective memory is General Amherst's postscript to his colonel in 1763 wondering whether to introduce smallpox deliberately among hostile Indigenous nations, the follow-up plan from Colonel Bouquet involving blankets, and the general's seeming assent. Whether such policy was carried out thereafter on orders from these high authorities is unclear, but British soldiers at Pittsburgh had already the month prior given Lenape leaders blankets and a handkerchief from the smallpox hospital, sparking an outbreak. Key correspondence has mysteriously gone missing, but it would seem Amherst was aware of and tacitly approved this attack.[64] Even if not a deliberate strategy used consistently during North America's proxy imperial wars, unwitting infection through fomites was an established concern. A French delegation tried to lure the Cherokee away from their alliance with the British in 1756 by suggesting that the governor of South Carolina's gift of a fine red coat "was not all," the underlying insinuation being that the coat was infected with disease.[65] An Odawa retelling of the 1757 outbreak links the sickness to a tin box sold to them in Montreal, which was opened only to find ever-smaller tin boxes within, the smallest an inch long with "nothing but mouldy particles" inspected closely by several who then fell ill.[66] Empiric understanding of the risk stretched as far back as 1639, without germ theory, when Father Le Jeune in Quebec wrote to Louis XIII in congratulations of his new heir born the year prior. In recording the appreciation of some converted Indigenous people of the French clothes the king had sent in their name, the missionary notes they offered in return a small set of clothes in their fashion to the new prince for his "amusement" to see how children in Quebec might dress, for they would not pretend to be able to give anything of worth when the newborn had so much. But Le Jeune expresses discomfort in sending the gift "as smallpox greatly prevails among our Savages," even though he had had it in his possession from before the outbreak.[67]

For the role Amherst played in suggesting genocide through biological warfare, Indigenous groups worked with the city of Montreal to realize its 2017 commitment to rename the street honouring him east of downtown — just one street west of Wolfe and Montcalm Streets, which recorded the horrific smallpox deaths among Québécois children in the 1885 epidemic. The street officially became rue Atateken in 2019, for the Kanien'kéha word for fraternity, or "our relations," some 256 years after the general's correspondence. Even without a smoking gun of confirmed colonial orders to use smallpox as a weapon, the concurrent threats of war, disrupted livelihoods, and environmental degradation that came with colonization made the added burden of disease, decoupled from care, debilitating. Smallpox played a significant part in changing the balance of economic relationships, forcing Indigenous communities jeopardized by the loss of breadwinners into a dependency on the settler economy.[68] But it seems futile and almost meaningless to attempt to parse out what caused the most harm as the many tentacles of colonization encircled North America.

Smallpox's inexorable spread west from the St Lawrence has been well-documented, forever changing demographics. Garrulous disputes around death tolls from these outbreaks are legion in academia, but a significant chunk of mortality resulted from consequences like starvation, as livelihoods were disrupted when the economically active — with the most direct contact with the outside world — fell sick. Measuring excess deaths is a more appropriate method of understanding the impact of epidemic diseases, as even today not every infection is caught and many die without a diagnosis. Additionally, not every death in an outbreak is necessarily attributable to a confirmed infection but rather could be due to its domino effect.

The horrific epidemic that reached the prairies in 1781–1782 had actually started in Mexico City in 1779, killing 40,000 people there, and then followed the path of the horse trade.[69] It travelled south towards Guatemala, even reaching southern Chile in the 1790s, seemingly enabling the expansion of Spanish control there, but it also travelled north.[70] This first well-documented outbreak in the prairies decimated existing social groups, such as the Pegogamaw Cree, who were living at the confluence of the North and South Saskatchewan Rivers. They were essentially obliterated by the epidemic, with survivors presumably assimilated into neighbouring groups. In a reflection of the nuance in the way different nations experienced the epidemic, this outbreak among the Pegogamaw occurred about thirty years after the first French fur traders arrived from Quebec in 1753. Competition emerged the following year as the Hudson's Bay Company began to send traders, though commercial activity halted briefly in the wake of the conquest of Quebec in 1759. The Company established a permanent trading post in 1774, where furs were exchanged for imported tobacco, alcoholic drinks, and the brass crockery which had largely supplanted local ceramics.[71] Smallpox seems not to have been a major issue during this period. Might the relative halcyon period of thirty years suggest a generation of immunity, perhaps from previous exposure to the disease? There were accounts of smallpox along the Hudson Bay coast in 1720, 1738, and an unidentified epidemic in 1757.[72] But the Pegogamaw much farther inland must have escaped those and perhaps other outbreaks relatively unscathed until the 1781 outbreak decimated them.

The damage done as trading patterns coalesced around Hudson Bay posts in the Plains was extreme. Trade at Cumberland House, a newly founded trading post in the interior in the 1770s, now considered the oldest settler community in Saskatchewan, showed a climb in value until 1780 and then a collapse to almost zero in 1781, the year the smallpox epidemic took hold.[73] Few Indigenous people came to the post — and if they did, it was not to trade. A lack of bison also marked the 1780s epidemic in the Northern Plains. Unusually high variability in cyclical drought conditions in the Plains exacerbated the eroded nutritional status of the people, some of them attributing the diminishing population of wild meat to the cosmological balance of dynamic living systems: as humans died, so too would bison as there was less need for the creatures in the world.[74] The physiological stressor of chronic hunger would no doubt cause case fatality rates from specific diseases to spiral far above what they might have been in a more well-fed population confronting the same illnesses in, say, a European capital. The increased mobility that occurred to search wider for food sources may have also facilitated disease transmission as more groups came into contact with each other, though smallpox generally needed prolonged close contact to spread. Certainly, people congregating around trading posts in search of succour may have also unwittingly sparked onward transmission of the disease.

There were some effective interventions at the outset, though piecemeal. In 1782, Matthew Cocking, in command of the trading post at York Factory, spoke of the death of an entire "tribe" of people in the vicinity, save one child.[75] The fur traders took it upon themselves to look after the people with whom they had established commercial and then personal contact, sheltering, feeding, and providing care for those who were very sick. From the accounts of English traders, settler merchants did demonstrate some thoughtful management of fomites, exhibiting a pragmatic understanding of infectiousness, whether or not they understood germs as a concept. Quarantine was sometimes used in situations we would now consider inappropriate. When ships belonging to traders challenging the monopoly of the Company overwintered in Hudson Bay from 1746 to 1747, leading the sailors to develop scurvy from lack of vitamin C, the Hudson Bay traders forbade the Cree from bringing the competing vessels food, allegedly to protect the Indigenous community from smallpox. The sailors aboard too understood it as protecting the Cree from their "Distemper," which we now know is non-infectious. The Hudson's Bay Company probably simply understood it as smart business practice.[76]

Even farther west, along the Pacific coast, where there was no immediate direct contact with settlers, smallpox did inexorably filter through even the imposing barrier of the Rockies in the 1780s, probably having a particular impact in 1782, about a year later than in the Plains. Many stories around the Strait of Georgia make reference to dreadful, devastating epidemics. One Squamish telling of that time details the loathsome nature of the skin lesions that broke out. A Katzie story referencing the eighteenth century recounts the "wind" bringing smallpox to communities, devastating them — although importantly, they had heard news of its impending arrival beforehand — followed "not many years later" by the arrival of settlers. Vancouver's voyage in the Coast Salish territories in 1791 documented large numbers of deserted villages, probably abandoned for five or so years according to the level of overgrowth and human remains. Arguments that the epidemic actually was later, or a different one, are contradicted by the fact that settler visitors in the 1790s saw people carrying the stigmata of smallpox.[77]

Following this first major epidemic of smallpox in west-central North America, outbreaks grumbled on, fuelled by the increasing militarization of the continent. As the British tried to defeat the Americans in the latter years of the Revolutionary War, the French, unable to make much headway in the Caribbean, tried to attack British interests through Hudson Bay — with some success. The British trading posts were (at least temporarily) abandoned along the coast, the Cree readjusting to life without European trade, although disease remained. There were anecdotal reports of bones being found on the shores due to the high number of deaths as late as 1815.[78]

Smallpox proved to be one of the key events in the later establishment of British Columbia as a colony. In 1862, lax regulations governing incoming ships led to smallpox leaking out into the population from a vessel arriving from San Francisco. It made its way through the northern encampments of Victoria where Indigenous peoples lived, and the colonial government — possibly provoked in large part by fear of contagion — evicted people in the camps and sent them home. Smallpox thus spread across the region, contributing to an 80 percent decline in the Haida population over forty years.[79] Although rumour at the time claimed the colonial government wanted deliberately to infect Indigenous peoples with smallpox for a landgrab, it was dismissed as a hoax, but the end result suggests that it was not an inconvenient side effect. In fact in 2014, the government of British Columbia posthumously pardoned six Tsilhqot'in Chiefs after their hanging for murder in the 1860s for acting in self-defence. Settler traders working for companies in which the colony's attorney general had shares deliberately instigated smallpox outbreaks with the intent to claim the land, killing up to two-thirds of Tsilhqot'in communities. The traders threatened to spread disease further, leading the Chiefs to declare war. There is some suspicion now that the smallpox outbreaks occurred with complicit knowledge at the top level of the colony's government under Governor Douglas, with the trials of the Chiefs of dubious process as well.[80] But the end effect was clear. The myth of the dying race of Indigenous peoples was spurred on by these smallpox epidemics as gold miners and farmers swept in to clear unnegotiated land that became British Columbia.

Farther inland, the politics around the spread of smallpox continued as Canadian power consolidated through Confederation, with the disease beginning to feature as a concern of British military strategy in North America. Irish-born Lieutenant William Butler had been a member of the British 69th Regiment since 1858, which was stationed in Burma and Ghana. One of the regiment's major postings however was Canada in 1870, where it assisted in the defeat of the provisional government of Louis Riel in Fort Garry (Winnipeg). Another of his regiment's victories was the Battle of Trout River in the spring of 1870 in Quebec, against Irish republican raids launched from American territory. The following winter, Butler took a long expedition out to Rocky Mountain House in present-day Alberta as part of a tactical reconnaissance mission trying to understand the weaknesses the British dominion might have in its rivalry with the United States for supremacy on the continent.

The account of this trip is an engaging perspective on this part of the world during that time, although to be read with some scepticism given Butler's position in history. But of note, he took great pains in his report to the lieutenant governor of Manitoba to discuss smallpox, suggesting that the British were aware of the strategic importance of health conditions on geopolitical realities. He described how outbreak-devastated communities had been attacked by Americans hoping to exert territorial control, and he recognized that the policy of "clearing out" Indigenous peoples had become a practice of the settler state — although he does not directly implicate Canada. He reports that at least in Saskatchewan at the time, the general belief was that settler traders from Missouri had deliberately introduced smallpox into the communities of the Blackfoot Confederacy in order to establish control over trade and resources in the region.[81]

In Butler's narrative, the first major wave of smallpox in the Prairies was around 1820, although it is now considered that the second major wave of smallpox in the Prairies after the 1780s started in 1837.[82] The Cree had initially been mostly spared from outbreaks, but 1869 saw the beginning of a terrible spread of the disease in the nation, according to Butler, linked to skirmishes between them and the Blackfoot.[83] Whatever the cause, the disease moved rapidly and with a high mortality rate, although one pocket around Prince Albert, where there had been effective vaccination ahead of time by a missionary, was spared. Although vaccines had also been offered around the Edmonton area, Butler was of the opinion that it was not a very good inoculum, perhaps made ineffective by poor supply chains, and it was distributed when the epidemic was already well-entrenched within the community.[84] Butler called for the expansion of quarantine facilities to prevent the disease from entering into Manitoba as it spread in the North-West, and also said that he feared that unless vaccination were to be made compulsory, the Métis population of the Prairies would be slow to take it on themselves, although he does not elaborate as to why he thinks so.[85] When significant vaccine supplies finally arrived in Winnipeg for distribution among the territories, it was too late for settlements like Carlton House, between Saskatoon and Prince Albert. The board of the Hudson's Bay Company acknowledged in 1871 "with deep regret the fearful mortality" engendered by smallpox on Indigenous peoples, both First Nations and Métis.[86]

This "fearful mortality" that gripped the Prairies through the 1870s was not entirely an accident. A swirling health crisis fed mortality in the Plains as the unstable colonial economy collapsed with the disappearance of bison. Already vulnerable from no exposure for at least a generation, if ever, any immunity in the population floundered in famine. There is evidence that the Canadian government intended for people to die of malnutrition: Sir John A Macdonald, as Conservative prime minister (egged on by the Liberal opposition) was a principal architect in engineering food deprivation for Indigenous peoples to force their dependency on the Crown and consolidate Canadian control.[87] This pacification of the Prairies through deprivation, which included hare-brained schemes of work-for-food and training people on new reserves in agriculture that the Canadian government itself recognized as unworkable, was not particularly novel or surprising.[88] Creating famine is a common theme in colonial politics, used by the British in India and Ireland, since widespread hunger is often not the result of inadequate supply but rather of inequitable distribution of resources.[89] Even when food is relatively scarce, most communities worldwide usually know how to adapt to the occasional lean period. The Canadian government acknowledged that its rations were inadequate in quantity and quality and, when sufficient, created the medical complications that occur with sudden refeeding after starvation.[90] These sometimes fatal consequences are now widely understood, but given imperial familiarity with famine, this reality must have also been known back then. My parents recount that the women even in my great-grandmother's generation in India, with limited access to biomedical science, were aware of the dangers of too quickly feeding someone deprived of food, referring to it in Bengali by the quaint idiom *hité biporeet* — to do the opposite by doing good. In high-resource, modern settings, we are able to monitor these conditions closely, but even when I have worked in settings of acute malnutrition in deprived contexts without access to medical laboratories, we control refeeding in careful, measured amounts. The Canadian government may not have had the capacity to do this measured release, and perhaps an apparent withholding may have been untenable in the context of dire need.

One story of the "fearful mortality" in this period in what became Manitoba a few years later is particularly revealing. Joseph Alfred Norbert Provencher, a Conservative candidate in Quebec at the first federal election in 1867, played a key role in Manitoba smallpox history. Defeated at the poll, he was eventually appointed secretary to William McDougall, the lieutenant governor designated to assert Canadian authority over the rebellious region of the North-West. On Provencher's first unfortunate foray into the territory, he was captured by Riel, and though released soon after, had to seek refuge briefly in the United States. He returned east, but in 1871 was appointed immigration commissioner in Manitoba for the Department of Agriculture, tasked with further sealing control over the territory. He left for Paris in 1872 under the federal government's plan to seek more immigrants from France to the Prairies. In 1873, he returned to Winnipeg as superintendent for the Department of Indian Affairs, and on November 4, 1876, it was he who sent a telegram to the Ministry of Interior in Ottawa asking for permission to send a physician to a purported outbreak of smallpox among "Indians" in Lake Winnipeg. A terse response dated November 6 states that if the report were confirmed, the costs of sending a physician should be ascertained before any action taken. Provencher dutifully responded on the 15th confirming the outbreak, with the approximate cost of a physician's services. The next day, the response came saying that Lieutenant Governor of Manitoba Alexander Morris should be consulted, and only if he agreed could a physician be sent. Thankfully, the Ottawa department notified the lieutenant governor at the same time of its own accord, essentially deferring the decision on whether smallpox needed medical attention to someone else. Two weeks after Provencher's initial request, Morris confirmed to the Ministry of Interior that a physician had been sent to the Indigenous communities, another to settler Icelanders. This creaking centralization of decision-making over Indigenous healthcare services might seem exhaustingly familiar to anyone practising medicine in northern Canada even in the twenty-first century. On November 22, two physicians in the region sent a report saying that it was likely mild smallpox but fatal due to poor living conditions, listed as "bad food, want of ventilation," and stating that twenty people had died in the previous ten days, with reportedly only two left in the mixed Ojibway-Cree-Métis community of Sandy Bar after eighteen others had either died or fled. On November 25, Provencher received news from Selkirk that two families who had fled across the lake at the start of the epidemic had all died.[91]

In order to prevent further infection, Dr Lynch issued a health order that the property of affected Indigenous families was to be burned. It explains why when I look for the community online, it is impossible to find on contemporary atlases. The only hint is a beach named Sandy Bar on the shores of Lake Winnipeg. The health order effectively obliterated Sandy Bar from the map and opened up the area for settlers to establish control. The area was already under contestation prior to the smallpox epidemic. The Dominion of Canada had previously sent out land surveyors to mark out a reserve not just for Indigenous communities but also an Icelandic immigrant colony whose aim was to extend the frontier of Canada's model of settled agricultural life based on private property even farther into Indigenous territory. The Sandy Bar band, recently transitioned to settled life from nomadism, had requested that its territory be protected, but their plea had been rejected in order to make room for the Icelanders.[92] Indigenous peoples resisted the arbitrary assignation of belonging and territory, communities made to band together with little apparent logic to them but clear to the colonial government's agenda of expanding control. This process was accelerated by the ruin the smallpox outbreak, and the medical response, caused. Communities have been moved on the whims of the colonial government many times throughout Canadian history, but Sandy Bar was one that was burned to the ground on the orders of a doctor. Understanding this act as a medical one is one example of medicine's complicity with colonialism in Canada. The survivors of that community were not compensated by the government and simply told to relocate.[93]

This outcome was predictable, Sandy Bar's annihilation a telling microcosm of what had perhaps happened across North America. Icelandic settlers had arrived in the area in the summer, and although there had been some confrontation over land between the immigrants and local Indigenous people, there was also some cooperation, with both communities sharing the church. These gatherings may have seeded the epidemic. The story of Icelandic settlement is uncomfortable reading for an immigrant like myself because it demonstrates how much of Canada's official comfort with immigration — although of course initially racist in its implementation — is part of the heritage of dispossession of Indigenous territory. No ambiguity exists in the purpose of inviting migrants to Canada in the nineteenth century: the Dominion government highly subsidized the arrival of Icelandic immigrants in order to expand the settlement of European agriculture north beyond the then borders of Manitoba. Icelanders, as immigrants from an impoverished non-English speaking European nation, were lower on the racial hierarchy than the British but were nonetheless part of the project, footsoldiers to do the dirty work of empire, essential workers of an economy based on dispossession and extraction from other people's lands. No person of the colonial elite was going to do the frontline labour, but they would live off the profits they sent their migrant minions to find.

Iceland had known smallpox epidemics since the arrival of Danish visitors in the thirteenth century, as the island colony slowly began to fall under the sway of Scandinavian empires. An epidemic in 1707 would kill a quarter of the island's population.[94] As immunity waned in subsequent generations due to Iceland's isolation, further epidemics would be introduced from the Scandinavian mainland, although oral traditions preserved some knowledge of the illness. There had been an attempt to vaccinate populations by British and Danish colonial authorities in both Manitoba and Iceland in the 1830s, but no formal program since then prior to the Sandy Bay outbreak. As the likely sub-optimally immunized Icelanders travelled through ports such as Quebec City to get to Manitoba in 1876, they were caught in the ongoing resurgence of the disease that decade and became infected.[95]

Icelanders in the settlements who had traditional medical knowledge were confused as to the diagnosis of the disease, either because they had not seen it before or it was a strain they could not identify. Or perhaps the disorientation of their new environment made it difficult to get their diagnostic bearings. Dr Lynch was the medical officer of Gimli at the time and attributed the outbreak of smallpox among the Icelanders to their isolation and incestuous intermarriages leading to poor physical stock. Projecting unabashed Anglo-Saxon racism, he did not think they had it in them to be western pioneers.[96]

An attempt at vaccination to stem the tide of the smallpox outbreak in the Icelandic and Indigenous communities around Lake Winnipeg proved to be ineffective — vaccine storage and transport were always a challenge. The Icelanders were subjected to a prolonged months-long quarantine that was widely condemned as too lengthy; one doctor noted that no Canadian would have been subjected to it, and when it was finally lifted, no one bothered to inform the Icelanders. But compared to at least 33 percent estimated to have died amongst Indigenous peoples, about 9 percent of the Icelanders died, largely children. Even though Icelanders were badly affected by the outbreak, their sanitation measures did not involve incinerating their possessions and property, like it did in at least five Indigenous settlements. The Icelanders merely had their homes thoroughly disinfected.[97]

Voluntary adherence to public health measures in other Ojibwe communities in the Lake Winnipeg area protected their communities from smallpox, of whose dangers they had by then become acutely aware, but conversely also furthered the colonial government's goals of keeping them confined to their reserves, unable to venture out on traditional territories. It had the implication of undermining their health in other ways as access to nutrition deteriorated. A doctor at Fort Alexander (Sagkeeng) noted that there was severe food insecurity, but the colonial authorities did not respond to his request for more support. He also ran out of vaccines so was unable to offer much in that realm either.[98]

Age-old squabbling over jurisdiction, which seems to be as core a part of the Canadian state as colonialism and extraction themselves, was also part of the discussion over the extension of quarantine of people and goods entering Manitoba from the then North-West Territories: the provincial government of Manitoba thought it effective and necessary, but in response to its request for funds for a quarantine centre at the border, the federal government stated openly that it was the responsibility of individuals to avoid disease themselves. There was some control of the flow of goods and people from the north into Manitoba, with people's belongings sometimes burned. But this smallpox outbreak gave the government of Canada an excuse to extend control beyond Manitoba by establishing the Keewatin Board of Health to manage smallpox on the unnegotiated territory outside of Manitoba's borders. Since health measures also involved controls on issues such as trade and migration, considerable slippage with how the body was named became almost natural; as jurisdictional creep began to set in, it was sometimes referred to as the Council of Keewatin, the reference to health dropped, stretching Canada's reach.[99] Both Provencher, the superintendent for Indian Affairs for Manitoba, and Governor Morris were appointed to the board, which came abruptly into being on November 25, 1876, about ten days after the outbreak was initially confirmed.

Given how central health has become to the Canadian sense of nationhood in the last five or six decades, in the afterglow of history, we have the tendency to mythologize its interventions as benign. But as Canada established itself, health was used in myriad ways to extend colonial authority over territories outside the purview of the Canadian state. Dr Lynch's recommendations as a medical officer seemed solely to ensure that Canadian state policy be followed, raising the thorny issue of dual loyalty in healthcare professionals, where clinical judgement, rather than being independent, is put to the service of another authority. Dr Lynch was not the last, as this tension in clinical practice continues in many ways today.[100]

The conflict is obvious within situations like prisons, detention centres, and immigration controls but remains relevant when working in healthcare services within a colonial context. Doctors in Canada have been historically reluctant to become employees of the state in a true national health service like the one in the United Kingdom. When Tommy Douglas first proposed this model in Saskatchewan, doctors began a strike in the province, mainly concerned about losing income if they became salaried public employees rather than businesspeople setting their own fees. The public insurance system currently dominant in Canada was the result of the compromise Saskatchewan negotiated with the doctors, allowing them to bill fees to this insurance fund for their services. Canadian doctors today are thus largely (but not totally) private contractors of a publicly held insurance system: most are not formally constrained by a government employer. While this arrangement limits the true universality of care, it does preserve some clinical independence. This arms-length relationship can be nominal as governments may decide not to reimburse certain acts of service offered by independent providers, for example. But it does allow doctors freedom to make decisions without too much bureaucratic impediment to the care of their patients.

But even with this veneer of autonomy, practice does have an uncomfortable interplay with government policy, especially if professional interests associated with income and status are ensured by collaborating with the government to achieve its goals. In Canada, this conflation was most apparent during the years of the tuberculosis sanatoria, as we explore later. Thus, although doctors in Canada as a professional body could in theory resist state authority, we often find ourselves assisting in government objectives simply because doing so cements our own power. At its most extreme, the profession has been implicated in medical oversight of torture in apartheid South Africa and racist syphilis experiments in the United States.[101] On a much more mundane scale in our daily work, we may uphold the objectives of the state even without explicit intent.

For example, in my routine care of children, I monitor their development. I ensure that they have appropriate motor, cognitive, social, and language skills for their age. I flag milestones that are not met as concerning, even if the parents I encounter, often racialized or Indigenous, might not be worried that a child is not speaking in full sentences yet. "They will eventually," they have sometimes shrugged. Children in multilingual contexts might speak later since, while deriving immense benefit from the stimulation, their brains process the complexity of language more slowly. But even if the concern is flagged for much longer than might be expected in multilingual contexts, making therapeutic interventions advisable, the parents I work with have sometimes been unconcerned if their children do not meet milestones set by Western doctors, embracing diversity in ways children might be in the world.

These responses have made me question my own professional concern. Where does it come from? Why do we measure children against these standard curves, and to what normality do they aspire? Are we concerned that a child is not speaking, for example, or are we concerned that a child will then not function well in school, which will then limit their ability to participate fully in the economy we have designed? Or are we concerned that the world will not be able to understand what they offer? What standards are we measuring people's health outcomes against? Who decides what is "normal" in people's bodies — and why do they decide it? Whose interests does this normality serve?

These questions lead to other ones, all deeply discomforting for a doctor. If standards to quantify well-being are imposed externally, as they might be in colonial contexts, what choices do communities have in deciding the measures of their well-being, and where do doctors in hospitals and clinics stand in this relationship? Are we ensuring our patients are able to lead healthy lives, on their own terms? Or are we making them better candidates for recruitment into the demands of dominant society? And so, when we decide we are acting in the interests of the "public's" health, who is the "public" is in these conversations — whose health has mattered most?[102]

Almost three hundred years after it first arrived, smallpox continued to wreak havoc in northern parts of North America into the twentieth century. When my great-grandfather half a world away was a young boy in 1901, there was a smallpox outbreak on the Six Nations reserve. The outbreak crystallized roiling tensions around medical care in the community. Even before the epidemic, colonial doctors noted that members of the community who practised Longhouse traditions, as opposed to Christianity, would consult their own medical practitioners first before turning to colonial healing methods. Doctors were vague about what exactly they did not like about this process, except possibly that it challenged their power — and their income. And certainly, the use of colonial medicine was not threatened, a petition even having been brought to the Haudenosaunee Chiefs Council four years prior that the community hire a third physician, revealing a demand to engage with it, though the request was eventually rejected by the Council.[103]

When smallpox erupted, traditional medical practices may not have been equipped to deal with a disease that was a relatively recent newcomer to the continent. On the whole, adherents of the Longhouse seemed to welcome vaccination, responding favourably to the federal government's call to be inoculated. Indeed, the first patient of the smallpox outbreak in 1901 was a Chief who followed Longhouse practices who asked for the colonial doctor from a neighbouring town to come see him. Settlers too made use of the diversity of options, as there was apparently an "Indian doctor" around this time who would travel to Kitchener-Waterloo to treat white patients at their request.[104]

Once smallpox emerged in the community, isolation was imposed on the households concerned — and contested. On the orders of Dr Peter Bryce, whom we encounter again later, at Ontario's Board of Health in Toronto, patients were cohorted, with tents erected to shelter suspected cases and those recovering separately, in line with epidemic management principles to this day. Guards charged with enforcing the quarantine were also given a tent, and arrangements were made to prepare for a widespread systematic vaccination campaign. Food was delivered by shopkeepers to the edge of the quarantine area and was picked up by families. Vaccines were procured to start what we would now term ring immunization, prioritizing those in closest contact to the outbreak. Several settler cities in Ontario, including Hamilton, immediately placed bans on reserve residents travelling to them. The Six Nations Board of Health was dispatched urgently to neighbouring towns, on which they depended for many supplies, to emphasize that all necessary measures of public health control had been put in place in the affected portion of the community and there was little chance of spread to all of it. Hagersville and Caledonia lifted their bans shortly thereafter, but Toronto and Hamilton persisted with their ban for another couple of weeks, stretching out travel restrictions on people from Six Nations perhaps longer than strictly necessary.[105]

Even after three hundred years of the circulation of smallpox in the Americas, there was dispute over the diagnosis given the lack of microbiological confirmation. A roughly contemporary outbreak in Hamilton where conflicting diagnoses of chickenpox and smallpox had been proposed fuelled scepticism about the pertinence of containment measures by those in Six Nations most harmed by them. As we see to this day, the ambiguity inherent to evolving health situations can cleave communities along pre-existing lines, as people choose which sources of information they believe. Within the context of colonial relations of mutual mistrust, the diagnostic uncertainty fuelled opposition to authority. Eventually, organized resistance in Six Nations, particularly by Longhouse members, to public health measures was channelled into a petition to the federal parliament, alleging that the smallpox diagnosis was an error that was perpetuated to procure funds from the Council's budget to employ the doctor's son, who had been on leave from a medical internship in Montreal. Members of the community suspicious of doctors as agents of governmental authority saw practices of obvious professional self-interest as confirmation of their doubts. The doctor's previous demands to build a hospital on the reserve at the expense of the Haudenosaunee Council made him seem like he was meddling in internal budgetary affairs. He also refused to live on reserve, as he wanted to maintain his private practice in the settler town of Brantford, even though it was the desire of the Council, which employed him, to have him be resident. But the federal government had rejected the Council's right, as employer most directly responsible for the contract, to insert clauses in line with this wish. Disagreement with medical decisions this particular doctor had made also influenced general doubt about his role in the community and thus fed concern about nepotism when his son arrived as apparently the only available doctor willing to manage the epidemic in the region, even though the father had initially objected to him taking up the position.[106]

This conflation of public health authority with the aspirations of the settler professional class has disquieting reverberations for me today. Even if not personally implicated in the conquest of land, it can still serve personal gain, no matter the cost and consequences for the people involved. Even today, one of the big difficulties for isolated Indigenous communities is to maintain physician services when this labour is imported from elsewhere, such as in my case. I primarily serve one community in the Cree territories on a part-time basis, and then work elsewhere through a variety of settings in the North, but my personal life remains based in the city to which I immigrated over two decades ago. Even though communities have grown, and healthcare needs have become more complex, the nineteenth-century tradition of visiting doctors in many Indigenous settlements continues, with few positions funded for permanent doctors in the communities. It is also difficult to retain professionals whose lives are based farther south. Communities have pushed back, especially in recent years, insisting on the importance of more permanent healthcare staff, ideally homegrown. They are actively partnering with medical faculties to train people who will demonstrate commitment to their care.[107] In contract negotiations, Indigenous health authorities, with more autonomy nowadays, may ask doctors to spend more time embedded in the communities, with which on political principle, I agree. The cost of surrendering my established social support system to work elsewhere for professional satisfaction is part of the reality of any migrant worker, though entitled healthcare professionals like physicians might balk when that balance is shifted away from them "having it all." Perhaps it is easier for displaced migrants like me to make that decision anyway, given that we are uprooted regardless of where we may be in the country. Perhaps this reason partially explains why many healthcare workers in northern Canada are new immigrants — not unlike Icelandic farmers in the nineteenth century.[108]

In 1901 in Six Nations, medical power was an established part of this history of relationships between federal government and Indigenous nations. Not only were the doctors dubious, but people, particularly those who held anticolonial language, belief systems, and worldviews, were also wary of the Board of Health, perceived as an unelected clique extending even more authority over the livelihoods and lifeways of the community through containment measures, which were beginning to have serious financial implications. Such patterns are not unlike responses seen elsewhere across the world as colonial medicine tightened its grip, but the account of the Six Nations' reaction to the crisis suggests that they simply used established means of resolution and conflict management, requiring no new structures or processes to deal with the aggravation. This brush with colonial authority was thus routine, and the community responded to it as it habitually would.

As the fallout from the epidemic, even though generally controlled, began to ripple across the region, a Methodist reverend in Brantford made the comment that the smallpox was the result of the "deplorable conditions, morally and sanitarily of the Six Nations," an equivalency drawn between morality and health outcomes that has long been a trope. The colonial Indian agent did make an effort at defending the community, but the Chiefs Council wrote back forcefully, saying that the reverend would not be welcome to minister in their community. Cases continued to pop up intermittently, as people actively ill with smallpox were hidden from health authorities. At one point, there were concerns that the doctor from Montreal was transmitting the disease, given his travels to Brantford to attend to smallpox patients there too. Doubt among people in the community that smallpox was at play may have contributed to hesitancy in reporting infections, as well as the inconvenience of public health measures that doubtlessly would be imposed upon households if smallpox were declared, with minimal supportive measures to compensate. The epidemic was actually beginning to take hold in surrounding settler communities as it died down in Six Nations. The possibility that migrant workers from Six Nations who worked on farms in these areas would bring the disease back to the reserve was beginning to become a concern, as was the cost of all the control measures. Flares of the disease continued through the winter into the spring of 1902, with periods of up to two or three months of no active cases, suggesting continued underground circulation, or introduction through migrant workers' travel to or from places where smallpox was also growing, before it finally died down.[109]

Similar to syphilis, debating the history of smallpox epidemics is perhaps more telling about the colonial venture than the disease itself. Academic scholarship centuries later still quibbles about whether smallpox killed 20 or 50 percent of the population. Of course, this quest for "truth" is not necessarily nefarious. Sometimes it highlights the resilience of populations in the face of great oppressions and recovers lost understandings of both science and society. Indeed, one of the first major works to revive the issue of demographic disaster through disease argued forcefully that the devastation caused by contact was much more severe than previously imagined. Dobyns' 1983 assertion that the populations of Indigenous nations prior to 1492 were much larger than initially presumed certainly challenged some long-held beliefs about the relative emptiness of the American landmass.[110] Debate on the impact of epidemic disease on Indigenous peoples galvanized the field of precolonial history in the Americas.[111]

But the fact that scholars late into the twentieth century continued to address this question suggests a struggle over narrative, reshaping and reframing it, more than it is about disease processes and epidemiological fact. As late as 2012, authors Carlos and Lewis tried to unpack historical data from four different vantage points to argue that the smallpox outbreak in the 1780s on the Prairies was not as destructive as presumed. This phenomenon speaks to me more about twenty-first-century neuroses of assuaging post-colonial guilt than it does about the time of first contact. Depending on what political aims are served, tolls from epidemics are inflated or deflated even today. The volume of goods trading rebounding within a few years following the crash of 1781 is taken as evidence that Indigenous traders might not have been badly hit. The researchers acknowledge that this interpretation sidesteps several issues of the colonial economy: a relatively new trading post might take time to establish appropriate trading networks and thus still see continued growth as it became more known, especially as demand from Europe to extract resources from the colonial hinterland did not abate, perhaps then resulting in higher amounts of traded goods in the currency of made beavers, despite population decline.[112]

While at first, I thought this approach attempted to minimize the suffering of colonization, on later reflection, I realize that it bolsters the argument that accidental epidemics were not an adequate explanation for the outcomes of colonization. If demographic devastation from disease alone did not account for the disruption communities faced, active colonial agency had to make up for the rest. In any case, so many limitations to these tentative reconstructions of outbreaks render them dubious: estimations of beaver populations and the hunting effort of populations two centuries ago to derive a sense of what may have happened then stretches into the territory of conjecture. Crude mortality rates may serve as a proxy marker for the severity of a disease but do not tell the whole story of its burden on communities: a 1 percent fatality rate can have searing impacts.

What are the survival chances of a child who overcomes a disease but whose caregivers all die? How do families fare when breadwinners are no longer able to bring sustenance due to disability if they have no access to new skills? Who do settler accounts not count when people invisible to them might have faced a differential impact of disease? Indigenous people engaged in the fur trade might have been relatively well-off and well-fed as the trade gave them a source of wealth. What of others who, though shielded from direct contact with Europeans, may not have had the same resources to withstand infection? Children were particularly vulnerable to smallpox, and their deaths would not be reflected in trade data. There would also be no immediate account of the demographic pressure from the increased rate of miscarriage that occurred with smallpox. What are the chances of surviving a severe illness when malnutrition takes hold? In cases where mortality was low, do we have any sense of previous exposure to the disease or immunizing events? How do we decide whose rates of mortality were standard for smallpox, or even acceptable, and why?

Contemporary academic reconstructions can also seem to undermine Indigenous accounts of what occurred. Why would we consider extrapolated proxy phenomena analyzed two centuries later based on assumptions of how much an average Indigenous male in the Plains might eat in the winter in the nineteenth century as somehow a more reliable depiction of what transpired than an oral telling of the events by descendants of that community passed down through generations? The belittling of lived or perceived experience speaks a lot to our preconceived assumptions of what is "truth," as though the impact of actions — on how people felt or internalized an event — is not a part of that truth. Written records unmediated by settlers are limited about how, in that time and place, Indigenous peoples experienced the outbreaks or the response — or the lack thereof — provided by settler individuals and authorities. But this filtering of what actually transpired through colonial documents deletes a lot of other information. Other ways of knowing, backed by the weight of historical emotion, may have more real-world consequences than determining whether 20 or 70 percent of a population died. In medicine, we know memories are held in the body in places beyond the brain, where words and numbers cannot reach.

Anthropologists have dwelt on the particularities of Indigenous custom or practice as an explanation of high smallpox fatality rates in the region. Curious obsessions feature in the literature, such as focusing on the fears Indigenous men might have had of smallpox-related scarring having a huge impact on their social and economic functions.[113] Aesthetic standards have always been a means to establish power and dominance, but it seems unlikely that vanity was a consistent enough concern among communities that were going through a series of transformative crises to be noteworthy. And why variations in managing symptoms like fever should make a particular impact in the Americas is unclear: the use of a sweat lodge or a cold stream bath seems irrelevant to mention as having more of an impact on mortality than folk practices to treat fever apparent in Europe for centuries, which included bloodletting as the pinnacle of its medical offerings, endorsed by some of the finest physicians around the time settlement of the Americas began.[114] Experienced supportive care might have made a difference, however, if afforded to the afflicted by knowledgeable settlers.

Indigenous unfamiliarity with novel disease contributing to death rates has also been advanced, focusing on community practices where many people gather around those stricken as sources of super-spread, as ties of kinship and solidarity obligated that the ill have care. State-based healthcare systems are after all not the only mechanism for succour in sickness. The argument that this behaviour had an extensive role in the decimation of populations is a little sad because it suggests a contrast that banishes Europeans to the comparative role of heartless heathens who apparently did not love their families enough to care for them when they fell ill. While Europeans might perhaps have been aware of the need for isolation in smallpox outbreaks, the distinction seems somewhat essentialist. Similarly structured societies in India, for instance, where kinship was paramount, had learned to deal with smallpox, isolating the cases and allowing them to be cared for only by those who had known immunity. Elaborate rites around variolation show that traditional practitioners in India were aware of what could happen if the disease escaped into the general population.[115]

This background would not have been available to Indigenous peoples in the Americas, but some communities learned to adapt and so were not passive victims trapped in tradition in the face of the pox's onslaught. There is evidence, for instance, that Cherokee medical practitioners used seclusion, an important tool within their worldview, asking people to remain in fields outside villages when smallpox was a threat. Romantic notions of the Americas as somehow devoid of infectious diseases prior to European contact are fanciful, and although there might not have been many epidemics, the existence of communicable diseases in some form was probably known to Indigenous peoples. Patterns of spread would become empirically evident to anyone with a keen sense of observation given smallpox's transmission only when symptomatic, although connections can be obscured in the chaos of crisis. The Cherokee also quickly adapted to the reality of settlement by Europeans and their illnesses, advising their citizens not to travel to areas with known disease and to avoid settler towns for multiple reasons, including outbreaks. And as any dynamic, responsive community that would learn and adjust to changing circumstances, they created new rites that shaped their conversations with the spirit world, cutting entire villages off from the outside world in rituals to fend off smallpox, which had practical implications in limiting the spread of the virus by the standards of contemporary biomedicine.[116]

But in essence, a focus on anthropological causes of mortality seems to me designed to distract. This othering gaze detracts from material causes of high mortality from outbreaks — things we know we can address — and diverts attention away from the actions of settlers. Infectious disease thrives on close contact, and the spread of acute, directly transmitted illnesses is accentuated by times of congregation and density, which may happen only intermittently in a thinly populated area where mobility might be constrained by large distances or long periods of thawing and freezing, such as northern North America.[117] Smallpox needed a concentration of susceptible people to take hold. But as cities developed — and in the case of North America — as nomadic life became more centred around gathering at trading posts — pathogens also profited from the change, especially as the tentacles of trade began to bring diverse ecological regions of the continent under one economic system. Tracking the virus in and of itself is not useful in isolation without tracking the structures of colonization. Late into the twentieth century, debates persisted on the role of intrinsic genetic factors in the immune responses in contemporary

Amazonian peoples to novel disease threats, with geneticist James Neel warning against "invoking genetic susceptibility to explain poorly understood situations," when it is clear that we do not need genetic causes to understand what happened to Indigenous peoples in the Americas: the knowledge we have already is explanatory enough.[118] Protection comes not from blood alone. Pinpointing demographic decline to purely biological processes overlooks the fact that health is a state of being that is an outcome of a complex network of determinants, not all of them immediately related to physiology and anatomy.

Just as its introduction, the end of smallpox in North America is intricately tied to colonization. Apart from stocks of live virus held in Atlanta and Koltsovo, smallpox may be gone, but the vaccine has not been consigned to history. Routine vaccination against the virus stopped in the United States in 1976, but the US Department of Defense reinstated its use in 2002 to select military personnel as fears of the virus's use as a biological weapon grew.[119] The utility of the vaccine to advance strategic aims however goes back a long, long way. And understanding its use in the North American context during the establishment of European settler colonialism reveals much about the way healthcare services rolled out across the continent.

Prior to the birth of the vaccine, given the tortuously long relationship humanity has had with smallpox, societies across Eurasia and Africa had developed ways to manage outbreaks, both in treatment and prevention. The intricate processes of variolation in China, India, the Middle East, and Africa were among these indigenous forms of inoculation whereby carefully controlled infection was introduced to induce immunity. In parts of Wales in the 1600s, people would pay for the scabs of those recovering from smallpox to be rubbed into their skin, which seemed to give them a mild case and lifelong immunity thereafter.[120] In Scotland, a more elaborate method of tying a smallpox-infested thread around a child's wrist was the preferred method. Many places referred to the procedure by some variation of "buying the pox," suggesting common origins.[121]

But it is Lady Mary Wortley Montague who is credited with bringing variolation to the forefront in the United Kingdom in 1721, after having seen it during her husband's diplomatic posting in Istanbul. It did not take long for it to cross the ocean to the settler colonies in North America, where smallpox had by then been established for a century.

One entertaining account of the debates around the value of variolation in the Americas is by Arthur Boylston, a pathologist who does not openly profess any relation to the Boylston who would become a key feature in the drama.[122] In this narrative, Boston, the largest town in North America with 11,000 people, had already known two major smallpox outbreaks by 1721. In that year, a ship from the West Indies breached its requirements for quarantine, and smallpox escaped into the community. Authorities eventually gave up on the prospect of isolating households once the outbreak overwhelmed their capacity to trace infections.

As the epidemic continued to rage, the story goes that Cotton Mather, one of the leading Puritans in the region, then most famous for his implication in the Salem witch trials some thirty years prior, had read published papers explaining the process of variolation in Constantinople (Istanbul). He had been intrigued as Onesimus, who hailed from what we consider now to be Liberia and who had been sold enslaved to Mather in 1706, had shown him his own scar of the process in 1716, confirming its reality. Mather became a huge proponent.

Onesimus was recognized three hundred years later as one of the best Bostonians of all time for his teaching.[123] But at that time, the focus was on Mather, then in his late fifties, who approached physicians in Boston to try to bring variolation to North America. One of them, Zabadiel Boylston, started to experiment with the procedure among his household and those of nearby friends. The danger of variolation was that if done inappropriately, it spread the disease to other people, and there was great opposition to his approach. People were appalled that previously protected neighbourhoods might now be susceptible.[124] The belief that smallpox outbreaks were part of divine will, certainly useful when it came to clearing the land for settlement, also complicated preventative efforts.

The debate escalated, becoming acrimonious. A French doctor claimed to have seen experiments with variolation go horribly wrong across Europe, pitting this paragon of European authority against the word of African slaves and Turkish heathens. The reliability of African knowledge as a source of medical practice was a considerable part of the dispute. The most vociferous opponent was William Douglass, who was the only formally trained physician in Boston at the time. The *New England Courant*, one of the city's earliest newspapers, published its first issue in August 1721, which noted the requirement of all vessels from France to quarantine on arriving near Boston due to a "contagious distemper" that had broken out on the Mediterranean coast and also included a piece by Douglass on the issue of smallpox inoculation. He used the fact that variolation could potentially spread disease to suggest scathingly (well before Amherst) that perhaps the military should consider variolation as a means to defeat the Abenaki, paying inoculators to unleash epidemics. Interestingly, Douglass also makes reference to the fact that smallpox should be twinned with "Negro yaws" — one of the nonsexual syphilitic diseases, for which African peoples also historically used inoculation to promote immunity to it later in life.[125]

Mather had to convince Boston that it was fine to learn about medicine from other parts of the world — just as Americans had learned about tobacco and rattlesnake bite treatment from Indigenous peoples. Boylston continued to find willing participants in the inoculation practice, until one died several weeks into his experiment. The cause of her death was debated furiously. But during the ensuing backlash, news came that the British royal family had granted permission of a trial of variolation in prisoners which went well, and interest rose again, this time among more affluent families in Massachusetts. The stamp of European authenticity was beginning to supplant the words of Muslims and Africans.[126]

In London, six prisoners had been experimented upon in Newgate Prison — an infamous place that would shortly thereafter be closed after its tenure of almost six centuries. The story of their consent — or coercion — in regard to undergoing this procedure, which was considered investigational at least in England, has been debated extensively. There was already precedent of experimenting on prisoners for health interventions even in 1721. Initially the historical record of the Newgate variolation trial considered the incarcerated people to be mainly on death row, largely for property crimes, including John Cawthery, who was accused of the theft of two wigs. But in fact all of them were actually facing the sentence of transportation to the American colonies — a punishment so horrifying that apparently some would prefer potential death by smallpox, though Richard Evans was found to have lied when he swore he had not had smallpox before as the inoculation simply had no effect on him. Mary North, another prisoner turned experimental subject, behaved in ways that suggest she would have been someone I would have liked to befriend. Sentenced to transportation once, she was in Newgate again for either somehow evading the initial deportation or inscrutably managing to return to England. The record notes she resisted her second arrest "using the most wicked expressions." To the dismay of the people running the study, she was more concerned about whether the lesions would scar her pretty face than she was interested in her serious crimes. And she also did not follow the rules by "unaccountably" washing in cold water one day, which seemed to be a medical no-no.[127]

One unnamed woman who had been identified as a potential candidate for the experiment ended up contracting smallpox before she could be inoculated. But for the others it was clear that variolation worked. Consent of course was questionable, although in the furious debates that ensued between the pro- and anti-variolation camps in London thereafter, people noted that the "criminals" being able to choose their punishment was indicative of informed consent, as the subjects could weigh the risks between social exclusion across a cold, impassable ocean and wilful infection with a fatal disease. In either case, the royal family pardoned the experimental subjects — including Evans, who was retroactively assigned the role of control subject. At least two of them though — John Alcock (who at one point burst all his pox with a pin to the chagrin of the experimenters) and Elizabeth Harrison — were back in Newgate awaiting transportation to the colonies within a few months. The latter, who had shown the least reaction to the inoculation apart from Evans, had even been paid extra to attend a smallpox-infected school in Hertford, where she had to nurse those stricken and even share a bed with a patient to prove that she did not fall ill after the inoculation.[128] It is actually quite surprising that they were not more ill given the abominable conditions of the Newgate cells at that time, but they were also visited by a merchant from Turkey, who assured the doctors that the course of their reactions was very similar to what was known in Istanbul.[129]

By March 1722, seventy people had been variolated in England with no adverse events. In April that year, two young princesses of the royal family were inoculated through variolation, sealing the acceptance of the practice. But by May there were two deaths — unclear if related — and London too fell into debates about variolation as Boston had done. Questions regarding whether the practices of old brown women in far-off parts of the world should sway England abounded. While scientific concerns certainly prevailed in the discussions — including valid ones about appropriate dosing, inoculum quality, procedural standardization, and complications related to other infections — moral and religious ones were also apparent, including the somewhat puritanical idea that faith could not be tested without disease, and if illness were prevented, sins would go unpunished. This thread of rhetoric has continued well into modern-day discourse, attributing illness as the logical course of individual failings rather than the product of processes shaped by biology and society, such as diabetes being the failure in eating well, when it is access to appropriate foods that determines people's capacity to eat well. One opponent of the variolation process, Isaac Massey, was worried that since smallpox often caused miscarriage, the deliberate infection involved in variolation would be used as a means of abortion, which he notes might be done with the good intention of wanting "to preserve a repenting young lady's reputation," but still to him could not be justified before divine or human authority.[130]

Proponents of variolation in London fought back. Why was there so much fear of variolation, they asked, when English medicine had clearly adopted beneficial treatments from abroad before: one commentator noted that England had happily adopted quinine bark for the treatment of malaria, a product transmitted to Europe "by a barbarous Indian."[131] Why the opposition then to variolation's benefits?

The debates in London were significant for the evolution of smallpox prevention in North America, as Boylston in Boston turned out to have inoculated far more people than anyone in England ever had, and as the paradigm of quantitative evidence in medicine became more established, the New England data became key, supporting the role of the colonies as sites of scientific advance. Boylston's account was fastidious and detailed, and importantly for the time, his numbers concorded with English experience: accumulated results suggested that 2 percent of variolated people died in smallpox outbreaks on both sides of the Atlantic compared to 16 percent of people who were not.[132] The clear benefit of this form of inoculation was astounding. These findings were criticized by those who argued that the high mortality from smallpox was due to poor care rather than anything inherent to the disease and the risks of variolation were thus greater than the benefit. In England, as would become the practice in Canada, because of these uncertain risks, people would be more likely to inoculate when there was a confirmed outbreak, with the relative risk of variolation seeming less threatening when there was disease actively circulating.

The unfolding of these debates in the two metropoles obviously had an impact on the way variolation as a practice would be perceived in English parts of Canada. Already the conversations between the different parts of the empire were in full swing about how to manage disease, and Indigenous peoples would be caught on the periphery of these arguments, being swept into worlds that decentred their own. The transfer of knowledge from the Middle East to Boston through London shows that the exchange of knowledge across borders was rapidly accelerated by the consolidation of colonial capitalism. This process contextualizes how prevention of smallpox came to be part of the first healthcare services provided to Indigenous peoples by colonial authorities in North America. It was not simply the product of a benign benevolence nor the result of Western ingenuity but part of patterns of power. Resistance to variolation's advance was muddied by lots of personal political intrigue, but opponents also mobilized racism to advance their own agendas, suggesting that people using the wisdom of enslaved peoples could not be trusted.

By 1729, when smallpox came about again in Boston, even previous opponents of the procedure grudgingly came on board — especially now that there was enough legitimacy behind it that the intervention could command a fee — and the city managed to stem the spread of the epidemic. Indeed, as variolation became more elaborate in the West, even the person who first promoted it there, Lady Montague, wrote of her disapproval of the abandonment of the simple practice she had noted in Turkey to the increasingly aggressive methods put together by English doctors, with embellished protocols to prepare for the procedure through diet and medication lasting two weeks prior to the actual injection, often fuelled by fees for service. Boylston notes that in London variolation gradually became a means for the working class to secure employment, as proof they would be of less risk to their employers. Variolation was also used to protect the slave trade. And in 1729 itself, a missionary in the Amazon inoculated the Indigenous people among whom he lived to protect them after 50 percent had already died of smallpox. By 1737 in England, the idea of a generalized smallpox inoculation program was emerging in public discourse, not just confined to the advancing edge of epidemics. This process would diminish the vulnerability of smaller towns, which only had waves of outbreaks once previous immunity faded, as they did not have enough of a population to support continual circulation and thus a degree of herd immunity.[133]

Though such a policy was not pursued, in the approximately seventy-five years between the introduction of variolation to England and the development of cowpox-based vaccination which would supplant it, variolation began to expand throughout English society, including to Canada. There was greater resistance to variolation in France, which took about three decades to accept it as a practice despite there being evidence of folk customs of variolation in rural parts of the country. France's powerful Catholic clergy dominated discussion with arguments against interfering in heavenly plans. Once French nobility accepted variolation in 1756, summoning a physician from Switzerland to inoculate the Duc d'Orléans, second in rank to the king, the French parliament eventually allowed the practice, only to ban it again in 1763 when a smallpox outbreak in Paris was suspected to have been triggered by variolation. However, five years later, the ban was rescinded.[134] Portugal discouraged variolation for a long time, thus leaving vast swathes of populations under its rule in Brazil vulnerable to disease. By the time Portugal endorsed the intervention by 1799, cowpox-based vaccination was already being introduced to the world.[135]

British troops in Canada were thus largely variolated, and it was confirmed to be practised in Quebec City in 1765, after the province's conquest by Britain. By 1770, an army doctor (Latham) variolated 1250 people in Quebec City and Montreal.[136] Arguments were still raucous south of the border, with residual concerns about interference with God's will, and American colonies passed laws banning the practice. A smallpox outbreak among them contributed to their retreat from Canada in the hostilities of 1776, with the death of Major General John Thomas from the disease near Chambly.[137] When the first major documented outbreak of smallpox swept through the Prairies in the 1780s, little seemed to be done to stem its tide as it spread through Mexico and the United States. In Canada, the Hudson's Bay Company had probably lacked the infrastructure to halt previous epidemics but by 1782 was in a position to stem the spread of the disease as it approached, by imposing quarantine or isolation on vulnerable populations. The Company's instructions to all its workers were detailed, even requiring them not to approach any of the uninfected population after contact with ill people without changing and airing their clothes. Variolation, even though well-established among the British military stationed in North America at the time, as evidenced by the victories over American troops who were decimated by smallpox, was not offered to the Indigenous population by the Hudson's Bay Company for that outbreak. In fact, an attempt by a well-meaning hospital worker in eastern Canada to inoculate Indigenous allies to Britain during the Revolutionary War was actively stopped by his superiors, even though the British military benefited from the protection the procedure afforded.[138]

In the later major outbreak in the mid-1830s, at least one trading party in the United States did try to protect the surrounding population through variolation, but given one of its side effects was potential further propagation of the illness, this one-off piecemeal intervention was ineffective. The epidemic began to roil onwards from Fort Union in North Dakota, even with an attempted quarantine; a thousand Indigenous traders arrived despite it and figures suggest only 150 survived. A similar attempt by traders to quarantine a boat near Fort McKenzie in Montana was foiled by Indigenous people again insisting, according to settler accounts, on continuing to trade.[139] The account, while celebrating Indigenous agency, is a little uncomplicated in erasing the dissent and discussion within Indigenous communities themselves. News about the advancing epidemic had almost certainly arrived ahead of the wave, and the possibility of this disease taking on epic proportions in communities must have been known. However, the last outbreak, fifty years previously, had possibly been the first ever in the region, and perhaps there was no living memory of it, minimizing its potential in the imaginations of people who were also scrabbling for a livelihood in the changing economy of the Plains.

In 1796, after their previous official objection to variolation in Indigenous nations, British authorities allowed for members of the Haudenosaunee Confederacy in parts of Ontario and Quebec to be variolated just as established practice was going to go through a paradigm shift.[140]

Edward Jenner, himself variolated at the age of eight, is often lauded as the inventor of the smallpox vaccine.[141] But as is routinely the case in science, no idea originates without a community of learning and exchange, and other people around the same time were also considering similar concepts. Dr Fewster mentioned the protective power of cowpox from subsequent smallpox infection to Jenner when the latter was a medical apprentice in 1768.[142] Jobst Bose experimented with it in Germany in 1769, and Benjamin Jesty was exploring its power in England in 1774. A Mr Nash wrote about cowpox's protective effect against smallpox in 1781.[143] And of course, possibly thousands of milkmaids and the farming communities to which they belonged had been aware of their relative protection from smallpox for a long time. Edward Jenner extracted this folk knowledge that milkmaids with cowpox did not get ill from smallpox to put into a published tract on vaccination in the late 1790s. He is also presumed to be one of the first to have documented exposing those infected with cowpox to smallpox to see whether it actually was as protective as was thought, in a prototype of a scientific "experiment." Thus validated, the practice became adopted by the colonial establishment, touting a great "discovery" of Europe that was then distributed to the rest of the world out of imperial largesse. There was considerable nationalistic preening about the political and social climate in Britain that allowed the "discovery" by Jenner to take place.

The first smallpox vaccines in North America were administered in Newfoundland in 1798 by John Clinch, a classmate of Jenner's in medical school, who was working as a minister in Trinity. He received another shipment of the vaccine in 1800, the year Jenner's treatise on vaccination was published.[144] In mainland Canada, the practice did not arrive in Quebec City until 1801. Perhaps the first wholesale effort at vaccination in the Americas started in 1804 when King Carlos IV of Spain arranged for massive vaccination in the American colonies, around the same time as the British were vaunting its use in the jewel in its crown in India. Puerto Rico was a particular target of the Spanish monarch, though for both logistical and political reasons many Puerto Ricans did not travel to the cities to avail of this gift from the distant imperial monarch. When the United States took over, one of its first acts, no longer concerned about interfering in divine will, was to engage in a compulsory vaccination program against smallpox in an effort to demonstrate the bounty of its civilizing influence — an attempt which was not entirely successful.[145]

Spurts of activity around vaccination in North America began to coalesce. Thomas Jefferson had instructed the Lewis and Clark expedition to carry inoculant with them on their travels and had persuaded a number of Indigenous leaders to be vaccinated upon their visit to him in 1801–1802. Whether this persuasion was real or more like coercion is unclear, but the American and Canadian states began to take the role of distributing this seeming miracle of

European medicine among Indigenous peoples. With the advantage of being safer than variolation, it displaced the older, more "foreign" practice quickly.

In 1803, the missionary working with the Abenaki at St Francis in Quebec requested of the superintendent at the Indian Department at Montreal, John Chew, that vaccination be provided to him and the Indigenous people around him. In 1804, a report at the Royal Jennerian Society for the Extermination of the Small-Pox by the Extension of Vaccination suggested that Indigenous people somewhere in Canada had travelled many hundreds of miles to receive the vaccine.[146] As variolation once had, vaccination garnered royal patronage. The Royal Jennerian Society in the United Kingdom in the early nineteenth century not only had honorary members from royal families across Europe, including Russia, Spain, Austria-Hungary, Bavaria, Denmark, Netherlands, and France, but also claimed among its members presidents and former presidents of the United States, rajas of puppet princely states in India, authorities in Baghdad, and importantly, Chiefs from all member nations of the Haudenosaunee Confederacy.[147]

The Society in this way was not unlike global philanthropic giants of today, such as the Gates Foundation, earning the cachet and the goodwill of elites and authorities who wish to be associated with its benevolent works. And indeed, good work it was — smallpox vaccination was a development in the nineteenth century that made eventual eradication in the twentieth century a reality. In 1807, the government of Canada (the British Crown) delivered Jenner's treatise on vaccination to the Haudenosaunee Confederacy, indicating that an attempt had been made to vaccinate the people of the communities but they had been out on a hunt at the time. One of their Chiefs died of smallpox soon after, and the message from the Chiefs Council to Dr Jenner through the channels of the Canadian government expressed gratitude for the gift that the Great Spirit had shown to Dr Jenner to share with the world. Significantly, the Haudenosaunee acknowledgement publicly credited the Great Spirit for choosing to share the wisdom of vaccination with someone on the planet, not specifically praising Jenner himself. This outlook of knowledge being universal and available to all is revealing, in contrast to British insistence that it was a product of their regime.

The Council also mentions "the man of skill who is employed by the great father to treat them when sick and wounded," probably the doctor appointed by the federal government, to whom they entrusted the volume on vaccination against smallpox.[148] The wording of the letter to Dr Jenner demonstrates how the Council of the Haudenosaunee Confederacy viewed their colonial counterparts, at least when speaking politely in the company of the British, in English translation. In English, the word used for the Crown was "father" — and there have been extensive discussions about the use of the term in Indigenous diplomatic traditions as they negotiated treaties.[149] English meaning may not accurately represent the implications of kinship the Haudenosaunee parties used when referring to the treaties, as they also clearly referred to the Crown as the sovereign of the British, and not theirs. In contemporary eyes, the term may ironically reflect the paternalism inherent in the British approach to treaties with Indigenous peoples.

Burgeoning systematic vaccination began to be established in Canada from a source that we would now perhaps consider unlikely: the Hudson's Bay Company. The trading company's objectives were possibly derived from the political economy of their operations: having suppliers of the goods that they traded for profit in Europe die in sweeping epidemics needed to be addressed. It might have been benevolence, but crude considerations of finances were not irrelevant.

After the initial attempts at vaccination in the early 1800s for Indigenous people around Montreal, a subsequent more organized initiative occurred in the Red River Valley in 1811, organized by Lord Selkirk, who was a major shareholder of the Company. He was in charge of setting up an agricultural settlement in the Red River region (the eventual Winnipeg) and used vaccination as a way to win over Indigenous peoples, showing how healthcare services have deliberately been used as appeasement for the colonial endeavour. Selkirk's words in correspondence to his employee to describe a strategy along this front included, "Perhaps by judicious management on the part of the interpreters, they may be made to entertain very high ideas of the power of those who have such a command over nature." For many Indigenous peoples in the region at the time, the devastating epidemic of 1781–1782 was thirty years prior and so probably within living memory.[150]

In contrast, in the east, government infrastructure of the established colonies made an effort to promote vaccination more generally through public funds. In 1815, the Quebec assembly passed a bill attributing £1000 to encourage the practice of vaccination across the province: the four administrative districts of Quebec were to use the sums to pay for physicians to visit parishes, with fifteen days' notice, during the summer to provide the vaccine to anyone wishing it. This framework reads as one of the first signs of a public healthcare service. The law specified that the doctor was not to accept any other payments. The doctors would also have to report to the legislature on the prevalence of endemic disease in the districts they visited. Some of the money was also to go to advertising the act to a wide variety of public officials, with a note detailing the advantages of vaccination.[151]

Considering that step not enough, six years later, Quebec established the Vaccine Bureau. This shift was deemed necessary as there had been some public suspicion that the vaccine provided thus far might have been ineffective, and so the province stepped in to better regulate its distribution and administration. The intricate procedure of the injection as suggested by the Vaccine Bureau was unlike what we would expect nowadays from a vaccination. The process involved close monitoring for days to watch for the development of the first vesicle suggesting effective inoculation, although evidence from Europe at the time suggested that two vesicles were important. Instructions were given to the doctor about how and when to administer second doses (carefully regulated by timeline depending on the clinical evolution of the first vesicle).[152] Despite this effort early on, as we shall see, bitter social divisions would limit Quebec's ability to control the disease sixty years later in Montreal.

Another organized vaccination program of Indigenous communities in Canada was in 1820, when there were reports of significant deaths west of Lake Winnipeg — which turned out to be due to pertussis and measles, but nonetheless, spooked Hudson's Bay Company colonists undertook widespread vaccination against smallpox. The United States federal government tried to institute an immunization program in 1832, with funds appropriated via the Indian Vaccination Act through to 1839 for the use of the Office of Indian Affairs for this purpose. But the limited capacity and infrastructure of the American government in the west stymied any effective implementation of this perhaps well-meaning law: federal agents of Indian affairs only occasionally visited their posts. The commercial imperative of the Hudson's Bay Company meant they had permanent employees stationed across the western Plains and thus had the capacity to engage in a more thorough immunization program. The Company's established communication networks, necessitated by its profit imperative, were also key, and certainly something imperial corporations had learned from long experience in the East, such as in India and Indonesia. The US federal government only heard of the devastation of the 1837 epidemic six months after it peaked, and when it tried to catch up with vaccination afterwards — belatedly — it still had to rely on individuals acting in good faith to extend the reach of the program.[153]

Vaccination slowly became established in Canada, though perhaps not always with proactive state encouragement. In 1836, Peter Dease of the Hudson's Bay Company had begun a comprehensive vaccination program of all First Nations and Métis people in Fort Chipewyan and Fort Resolution, even before there was any knowledge of the smallpox epidemic arriving from the south the following year.[154] Another example is the chief factor at Swan River trading post, William Todd, who was also an experienced physician. He probably received his medical training around the period the vaccine was developed and was influenced by the debates around its efficacy at that time (although of course such debates continued in many circles in Canada for decades).[155] He himself was known as "Picotte" due to the scarring from his own tussle with smallpox.[156] He may have been unaware of the role he played in the greater political chess, but he acted decisively with aggressive vaccination locally in advance of the epidemic of 1837. When the first reports of an outbreak reached the trading post in September, there was considerable conflicting information about the exact nature of the disease until December, when the epidemic was conclusively identified as smallpox, by which time it had already swept through much of the region. The importance of someone with health knowledge and tools being accidentally the first person to be aware of the epidemic was fortuitous. The Company had already made vaccination available to many outposts, but William Todd was particularly successful in protecting Swan River through his pre-emptive action out of an abundance of precaution, perhaps facilitated by the reputation he might have had among Indigenous people in the region as a healer worthy of trust.[157]

In its role as surrogate colonial state, the Hudson's Bay Company continued to ship cowpox vaccine from London through its wide network of Canadian trading posts after this major Plains outbreak of 1837. In 1838 and 1839, after the epidemic was largely staved off in Canada, with vaccine supplied from head offices in both Montreal and London, the map of the Company's vaccine distribution program looked in many ways as essentially a map of modern Canada, even before Confederation or the railroad. Distribution trails tracked westwards from Montreal, Moose Factory, and York Factory. Vaccines reached as far west as Fort Simpson and Edmonton. There is some suggestion that the vaccine even crossed the Rockies toward the Pacific coast (or arrived directly in Victoria by sea). The campaign was assisted by the Company's employees across the territories. However, now with some baseline immunity, outbreaks were less threatening, and Company employees only provided the vaccine, not as part of a concerted pre-emptive program, but as an intervention in the face of an approaching epidemic, such as happened in Fort William (Thunder Bay) in 1842, when an outbreak occurred near Sault Ste Marie. But this policy was not entirely favoured by central authorities in London as it did not build up sufficient immunity.[158] Initial stories painted the Company's intervention as one of benevolence and compassion, some noting that it was an attempt to prevent conflicts between groups. This trope of the magnanimous colonial force, with benign goodwill towards the savages who knew not what they did, was common elsewhere in the British Empire too. But the self-serving nature of the work was clear — disruptions to trade were not good for profit. And thus began the workings of Canada — and the early signs of our healthcare system.

In 1840, Great Britain banned the practice of variolation to make way for vaccination: variolation certainly had its inconvenience when compared to vaccination in that it could cause localized outbreaks of active disease. We continue to confront similar consequences with a version of polio vaccination which, though convenient to deliver as an oral dose requiring less paraphernalia than an injection, sometimes lets the virus escape into the ecosystem through sanitary waste. If baseline immunity from vaccination is otherwise low, this source has been known to cause rare outbreaks that still circulate in parts of the world.[159] Variolation could also transmit other communicable diseases.

Vaccination had the added benefit of being a made-in-Britain solution that glorified the story of imperial progress over the hackneyed superstitions and traditions of the colonies, and so the pressure to outlaw variolation accumulated. A Quebec City doctor in 1847 noted that Jenner's work was celebrated not only in all Christendom but also by "Jews, Turks, and Heathens." A note from doctors at Hôtel-Dieu that year shows that there was a general fear of migrants bringing back the disease and that there was also a new concern that vaccination did not produce lifelong immunity, like the infection itself did. But nonetheless, vaccination continued, with the sisters running Hôtel-Dieu setting up for vaccination to all who wanted it at noon on Wednesdays and doctors being able to collect the vaccine as well in case they wanted to administer it to their patients in their community practices.[160]

Variolation was outlawed in Canada in 1853 to allow for the dominance of vaccination. The third major outbreak of smallpox in the Prairies was in 1870–1871, after eastern Canada confederated, but with pre-emptive vaccination starting in Winnipeg before there were any cases, it was a considerably less bad outbreak in that region. But as Métis moves towards self-determination made the Canadian government nervous, political crisis rocked Manitoba, hampering vaccine distribution, and mortality increased towards the west.[161] At this point in history, protection from the outbreak was becoming reliant on the creep of Canadian control. Smallpox, profiting off the trade and traffic that increasingly crisscrossed the continent, spread quickly, but liberation from this plague followed these routes too, highlighting the dependency into which Indigenous nations were drawn under the ever-growing reach of extractive capitalism, centred in Euro-American metropoles. Disrupted ecosystems not only exposed Indigenous peoples to new risks, but their means of livelihood spun outside of their control, forcing them to rely increasingly on access granted by the colonizers for necessities of life.

In the 1870s, when the Grey Nuns in Saint Albert, just north of Edmonton, heard about the approaching outbreak of smallpox, they knew they had to act. A small committee was set up as a board of health whose sole task was to combat the epidemic and then be dissolved. The board was focused on commerce-related measures — traders had to demonstrate scars suggesting vaccination, and to cross the river into the territory people had to engage in a ten-day quarantine and pass a medical inspection. The largely Indigenous population had been thoroughly surveyed and censused, so it was known that a third of the people died (about a 50 percent case-fatality rate) with that outbreak in the Fort Edmonton area. The board was recreated in 1876 when another smallpox outbreak approached the city, but a permanent one was not formed until 1892, when the recurring outbreaks were deemed to require more consistent monitoring.[162]

A concerted effort by the federal government to vaccinate people with its own medical personnel in the southwest Prairies in the 1870s greatly dampened smallpox mortality in the region, but the program was cut in favour of letting doctors attached to the police and other practitioners do more haphazard vaccination, allegedly in the best interests of Indigenous peoples, and naturally, the government's purse.[163]

The major outbreak in Montreal in 1885, to which I referred earlier, was a particularly important moment of contestation over smallpox vaccination globally, particularly due to the influence of imperial British politics. As the technology around vaccines developed and evolved, with trial and error of empirical science, there were some vaccine failures. Nowadays we would ascribe some of these faults to incorrect storage or imperfect quality control in production. But longstanding suspicions between the French majority and the English ruling class in Montreal, as Canada's metropole at the time, fuelled annual mortality in smallpox far above the rates in London and Paris.

Certainly, in the 1870s, a significant number of physicians in Montreal were concerned about the quality of the vaccination program in Canada. It was erratic, with no clear pattern of protection from contracting smallpox. Jenner's assurances that, like variolation, vaccination with cowpox infection granted lifelong immunity to smallpox proved to be inaccurate. And indeed, cowpox was actually a very rare disease among cows, so to find the original material to inoculate was a challenge.[164] Early vaccination was dominated by the arm-to-arm method, in which cowpox matter from the lesion that erupted in one person after vaccination was used to immunize the next. This process, which would make us squeamish today to say the least, also required a steady supply of nonimmune children. In India, colonial subjects of oppressed castes were used as available instruments for this work of transmitting and carrying the virus across communities. Sometimes children would be used to transfer the vaccine during a long ocean voyage. A major concern emerged that it transmitted other infectious diseases as well in doing so, syphilis and tuberculosis being the other primary concerns of doctors then.

Dr Coderre was a prominent Montreal physician who first gave a speech opposing vaccination in 1870 after two of his eleven children died following the procedure. A widely respected doctor whose stance did not dent his reputation, he began to view the data emerging elsewhere in the world with scepticism, saying that what people were actually counting was improved smallpox outcomes once caught — since even data in Paris did not suggest that vaccinated people contracted smallpox any less than those unvaccinated. What was actually happening, according to him, was that people were surviving it better due to better social conditions not because of the vaccine. Although Coderre's resistance to vaccination was likely more due to concern about the way it was practised, he also showed a degree of sophistication in understanding infectious outbreaks that still has some pertinence today. Coderre was never fully convinced that all possible factors that may influence outbreaks were explained, wondering (though incorrectly) whether sporadic outbreaks were linked more to continued exposure to zoonotic transmitters that were circulating in the wild rather than any particular human factors, such as low collective immunity.

All of these points were academic in Montreal until the possibility of obligatory state-mandated smallpox vaccination became an issue in an effort to control the city's record on outbreaks. Hingston in 1875 had become mayor of Montreal and used smallpox to organize public healthcare services in the municipality. He intended to follow England's example with compulsory vaccination, countering Coderre's anti-vaccine message in francophone quarters of the city with his own advertising campaign. But as smallpox improved in the city for multiple reasons of its own accord, the debate was left unresolved. Spotty protection from infection led eventually to the devastating 1885 outbreak, which was the worst in settler Canada.[165]

In comparison, in neighbouring Ontario, an outbreak in Hastings County in 1884 allowed the newly constituted provincial Board of Health, led by Dr Peter Bryce, who would also respond to the smallpox outbreak in Six Nations in 1901, to move into swift action when the local county health authorities fell ill. Travel restrictions were instituted, public gatherings in the county banned, and medical students engaged in a door-to-door vaccination campaign. The outbreak did not spread as a result. Given the lack of any provincial health authority in Quebec until 1887, in 1885, Dr Bryce decided to overstep provincial jurisdiction by sending inspectors to examine all passengers and goods entering Ontario from Montreal for smallpox.[166]

Canada's smallpox vaccination production became a lynchpin in the global eradication program in the mid-twentieth century. The initial vaccine farms where cows infected with cowpox were still used to produce inoculant were in many ways the launchpad of the country's pharmaceutical industry. The use of these farms rather than human-to-human chains reassured people about being exposed to other diseases and also provided a degree of quality control, although the idea of inoculation with animal strains offended others.[167] Propelled forward by the 1885 Montreal epidemic, Canada's smallpox vaccination production started to grow, much of it eventually coming from one farm west of Toronto, where a plaque to the Ontario Vaccine Farm still stands in Palmerston, Wellington County.[168] From 1885 to 1911, Dr Alexander Stewart, a general practitioner, ran the farm until he died, when it was taken over by H.B. Coleman. By the First World War, vaccine production was largely taken up by installations in the United States.

The Connaught Laboratories, founded in Toronto in 1914 as the premier Canadian public health institution, not unlike the Pasteur and Lister Institutes, initially devoted itself to the control of diphtheria, which killed thousands of young children. That enterprise eventually took over production of the smallpox vaccine in Ontario.[169] As the organization and its capacity for vaccine production grew, it would eventually become the reference point for the World Health Organization (WHO) program for smallpox eradication in the Americas in the 1960s. Dr Paul Fenje, a recent Serbian immigrant to Canada, became central to the work, though he had been initially hired to work on the rabies vaccine, given a terrible outbreak in the Northwest Territories that spread through Inuit dog packs and into Ontario over a decade, infecting wildlife, domesticated animals, and humans.[170] He was pulled from the rabies work to support the WHO program, although Canada's official role in this regional solidarity was somewhat fraught, as the country only reluctantly joined the regional chapter of the WHO (Pan-American Health Organization) in 1971, and the Connaught Laboratories' collaboration with Brazil's vaccine laboratories ran for a long time without government involvement.[171]

The healthcare system may be a symbol of nation-building for some, but it may not have inspired fuzzy feelings of warmth for all people in Canada at all times. The first Canadian healthcare services afforded to many Indigenous peoples — the missions of the Church and the vaccination by the Hudson's Bay Company — were clearly linked to the colonial enterprise. The Hudson's Bay Company saw traders from Quebec as competitors for a long time, even after its conquest. A lot of their accounts of smallpox epidemics were part of monitoring interactions with rivals, keeping tabs on their movements. Health outcomes were documented as an extension of a great degree of commercial surveillance, especially given the immense impact smallpox had on the trading relationships that Indigenous peoples developed. Lieutenant Butler's detailed account of outbreaks was part of a military surveillance mission to cement British control over central North America. In their struggles against the disease, Indigenous nations found vaccination one of the few survival strategies available to them, even if offered by the colonial government, because there were otherwise limited opportunities, as resources available to them eroded, to develop their own management systems for this disease.

This evident foundation of the commercial imperative, in souls, in land, or in furs, for colonial healthcare interventions makes me reflect on my current role in the healthcare system in Canada. Missionaries, merchants, and the military played a role in entrenching healthcare colonialism. The benign magnanimity of "serving" Indigenous communities is a way for many settlers, especially more recent immigrants buying into the Canadian dream like me, to make good with a state whose agenda will never be liberating. The very point of Canada has been to settle other people's land and to seek out its resources. Indigenous peoples have to navigate their survival through this constant reality. Healthcare services are part of this settlement the federal government imposed on Indigenous nations to coax them to stay on small parcels of their original territories. We could argue that I am a continuation of that Hudson's Bay Company tradition of health surveillance to maintain Canada's commercial interests. The medicine chest clause is a tainted offering. And I am part of that imbalanced exchange.

In building a more robust, responsive healthcare system in Canada, we need to incorporate lessons of its birth in this background of tumult and turmoil. Wars that were formative for the development of North American nation-states fuelled smallpox and its response: prisoners of wars, refugee flights, badly practised variolation, all triggering outbreaks.[172] Contagion was a part of the confusion that Indigenous communities faced, but it served as a critical warning sign of a larger upheaval. In an ordinary household in an unremarkable village outside of Kolkata, gnawed away by smallpox for perhaps millennia, the arrival of the disease in my grandmother's household was perhaps routine, part of a known cycle, framed by ritual and experience. In a similar household in North America, new and everywhere, the disease's disruption was but a symptom of the swirl of colonialism's looming chaos and unknown.

Tuberculosis

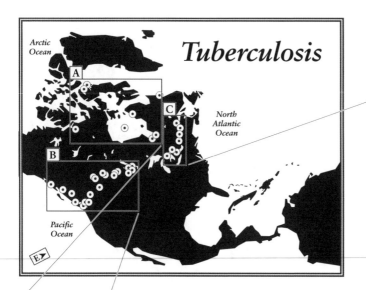

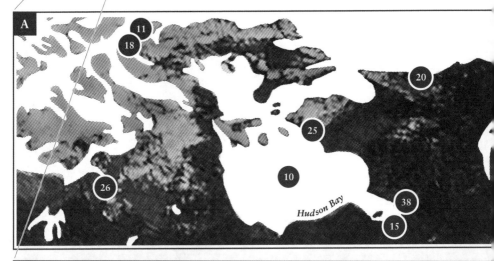

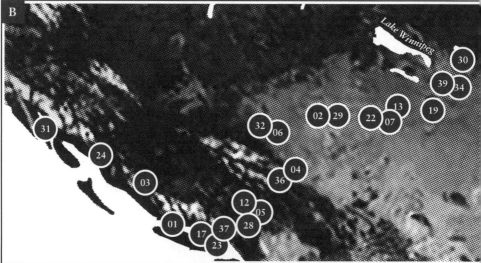

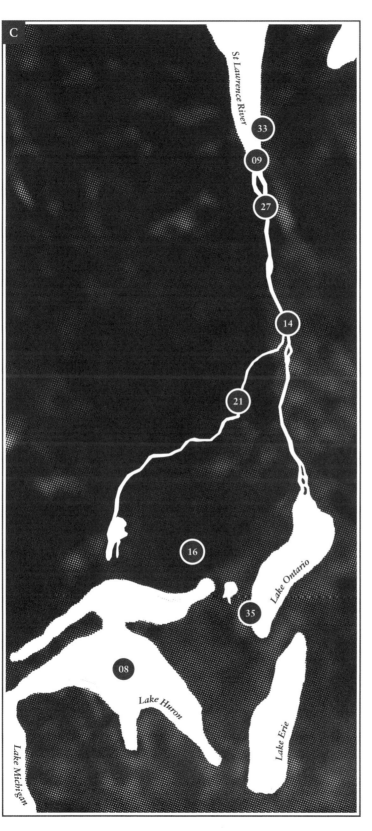

Locations

01	Alert Bay
02	Battleford
03	Bella Coola
04	Calgary
05	Chilliwack
06	Edmonton
07	Fort Qu'Appelle
08	Great Lakes
09	Grosse-Île (Quebec)
10	Hudson Bay
11	Ikpiarjuk
12	Kamloops
13	Melville
14	Montreal
15	Moose Factory
16	Muskoka
17	Nanaimo
18	Nanisivik
19	Ninette
20	Okak (Labrador)
21	Ottawa
22	Pasqua First Nation
23	Penelakut Island
24	Prince Rupert
25	Puvirnituq
26	Qingaut
27	Quebec City
28	Sardis
29	Saskatoon
30	Selkirk
31	Sitka (Alaska)
32	St Albert (Alberta)
33	St Lawrence River
34	St Vital (Manitoba)
35	Toronto
36	Tsuut'ina
37	Vancouver
38	Waskaganish
39	Winnipeg

4

Tuberculosis

Prior to my admission to the United States as a university student in the late 1990s, I was screened for carrying latent tuberculosis and tested positive. The nurse had injected the purified protein extract derived from the bacteria into the skin of my forearm, and two days later, I had an unmistakable result: a red swollen patch of a size that could not easily be explained away by reasons other than that the bacterial culprit must lie, though probably inactive, within my system.

As a child I had had the Bacillus Calmette-Guerin (BCG) vaccine, which can make the test turn positive as the immune system registers its response as though you were exposed to the actual bacterium. But usually the immune memory of the BCG fades past childhood. The vaccine leaves a tell-tale pockmark where it is administered in infancy, which I still have high on my left shoulder, stigma that easily identifies me as hailing from poorer parts of the world, a sly wink of camaraderie that exists between us, the migrant diseased. As vaccines go, it is quite imperfect: while the inoculation is known to decrease risk for serious tuberculous complications in children, it has variable ability to confer significant immunity in the long term and has limited, if any, impact on transmission.[1] It is used in many parts of the world where the risk of paediatric tuberculosis death still exists. It has not been in routine use in Canada since the 1970s and only continued exceptionally in some communities into the twenty-first century, such as in Nunavut.[2]

About one in four people on the planet today is presumed to be a carrier of tuberculosis, but only a minority — approximately a tenth of those — fall sick and transmit the disease.[3] Catching tuberculosis is difficult unless conditions promote it. It takes prolonged exposure to be infected by the bacteria-laden aerosols lingering in the air from the cough typical of someone with active tuberculosis in the lungs: good ventilation disperses the particles,[4] and sunlight's capacity to inactivate tuberculosis bacteria has long been known.[5] If the bacteria do find their way into someone's lungs, most people mount an immune response to contain it, remaining well and not infectious. People whose health is compromised by malnutrition or other medical conditions may not be able to funnel immune system resources to stop development of the disease.

Back in 1998, it did not seem unreasonable that I might be one of those carriers of tuberculosis, having lived in India, which has by far the most cases of the disease in the world.[6] Skinny and small for my age, I might have been assumed to be a prime candidate to have an active infection as recent immigrants are among those with the highest risk of tuberculosis in Canada, although I had none of the classic symptoms. My chest x-ray showing no worrisome signs, I had a pleasant conversation with the doctor, who asked questions I found heartstoppingly personal about sexuality as part of her thorough assessment. Young and uncomfortable with myself, mistrustful of the consequences, I sidestepped the inquiries with half lies, invention a form of active agency. The link between active tuberculosis infection and HIV was known even to me at that point, and I did not wish to discuss risk factors.

The doctor — kindly, older, white — explained that she thought it unlikely that my highly positive reaction was due to the vaccine as an infant so long ago and more likely to be due to exposure later in life, or that in other words, I was a carrier. She suggested that I undergo the months-long treatment to eliminate the probable latent infection. This intervention is considered significant in Canada in its public health control of tuberculosis. At that point, I had little sense of the disease's trajectory in the country over the centuries, not understanding the layers of history which lay behind that invitation to medicate myself for several months. In Canada, where the burden of tuberculosis on average is now relatively low, elimination of the disease seems like a feasible public health goal, suppressing the possibility of outbreaks to the maximum. Having beaten back the disease into a few corners, contemporary Canadian public health policy promotes aggressive action in treating those who are carriers, even though they are not sick and not contagious, to limit any possibility of active tuberculosis rearing its head later in life.

I was easily cowed by authority: young, brown, new to the country, raised in a family that toed the line, unhappy with my own queerness, unaccompanied by any advocates. But I also had a lot going for me: a comfortable home, access to good food, basic scientific literacy, and fluency in the language. I understood what was being offered to me, although I found it mildly ridiculous. As mentioned, India has the world's highest number of people with active tuberculosis — treating those who were actually sick was a priority there, not people who maybe one day in the future might fall ill. In all likelihood, I would have pretended to accede to any doctor who had been more forceful or intimidating, but I would have then found ways not to cooperate: not filling the prescription or attending follow-up appointments, behaviours in a patient that my colleagues now would consider "uncooperative" at its mildest.

But with this gentle physician, who gave me some space to feel brave, I declined the intervention for reasons I thought were acceptable. Even now, twenty-odd years later with medical training, I would hesitate before I made another choice. I felt generally well, and although it was impossible to predict, believed that I was not someone who would likely develop active tuberculosis, with my touching middle-class faith that the socioeconomic dynamics that supported my immune response would continue in perpetuity. The antimicrobial regimen offered then for latent tuberculosis treatment was much lengthier and more rigorous, with more risk to the liver, than the one that evidence nowadays suggests is just as effective. I was perhaps reluctant to risk my own hepatic health for the goals of the Canadian state.

But my main hesitation was that I thought it was silly to treat latent tuberculosis in me when it was likely that I would be reexposed. I saw myself returning to India often, and although I did not expect to be in close proximity for extended periods of time with people with active tuberculosis — at that time I had little idea I would eventually become a healthcare worker — I did not see how treating myself once would prevent me from contracting it again. I was not even completely sure that I was an actual carrier since even in 1998 tests to identify latent infections were still crude and clumsy. An online clinical tool that has since been developed suggests that it was about 37 percent likely that my positive test was a true positive, supporting my interpretation then that it was more likely I was not a latent carrier. But the algorithm also notes that my chance of developing liver side effects from eradication treatment would have been essentially zero.[7]

I understand all these years later that public health interventions are more about attenuating risk for the larger population than they are concerned about my own individual trajectory with the infection. As a professional now, I would probably encourage patients in a similar position to take the treatment, although knowing my own choice, I would sympathize with people who declined. More significantly, I comprehend why many people who have an even more precarious relationship with the medical system than I did might balk. While treatment of active (infectious) tuberculosis can be enforced by the legal system in Canada, latent tuberculosis cannot as it is not a direct danger to anyone's health. It is entirely probable that most people with latent carrier status will not ever develop the active, infectious disease in today's Canada, where nutrition, housing, and immune status are generally robust. Treatment of latent tuberculosis simply reinforces a shield of security to ensure that there are no runaway eruptions of disease.

Perhaps vindicated that I did not take the treatment, I did end up working in contexts with close proximity to people with active tuberculosis, for instance, in South Africa during the height of the HIV epidemic, years before I considered medical school. In the early 2000s, the disease was making a resurgence across the country as people's immune systems faltered. Tuberculosis became an easier way to discuss how people died, rather than engaging with the stigma of HIV. In a tiny farm school where the principal had just died of unclear reasons, I met with the acting head teacher and a number of her colleagues to discuss an HIV awareness session with the students. The conversation was tortuously stilted and hostile, the teachers stiff and quiet as I, insensible and determined, prattled on in self-righteous conviction, appalled that they seemed to think that HIV was not a major problem in their area. In one exchange that I wince at now, frustrated at the lack of progress, I asked abruptly, "How did the principal die?"

The successor looked down, "They say tuberculosis."

I snorted with a triumphant gloat. Although I eventually wore them down to the point where we had permission to speak to the students at the school, I certainly made no friends. Statistically speaking, of the six South African adults in the room with me on that day twenty years ago, two of them were HIV-positive and aware there was no treatment available to them then: a diagnosis meant death. I know now, mortified by my oblivious missionary zeal then, that the stiff quietness was fear. My heart still breaks that one of those teachers pulled me aside privately later and asked me how she could protect her children. When I asked if she had been tested herself, she shook her head with impatience, and even then, I noted the resignation, "It doesn't matter about me. What about my children?"

Encounters with tuberculosis continued as I began clinical training. One of the clearest memories I have from a month's rotation at the Calcutta School of Tropical Medicine was a clinic visit of a young woman who was complaining of crampy abdominal pain with bloody diarrhoea over many weeks. My supervisor asked me what I thought, and uncertain in my early training, I quavered and said, "Well I'd say maybe Crohn's disease ..." but he shook his head, amused at my Canadian repertoire of diagnoses. Tuberculosis, he said. In India, it was almost 90 percent certain that it would be intestinal tuberculosis, a possibility that occurs after someone recovers from active tuberculosis infection in the lung which may have gone unnoticed. The germ disseminates and eventually, in its slow-growing way, shows up in peculiar places well beyond the lung. Given the burden of tuberculosis in India, my preceptor told me to consider the disease a potential explanation for every single patient's complaint. I recall this case distinctly as when the patient returned a while later with her biopsy results, it confirmed that she had not tuberculosis but Crohn's disease after all.

Many years later, when working on a paediatric ward in a small town on the River Niger, we often dealt with malnourished children who were not gaining weight. Testing children for tuberculosis can be quite tricky using conventional methods, and we did not have the facilities for the advanced investigations that would have facilitated diagnosis. Often if we found that children were not responding to malnutrition therapy within two weeks, we would start them on tuberculosis treatment on the empirical assumption that little else we could do anything about in our constrained context would explain such wasting. Almost without exception, the children would begin gaining weight after starting the anti-tuberculosis medications.

A tricky situation would be in cases where a child under six months would not be gaining weight. At that age, where exclusive breastfeeding is the best medical therapy for poor weight gain, exploring diagnoses such as HIV or tuberculosis might be the only way forward. But given the practical impossibility of testing the baby for the latter, we would test the mother, the logic being that the baby's closest contact for infection would likely be the breastfeeding parent. If the test there turned out to be positive, the chances were that the child was infected too.

We diagnosed such a case once, although the testing was almost unnecessary, because the mother was actively coughing up blood into our unmasked faces as I examined the baby in our austere hospital. We had tried to isolate her away from the busy main ward into a room where there were fewer patients. I am not sure it did any good because the wards in general were open to balconies with plentiful fresh air, but this tiny isolation chamber at the end of the corridor was much stuffier and had a lot less of the natural light that might have been helpful in reducing spread.

These experiences of tuberculosis far away may seem to have little to do with the history of colonization of North America, but this disease was central to the way Canada formed and functions. In parts of the North to this day, as in India and sub-Saharan Africa, we can still diagnose tuberculosis commonly. But the story of how this prevalence came to be says as much about twentieth-century Canada as it does about the *Mycobacterium tuberculosis* organism itself.

Tuberculosis has a longstanding relationship with the human species. It emerges from a peculiar family of bacteria, unrelated to many other routine infections, though one other species on the same family tree branch as tuberculosis causes leprosy. The prefix *myco-* refers to fungus, given the confusion it initially generated for seeming to grow the way mould does. We know now the germs are bacteria, but they are difficult to identify through the traditional microscope method called the Gram stain. Thus, if tuberculosis is suspected, physicians need to ask the laboratory specifically for a stain that gives mycobacteria another technical name used to describe them: acid-fast bacilli.

Under the microscope, with a particular set of chemicals used to stain them to become visible, mycobacteria often show up as a pretty pink, a construct of laboratory techniques. The mycobacteria are strikingly slow-growing — both leprosy and tuberculosis take months to years to incubate in people with well-functioning immune systems, compared to days for many other bacteria. In a laboratory setting, it can take weeks waiting for sufficient growth in the microbiology dish for mycobacteria to be definitively identified compared to two to three days for other bacteria. Thus, beyond staining alone, clinicians again cannot rely on routine laboratory techniques to monitor for mycobacterial growth if they have a suspicion for the diagnosis. A chest x-ray, however, can be telling for an active infection, either present or historical — if you have easy access to one. X-rays were initially used for mass screening of tuberculosis in Canada, with Saskatchewan as pioneer. Melville was the first place in the country, in 1941, to undertake a mass formal survey, and in 1948, 96 percent of people in Saskatoon underwent testing, although the incidence of tuberculosis had already dropped extensively by 1945. In the 1960s, about 75 percent of British Columbia was screened for tuberculosis.[8] But then, tuberculin skin tests, such as the one I had in 1998, were found to be the cheapest option. They could detect latent infections, and then also avoided the considerable infrastructure required for mass x-rays, which would only really find old or active tuberculosis anyway, with latent carriers unidentified. However, by the 1960s, the discovery that tuberculin led to lots of false positives, perhaps due to the presence of other bacteria in the same family, complicated matters for a long while. We only managed to address this concern partially about forty years later, in the early 2000s, with a blood test that can sometimes help to differentiate more accurately active from carrier status — which would have helped me when I reacted to the skin test back in 1998![9]

The tuberculosis germ has found a way over the centuries to coexist with us, thriving through human infection. As we have seen, in most humans, approximately 90 percent of them, the relationship is somewhat of a dead-end. The human immune system reaches a stalemate with the bacteria, and the germs are forced to live within walled-off granulomas in the lung, unable to be passed on to another host. This ending might be tragic for the individual bacteria concerned, but collectively as a species, the bacteria do not need much more for success, as human society has historically facilitated their work immensely. In the remainder of infected humans, the immune system is too run down by poor nutrition to fend off the onslaught of concentrated infected particles in poorly ventilated, dark housing to which people may be confined. Unable to keep the colony of pathogens at bay, the infection grows as the bacteria merrily reproduce, generating enough disturbance in the airway to cause the human host to cough reflexively in an effort to clear it, and thus passing the germs out into the air to infect others.

Tuberculosis is considered to have been part of the human experience for thousands of years, though there are disputes about whether it emerged 40,000 years ago around the time humans were travelling out of Africa or whether it was within the last 5000 to 10,000 years, its relationship with us being mediated perhaps through another species. The central role of cows in smallpox has a converse here as the bovine form of tuberculosis can instead easily cause infection in humans, as opposed to immunity. One argument even suggests that the human disease jumped from cows through a mutant evolution, but an alternative hypothesis holds the reverse as true: that the bovine disease mutated from the human form at the time of domestication of cattle. Another type of tuberculosis-like germ found widely in the environment can infect the immunocompromised, although that particular form is not known to be transmissible between humans.

Given the family of bacteria's worldwide presence in many different species, it seems likely that some form of tuberculosis did also exist in the Americas prior to the arrival of the Europeans. Bony deformities suggestive of infection with mycobacteria have been discovered in mummies in the landmass. Even despite the reservations one might have about techniques of study, archaeological finds of relatively recent times suggest that perhaps tuberculosis was endemic in the Great Lakes area prior to European arrival.[10] Various theories circulate about the disease jumping to humans from seals in Peru, or arriving with the Vikings in Labrador, or llamas and bison bringing the bovine form across a possible Bering land bridge. Even if tuberculosis was present prior to 1492 in the Americas, it was of a strain that is no longer dominant as the European variant has become the most prevalent.

Evidence from across the Pacific adds context to this picture. As the largest country in Polynesia, which was the last region of the world to encounter European colonization, Aotearoa (New Zealand) holds some fascinating insight. While it may at first glance seem unlikely, the tuberculosis strains found in New Zealand are shockingly similar to strains found in Quebec (which then spread westward across Canada toward the Pacific coast). French implication in both whaling in the South Pacific and the fur trade in the Atlantic perhaps seeded these outbreaks in Indigenous peoples in both the Americas and Oceania.[11] Whether these strains are the only introduction of tuberculosis to the region is unclear — some strains can quickly become dominant, displacing original strains, making it trickier to trace diseases to the source. Given the course of tuberculosis's time in human history, which rivals the intricacies of our closely entwined biological and social relationship with malaria, it will probably be difficult to determine the beginnings of tuberculosis in the Americas with certainty.

Notwithstanding its existence on North America prior to contact, the general understanding is that the disease spread massively with European settlement. In Europe, tuberculosis was already known as a disease of poverty and marginalization, with its appearance in critical moments of Romantic era cultural works, such as *Jane Eyre* by Charlotte Brontë in England in 1847, where significantly, an institutionalized child dies of it, and in Verdi's 1853 opera *La Traviata*, set in Italy, where a sex worker confronts the malady, its inextricable link to morality a leitmotif.

It would be some time before tuberculosis had the same impact in the Americas, but by the turn of the twentieth century, the disease would loom large in Canadian medical policy. It is possible that the disease became entrenched through repeated introduction with arriving settlers from Europe, but the late appearance of many of the worst tuberculosis outbreaks among Indigenous peoples implies that it took many decades after contact for conditions conducive to spread to take hold, suggesting that tuberculosis is the epidemic above all others that is symptomatic of colonial policy rather than accidental contact. Tuberculosis would not have made itself known as a widespread phenomenon in the Americas unless there were severe physiological stressors that led to immunosuppression. Malnutrition would be a critical factor among them. As the economy changed around them, Indigenous peoples often had to struggle with finding a livelihood in the new economic structures in which they were unwittingly caught up.[12] Poorly ventilated housing as well as lack of exposure to sunlight were also major contributors to the spread of tuberculosis.

Even before settlers became aware of the disease making inroads in Indigenous communities, tuberculosis dominated the medical imagination of the nineteenth and early twentieth centuries — and for good reason as it dominated the cause of illness for many people. To this day, addressing tuberculosis can have a dramatic impact on collective health. In 1899, prior to the era where antimicrobial treatments were available, one paediatrics textbook split its focus, with 54 pages on illnesses in the newborn infant, 125 pages on nutrition, and 130 pages addressing general respiratory illnesses. Tuberculosis had its own separate 135 pages.[13]

The infection was widespread in Canada, affecting marginalized settler communities disproportionately early in Confederation, but there are limited data on the rates in Indigenous communities prior to the massive institutionalization of children in residential schools. The establishments served as super-spreaders, but the disease must have taken root prior to that phase. By 1928, the Department of Indian Affairs in Canada was noting that the prevalence of tuberculosis in Indigenous communities was five times the rate of the general population. The department blamed the rates on the lack of nutrition but also on Indigenous communities having not learned "to make good use of the supplies to be had." Ignorance and the lack of education are also considered as reasons, but the department pointed mainly to the lack of immunity from prior exposure in Indigenous communities compared to white settlers as its principal, probably flawed, argument.[14] This theory has been used to explain why tuberculosis continues to linger in the Prairies and in the North to this day, compared to the Atlantic and Pacific coasts, which saw relatively earlier settlement from Europe. It wavers slightly in plausibility if tuberculosis was already known in the Americas, unless the European strain was novel enough to confuse otherwise robust immune systems.

In pursuing this line of inquiry, one study suggested that communities that had later contact with colonizers and higher rates of tuberculosis tended to be both more remote and have more overcrowded housing.[15] This finding raises the question of whether the high rates of tuberculosis were really caused by less effective immunity to tuberculosis due to later exposure to colonists, or simply by the resultant overcrowding from more recent land theft. The study offered that remoteness of communities from medical services seemed not to explain the differences in tuberculosis incidence because the very fact that the disease was being diagnosed efficiently even in isolated areas was an indication that government screening programs for the disease were effective. Although perhaps persuasive, this argument clearly does not mean the epidemic is better controlled. Diagnostic services for one disease alone as indicative of the strength of the whole healthcare system can be sadly misleading. As a healthcare practitioner, I know that the perversity of funding from governments and donors can mean that although malaria or HIV or tuberculosis might be easily identified, treatment for the illness, or for all the other everyday illnesses that may come through a clinic door, does not automatically follow.

All epidemics track a curve of their own, cases rising as transmission chains take hold and then ebbing as factors such as immunity and reduction of contacts with the sick sometimes spontaneously kick into effect. The time of the first outbreak may determine where along the curve a given community lies in its outbreak. Multiple factors can accelerate or brake its course. In the case of tuberculosis, factors like overcrowded housing may push communities along a very rapid trajectory of spread. The contention that tuberculosis to this day may simply be working its way through communities by the dictates of epidemiological models alone and will eventually burn itself out might be tempting. But I worry such fatalism serves to encourage passive inaction in face of the clear injustices inherent to the disease. Tuberculosis's propensity, like many infectious diseases, to affect the most marginalized disproportionately was apparent late into the twentieth century in Canada. In Edmonton, half the people diagnosed with tuberculosis in the mid-1990s showed up in the emergency room twice in the six months prior to their diagnosis, seeking care for myriad issues that were at that point not known to be related to tuberculosis. That cohort of patients was more likely to be older, have another condition (such as HIV), and eventually die of tuberculosis.[16] The half who did not have to use the emergency room prior to diagnosis clearly had access to other supports for their care and had better outcomes.

Ascribing these factors simply to the epidemic cycle is not the most productive way forward. In today's mobile populations, tuberculosis will not be eradicated here until it is gone everywhere. And even then, the bovine form continues to circulate discreetly in wild species in Canada, ready to leap back across to humans. It is generally believed that the disease was introduced to the wild from imported livestock, spilling over from European cows to deer and bison. Cattle in Canada are almost completely free from tuberculosis now, although there are sporadic cases, mainly in western Canada. These outbreaks seem to be linked to contact with wild animals transmitting tuberculosis back into domesticated herds. When bison were first reintroduced in Canada in the early twentieth century, after their near elimination on the Plains, the federal government response to the discovery of tuberculosis in that herd was to clamp down, not so much on the disease though hundreds of bison were slaughtered, but on the truth, forbidding veterinarians from admitting this reality publicly.[17] The ailing bison were perhaps inconvenient for the aims of commercialization and preservation of romantic settler idealizations of Canadian wilderness.

But animal tuberculosis has real repercussions on humans, with a case of active infection as late as the 1990s in one of the veterinarians responding to an outbreak in game farm elk in Alberta.[18] This case is a clear challenge to previous notions that cross-species infection historically occurred only through the consumption of cow's milk: airborne contamination from cows has obviously occurred too, especially in workers with very close contact with the animals, who then might have also spread it to their children. Canadian veterinarians today are unlikely to see tuberculosis in herds, which makes it harder to diagnose when it does appear, but aside from the well-being of the animals themselves, this need is a concern for human collective health too. Even if the general perception is that we have beaten tuberculosis back into distant enough corners of the North, of immigrant ghettos, of remote game parks, that it no longer poses a real threat to comfortable Canadians, it is evident that the belief that we are protected from an infectious disease active anywhere on the planet is naive to the extreme. No one is free if even one of us in chains, yes, but also, not one of us can be healthy if even one of us is sick.

In 1929, Saskatchewan became the first North American jurisdiction to offer universal free diagnosis and care of tuberculosis, a precursor to its later innovations in healthcare financing.[19] Universal tuberculosis treatment in Saskatchewan might have laid the groundwork for the way the first public health insurance program in Canada eventually rolled into the province about four decades later. Its tuberculosis program reportedly brought its death rates from the disease down to the lowest in Canada in the 1930s. The Saskatchewan example is revealing about the course of the epidemic in twentieth-century Canada and bears some study. Even though their healthcare services lie under federal jurisdiction, Indigenous people could also access this provincially managed coverage.

In 1911, as part of the wave of generalized mobilization against tuberculosis, the chief public health officer of Saskatchewan decided that it would be important to start a federation of local municipal organizations working against the disease, which became known as the Saskatchewan Anti-Tuberculosis League. Its ultimate goal was to build a hospital and a sanatorium in the province dedicated to treating the illness. As a partnership between this civil society fundraising and provincial grants, although interrupted by the First World War, a sanatorium was eventually completed at Fort San in 1917.[20] The federal government stepped in in 1918 to fund beds to house veterans with tuberculosis. By 1921, the sanatorium had rapidly expanded with beds dedicated to children and mothers who were unable to fund their care through private means. While therapies remained dubious, it did not hurt patients to be away from cramped homes and thankless jobs. Fort San was exclusively an institution for settlers for many years, although it would eventually grudgingly allow Indigenous people to be admitted as part of an arrangement to repay debts to the federal government.[21] Reports of abuse that are largely in line with colonial policies of humiliation and oppression emerge to this day.[22]

In 1921, Saskatchewan appointed the Anti-Tuberculosis Commission to explore the situation of the epidemic. It found that one in every eight women receiving a widow's allowance from the government had been bereaved by tuberculosis. More shockingly, in its sample of schoolchildren across eight districts, it found about half of white children showed exposure to tuberculosis but that almost every single Indigenous child did as well. At the teacher-training schools (normal schools), three-quarters of the students had signs of carrying tuberculosis, while 1 percent were active cases. Dr Ferguson, secretary of the Commission, noted that residential school admission policies played a role in damaging the health of Indigenous children. Additionally, although the consumption of unpasteurised milk was a known risk for tuberculosis spread, close contact of workers in abattoir settings in an agricultural context like Saskatchewan was also important, and the Commission became interested in the control of tuberculosis as a bovine disease.[23]

In response to these findings, the Commission asked that all schoolchildren be medically examined in Saskatchewan, with time set aside in the curriculum for health teaching, that clinics dedicated to tuberculosis be established, along with a travelling specialist to support rural physicians who did not have access to such a clinic, and that public health nursing services be expanded, with all nursing students required to have a three-month rotation in a sanatorium. In particular, the Commission suggested that there be specific focus on tuberculosis in Indigenous communities.[24]

This forward thinking is impressive even now. Twelve of the twenty-one recommendations of the Commission were carried out. Several Saskatchewan municipalities were already employing a full-time physician for work we would now consider as public health, with annual physical exams at schools in their jurisdiction, allowing for closer monitoring of tuberculosis cases in the community. Two further sanatoria were opened in Saskatchewan by 1928, and 10 percent of all beds in general hospitals that received provincial grants had to be reserved for tuberculosis patients, who would be treated by the travelling specialist. As soon as a sanatorium bed opened up, they would be transferred out of the hospital.[25]

The move towards universal free treatment became pressing despite this extensive investment. Although the infrastructure was built with lots of public money, the daily operations were privately financed, with patients paying about 80 percent of the costs to the Saskatchewan Anti-Tuberculosis League, except in the case of veterans, whose fees were paid by the federal Department of Soldiers' Civil Re-establishment. The first whispers of redistributing these costs came in 1920 as municipal governments became required to contribute to the League, establishing a pool of funds, separated by urban and rural status, to cover the treatment for patients who could not afford it.

It soon became clear that 90 percent of people requiring treatment could not afford it. Sanatorium treatment involved prolonged costs. Even people who were able to pay were impoverished by the long stays, especially when unable to return to work immediately due to the disease. Many people were hesitant to accept charity treatment, leaving them out and infectious in the community. By 1928, the municipal funds were already paying almost the entire cost for most people, aside from a small portion paid by the provincial government.

By 1926, a motion for free tuberculosis treatment was already being proposed at the annual meeting of the association of Saskatchewan's rural municipalities. It received only 3 percent of the vote. On its third attempt, in 1928, it passed, a testament to incredible organizing on the part of clairvoyant early advocates who

made this sea change possible in two years. The provincial government, also pressured by the urban municipalities, quickly acceded,
and as of New Year's Day 1929, anyone who had been resident
in Saskatchewan for six months who was suspected of having tuberculosis could have free treatment at a sanatorium, covered by
provincial and municipal funds pooled together. Veterans did not
have to meet the residency requirement.[26]

This policy change liberated many more people to seek care,
and Saskatchewan saw a surge in cases related to people being
diagnosed. Data from 1925 to 1930 showed substantial increase
in early diagnosis in the province. The League had also put on fundraising events to pay for physicians to do tracing, examining close
contacts of patients to recommend further x-rays and consultation
with the travelling chest specialist. The financial incentive made
physicians more eager to do the contact tracing, and as a result, patients started to receive treatment — such as it was — earlier. Even
though sanatorium treatment was not particularly effective, it did
provide opportunities to limit in-community spread of tuberculosis. With this concerted program, by 1933, the League believed that
it was in touch with almost all tuberculosis cases in Saskatchewan,
and there were signs that the peak in sanatorium hospitalization
was turning.[27] How individuals, settler or Indigenous, actually experienced the institutionalization may have been a different matter
beyond the policy success.

The dawning realization of the inequitable outcomes for
Indigenous peoples also led to some intervention in Saskatchewan.
Federal agencies worked with a health unit in the Fort Qu'Appelle
region to fund healthcare workers dedicated to tuberculosis control, which resulted in the mortality rate from the disease dropping
to half the average rate for Indigenous peoples provincially. The
League suggested that this focus of Indigenous service be extended
to all health units across Saskatchewan but also that all Indigenous
children found to have tuberculosis have their own separate board-
ing school — that is, suggesting a model of containment of infectious disease.[28] From a public health perspective, this approach is
what we might call cohorting, but it did not fundamentally question the model of the residential school. The idea of expanding
some residential schools into sanatoria had been around since

1907, when Dr Peter Bryce, of Hastings County smallpox fame and the chief medical officer for Indian Affairs in Ottawa at the time, had suggested it. In 1935, Dr Ferguson noted that segregation of active cases in Indigenous communities would have the same effect in decreasing the rates of tuberculosis as had happened among white settlers in Saskatchewan. Some churches also supported this idea by this time (perhaps due to implications for their funding?).[29] As improving living standards for settler Canadians, bolstered by the ongoing endeavour of extraction of resources from Indigenous land, drove tuberculosis rates down for them, the Canadian Tuberculosis Association, with physicians and sanatorium directors among its membership, shifted its attention to Indigenous communities as it sought continued relevance, and doctors began to insist on the value of racially segregated institutionalization.[30]

The federal government did support Saskatchewan's program by funding a travelling clinician in the 1930s to examine all children at residential schools, using the opportunity to cut four other physician postings at residential schools and reserves, thereby saving costs.[31] I now wonder how my own work as a travelling physician, like so many other doctors who work in Canada's North, shuttling in and out of remote Indigenous communities, emerges out of that history of federal tight-fistedness. Other factors have contributed to this structure of dislocated doctoring, but in medical school, I had not questioned the model of physicians travelling in and out of isolated communities, as I had just assumed it a routine part of medical service in the country — a normalization of the idea that a full-time physician in a remote small community was a poor use of resources. It even used to strike me as odd when people outside Canada were bemused by it. In reality, a full family practice today would be considered around 1500–2000 patients if primary care were all you were doing, ignoring the emergency cases that remote physicians have to handle. Even though there are changes in today's medicine that see better staffing of doctors in isolated areas, the paradigm of part-time physicians in Indigenous communities still lingers, embedded in patterns of selective federal austerity.

After communities launched a successful campaign to reverse attempted cuts to tuberculosis spending in Saskatchewan in 1937, the federal government eventually agreed to ramp up efforts to suppress the disease in Indigenous populations in Saskatchewan, not only for the benefit for their communities "but to protect the White population as well."[32] They at long last agreed to the policy of releasing children with active tuberculosis from residential school — a policy that had been suggested over thirty years prior — in order to limit transmission from child to child. Tuberculosis had first been demonstrated to be infectious in 1869, so presumably it did not take sixty-eight years for the federal government's understanding to catch up, but rather, this truth was inconvenient for the policy goal of obliterating Indigenous identity in children through institutionalization. The lost three decades since Dr Bryce's suggestion resulted in the rampant spread of the disease through the schools, which is an explanation for why tuberculosis, above all diseases, is not only the product of poverty but, in Canada, a consequence of colonization.[33]

Set above the banks of the Humber River in western Toronto is the West Park Healthcare Centre. Dedicated to serving the needs of people in Ontario who need rehabilitation, whether after strokes or amputations among many other diagnoses, the seemingly unremarkable nature of the complex of red and brown buildings in a quiet residential enclave belies its central position in Canadian healthcare history. Over a hundred years ago, in 1904, it began as the Toronto Free Hospital for Consumptive Poor. It was part of a wave of sanatoria opening in Canada, assisted by the Sanatorium Association, in response to middle-class panic at rates of tuberculosis in the country, concerns about morality of the poor dominating discourse on the disease. Initially a fashionable intervention for the elite to mimic trends in Europe, "taking the cure" involved attending a sanatorium for rest and recuperation in fresh air away from the city. It gradually became policy enforced on the less elite, a way to institutionalize the poor and the immigrant to encourage people to adopt norms of behaviour.

The import of the European conception of sanatoria with expansive access to the outdoors took on another meaning in the settler context. The first sanatorium in Canada opened in 1897 on land that became known as the Muskokas, from which Algonquin and

Huron-Wendat people were moved after the Free Land Grant and Homestead Act of 1868, which encouraged settlement for families that wanted to cultivate the area. Logging in the region was also facilitated by the government. Prior to that Act, the Muskoka region was considered for a large reserve for Indigenous peoples. But land around the Great Lakes in the vicinity of Toronto became too strategic, and by the 1830s, it became clear government policy to settle the land, the governor of Upper Canada (Ontario) at the time, Sir John Colborne, deciding that the Indigenous peoples in that region were to be moved to smaller or more distant reserves.[34] He is reputed to have increased the colony's population by 50 percent in three years by establishing an organized system of bringing in British settlers.[35]

With the land cleared in this way, Muskoka saw the world's first sanatorium that provided some care for free, where settlers could be subsidized to recover from a disease that would decimate Indigenous nations, on land from which they had displaced the very same nations. While the first 1897 Muskoka Cottage Hospital required payment for admission, this second sanatorium in the region accepted subsidized patients as long as they were not too sick. Eventually, as sanatoria expanded, the Toronto Free Hospital, which is now West Park, was the first to take in people even with advanced tuberculosis who were unable to pay fees.[36] It opened a wing dedicated to children in 1913. And even a century later, with a different vocation, it still has a tuberculosis unit as a support for difficult or complex cases of the disease in Ontario.

Hospitals in general in Canada transformed from places for the poor to places where the well-off could also count on dedicated medical care in the early twentieth century, as part of the broader reification of institutionalized Western medicine that occurred across the world. Developed as distinct from general hospitals, tuberculosis sanatoria were initially dedicated to use by settlers. Although wealthy people could afford to pay for extended sojourns in the countryside of their own account, early tuberculosis control efforts in Canada were focused on improving the poor as subjects and making them more amenable, pliant subjects to the desires of elites. Even with antibiotic therapy, which initially required regular injections before oral medications were developed, long institutional stays were often required. Aside from their ability to isolate people with infection away from their households, where a significant amount of transmission occurred especially in overcrowded areas, there is little evidence that the sanatoria provided much more than allowing people an opportunity to build up their immune system with good nutrition to fight the infection. Still, they were popular in the imagination of the charitable Canadian class as an institutional environment to reform character and citizenship. In the late nineteenth century, the state was beginning to assert its authority to legislate over people's lives in what had otherwise been a loose network of settlements connected almost solely through commercial links. Canada became eager to regulate what was considered appropriate parenting and schooling as a national concern. These interests cannot be seen in isolation from the demands of an economy that required a pliant workforce to serve the needs of the colony's aggressive, extractive expansion. Coupled with racial anxieties about maintaining supremacy, these considerations shaped the way tuberculosis sanatoria played out for settlers, focusing on marginalized people as needing character reform more than they needed care.

White women of means were at the core of this tradition of charity that involved nurturing solid moral fibre in the poor, unwashed masses. Children in distress or neglected due to the ill health or the lack of resources of their usual guardian were a convenient conduit to enact this vision of social reform through proxy parenting. In Toronto, one children's care home, starting off with six cots, gradually evolved to become the Hospital for Sick Children. After the First World War, this work done by white women of caring for neglected children increasingly became the work of public health departments as part of formal state functions.[37] This transformation took caring work away from families and private citizens and into the arms of the state through professions such as medicine and social work.

The first tuberculosis public health nurse in Canada started work in 1909, delivering care to patients released from sanatoria living in Toronto. In 1911, the same year the Saskatchewan Anti-Tuberculous League was founded, a dispensary supplying supplementary nutritious food to people with confirmed tuberculosis also started in Toronto. Medical interventions for tuberculosis became more aggressive, though we might question the value of some of them today. There was contemporary debate about such measures, but now treatments such as lung collapse, as was routinely done, seem dubious, with the possible relief of suffering counterbalanced by their side effects. But prior to antibiotics, there were few options other than rest and some surgical procedures as mainstays of therapy. It is unclear whether they actually improved outcomes, and there was perhaps a degree of empirical experimentation that was inherent to these efforts, physicians learning on bodies by trying to see if interventions worked. Once vaccination with BCG became possible, Quebec and Newfoundland were the only provinces to develop programs for mass inoculations against tuberculosis, perhaps largely due to their existence outside the influence of the United States, where the debates around efficacy of the vaccine were much more polarizing.[38]

Similar institutions for tuberculosis care in children emerged in New Zealand, Ireland, Britain, and the United States, for example.[39] Most of the Euro-American world established sanatoria care for adults as well, the first one in the world established in what is now Poland.[40] Sanatoria beds for the whole population in Canada grew in the period from 1938–1953, with available beds jumping from 9,000 to 19,000. But as antimicrobial therapy became standard in that period, within ten years after that, dedicated beds for tuberculosis were drastically reduced.[41] Although antibiotic treatment was first widely available in 1948 after being discovered in 1944, it was not used in an appropriate manner until 1952 or so, when its use began to be almost 100 percent effective in Canada.[42] But the expansion of tuberculosis institutions as part of the welfare state had its parallels in Indigenous territory, with a distinct trajectory through Canada's colonial history.

The spread of tuberculosis in Indigenous populations became a concern if they were going to be kept in sanatoria with white settlers. Indigenous patients were generally rejected, though Saskatchewan made exceptions for Indigenous people who were deemed worthy of having access to stay in "general" sanatoria. Discretionary admissions usually had to be made through the Indian agent after approval from Ottawa. As mentioned, Saskatchewan also maintained some forty beds dedicated to Indigenous peoples in a segregated wing at Fort San sanatorium as reimbursement of debts owed to the federal government, the health of Indigenous peoples a pawn in constitutional spats.[43] Even though Toronto was relatively distant from where many Indigenous communities had been relocated, estimates suggest that 5 percent of the children institutionalized at the sanatorium there were Indigenous. Even if not officially segregated, there was little regard given to the particular needs of these children, who were brought to what was allegedly a voluntary institution probably through the actions of the Indian agent, thereby cementing the link between the hospital system and colonial power.[44]

The "Indian hospital" became the solution to the problem of exponential tuberculosis growth in Indigenous communities, but with a reluctance to provide adequate care, they were another institution emblematic of Canada's entrenched racism. Care institutions with specific ethnic foci were not unknown in Canada, though they tended to be based in communities that lived around them and participated in their function, responding to needs the community themselves established. In 1918, nuns opened a temporary hospital to care for Chinese immigrants afflicted by the influenza pandemic in Montreal. When the need for those services ended, the community decided they liked having their own hospital and found money for premises in downtown Montreal. They asked the nuns to return to staff it in 1920, with the community funding it through their own donations until 1945. St Joseph's Oriental Hospital in Vancouver started off with similar missionary attention, although it was not until the 1940s that the community became involved in its administration and funding.[45]

When I visited Moose Factory in 2013, in Cree territory around James Bay, it was the first time I had to take a snowmobile taxi. I had gingerly stepped into the sled that had a makeshift windshield of plastic sheeting constructed on a loose frame pinned up on four sides. Even though I was hardened by northern Ontario winters, I was glad for it, though it was not very effective as the biting cold of the air flayed my face anyway as we bumped across the frozen water. I was struck by how uneven the ice surface was, still getting accustomed to this element that was so far from my childhood, and I was nervous that it was not solid enough. Spring was still a few weeks away in early March, and I noticed how water sloshed onto the surface of the ice, the snowmobile charging through pools of slush. I knew people closely monitored conditions to decide whether it was safe to use the iceways. I also knew water always rushed underneath any thick layer of ice. Still, desert-born that I am, my confidence wavered with each bump and icy spray on the winding ride on channels between islands to get to the community, relieved when finally on the other shore. My return trip to the mainland occurred during the shoulder season before the ice had truly broken up, and there was no direct safe surface route back to the airport. So, helicopter was the only way, lifting into the air vertically to look out towards the mouth of the Moose River as it emptied gloriously into the southern tip of James Bay's expanse.

Moose Factory sits on an island peculiarly split into a complex jurisdictional patchwork. Part of it is reserve, as would befit the Canadian government's historic tendency to confine Indigenous peoples to inaccessible parcels of land, from where the extraction of resources was too inconvenient to make it worth claiming for settlers. The unincorporated southern third of the island is where the Hudson's Bay Company's post was — the second in Canada after Waskaganish (Rupert House as it was known in those days), where I work mostly now on the artificial "Quebec" side of the bay. The non-reserve land was where other services, such as the Anglican church (still standing) built by the Company, were set up, as well as its residential school. The hospital would eventually be built on these unincorporated lands too. There has long been discussion of a bridge to link the island to mainland Ontario, but it was never in the federal government's interest to allow increased mobility.

As the tuberculosis epidemic began to grip the Arctic in the first half of the twentieth century, Moose Factory, with its strategic position at the base of Hudson Bay, became an ideal site for the federal government to establish a tuberculosis sanatorium that served that entire coast, including Inuit territory as far away as Puvirnituq. It was a large institution, labour to build it in the 1940s coming from all over the James Bay area, including from Waskaganish. The hospital rose not far from the residential school, which also brought children from across James Bay to the island. The hospital was not, of course, ideal for many people who were forced off their land to be institutionalized, the Inuit being largely the targets of this intervention, sent to many institutions to the south for apparent definitive care. Some estimates suggest that one in ten Inuit people living in Canada in the 1950s may have been removed from their communities to tuberculosis sanatoria.[46] The pressure on the institution in Moose Factory was so great that the hospital was not entirely set up with facilities when the first patients arrived, and staff had to put mattresses on the floor for them.[47]

Today, at least seventy years old, the hospital now known as the Weeneebayko General Hospital rather than the Moose Factory Indian Hospital, still functions, although there are moves to build a newer institution more responsive to the community's current needs on the mainland, so people now living in the large community there (Moosonee) do not have to take a water taxi to get to the emergency room on the island. I have worked there on a number of occasions, aware that this institution represents a particular part of a legacy of my profession in colonial Canada, with its interest to confirm its sovereignty in the Arctic in the era of the Cold War. From the late 1940s onwards, Canada made significant military investments in the North in its alliance with the United States against the Soviet Union, which lay across the Arctic Ocean.[48] But ensuring sovereignty over people was also a strategic consideration. Investments in education, housing, and healthcare reasserted ties of belonging, citizenship, and dependency on Canada among Arctic peoples.[49]

The Moose Factory hospital is emblematic of the tuberculosis sanatoria dedicated to Indigenous peoples in twentieth-century Canada, notorious features in the history of displacement and disenfranchisement that are not dissimilar to residential schools — children would be among those taken, sometimes for years. The confusion around asymptomatic tuberculosis patients also contributed to the terror associated with evacuation, as the logic with which people would be removed seemed inscrutable. Aside from worrying about their own health, people also had to worry about the health of their families, who might be bereft of a caregiver or a breadwinner, not knowing when or if they would see them again. People were misnamed, some were transferred back to incorrect home communities, and relatives were sometimes not told of the death of their loved one.[50] Even while away, the contact that patients were allowed to have through correspondence with their families was routinely placed under government surveillance.[51]

People would sometimes be so lost upon their removal to the south that they would not be able to reintegrate upon their return. For children, loss of language, loss of livelihood skills, loss of relationships with family — all were referenced as factors that had searing impacts on families due to prolonged stays in the hospitals in the south.[52] Like many other institutions described as "total institutions," such as prisons, tuberculosis hospitals might have consumed the entire person, regulating their way of being. Infantilized and overwhelmed, with sometimes entire childhoods spent in such an institution, people sometimes had to find bonds of surrogate family. Even when relatives, no matter if as close as parent and child, were placed in the same institution, policies could keep them apart — nominally for their own clinical good.[53]

The federal government did not actually intervene in the tuberculosis epidemic in the Arctic until 1946, when the Advisory Committee for the Control and Prevention of Tuberculosis among Indians was set up. The timing might have been a bit suspicious: Canada's benign neglect of the North had come home to roost in the wake of the Second World War. Serving as the "free world's" interface with the Soviet Union, the North became central to the federal government's geopolitical strategic interests in US–Soviet wrangling. Presumed Inuit physiological adaptation to cold became subject to racialized investigation as potentially useful in military strategy.[54] Prior to this period, Arctic regions had largely been beyond the scope of Canada's interests, with few resources that had any significant commercial value to extract. Even in

1958, some argued that Inuit populations were immunologically isolated from the global circulation of pathogens that cause upper respiratory tract infections (colds), like coronaviruses, adenoviruses, rhinoviruses, and enteroviruses, which would reportedly only occur when a supply ship came in to their communities, bringing up the viruses from beyond the tundra.[55] This understanding requires further study as some Inuit did at least intermittently have some contact with other peoples in the circumpolar world. Even relatively recent accounts of the beginning of the Inuit experience of tuberculosis make Scottish whalers the protagonist, out exploring the world, with the Inuit with their "Stone Age technology" portrayed as hapless, unwitting collateral beings swept up in the waves of history. Rather, they were a vibrant community that actively engaged in relations with others, compelled into navigating forces that were integrating their communities into a global economy that was based on wealth accumulation in Europe.[56] This myth of tuberculosis as simply an unfortunate byproduct of buccaneering Celtic adventures is false.

As proof of the naivete of such views of the Inuit as pristinely undisturbed, there were reports of tuberculosis outbreaks in the North as early as 1861. Living conditions had declined sufficiently in the early twentieth century that one surge was documented in written form to have happened among the Coppermine Inuit around 1930, by when it was estimated that already 25 percent of the population had succumbed to the disease. The first identified case there had been a man with spinal tuberculosis, discharged from a southern hospital because the federal government refused to pay for his care in the institution any longer since he was considered "incurable."[57] Just because he was the first identified does not mean that he is the first one to have had it, and indeed infection of the backbone suggests quite advanced tuberculosis. The doctor in the region at the time was refused funds by the federal government for medical supplies, let alone a hospital.

The 1918 influenza pandemic was brutal on Indigenous peoples — with some communities facing death tolls of 20–30 percent of the population. The community of Okak in Nunatsiavut (Labrador) reported the death of every single adult male between October 1918 and January 1919, during the second wave, which was particularly devastating worldwide. In the end, three-quarters of the community was dead. There is some speculation that underlying tuberculosis aggravated pandemic influenza deaths in Indigenous communities. The 1918 experience cemented the suspicion that healthcare from colonizers not only did not guarantee health but seemed ineffective in illness as well.[58] Even as tuberculosis began to be controlled in Indigenous nations farther south, malnutrition through the destruction of traditional subsistence livelihoods and the disintegration of fur-based commercial economies meant that tuberculosis took deep hold in Inuit lands. The forced relocation of the Inuit into permanent communities in the 1950s, partly done with the intent to assert Canadian geopolitical sovereignty over the Arctic, compounded lack of access to traditional food.[59] The deliberate slaughter of dogs by the federal government meant migration after the large mammals the Inuit hunted for food was no longer an option.[60] Coerced sedentary lives led to overcrowding, with massive amounts of transmission within the poorly ventilated spaces at home. Even the introduction of antibiotic treatment in the management of tuberculosis did not close the gap, which some authors explained away as isolation making distribution of medication difficult in the North, rather than as concerted neglect of any issue beyond immediate extractive or military strategic interest. After all, those Scottish whalers had got to the North just fine!

A hospital boat — part of the Eastern Arctic Patrol, a name which suggests that it was not primarily interested in health surveillance — would take people away from the region to the south at any suggestion of tuberculosis infection. Beginning in the 1920s, the *C.D. Howe* was the most famous ship to take on this task from 1950 onwards. Elder patients of mine living in the watershed of Hudson Bay who have generally avoided colonial doctors, have medical charts thin enough that documented care received from physicians in the 1950s is still easy to find. I suspect these notes are from doctors who might have travelled on such ships. I am fascinated by the services my patients received at that time, looking at their prescriptions of antibiotics with some wonder, since it was such a novel intervention then. In some ways, so many things have not changed — children still got ear infections and tonsillitis. But then there are medications and diagnoses at which I frown, trying to make sense of them: treatments we no longer use, conditions we have now renamed with evolving science. From the vantage point of medical practice today I wonder how much might have been missed. We have so much more to know now as doctors, only because we have so many more tools to dig deeper and so many more therapies to fix things we have decided are wrong.

Prior to the arrival of the formal federally funded healthcare services in the North, biomedical healthcare was dispensed by members of the Royal Canadian Mounted Police, traders of the Hudson's Bay Company, and missionaries. Although all these figures were highly symbolic of colonial incursion, they also had established human relationships in the communities. The ship was a significantly different experience and was backed up by brute forces of the Canadian state. Police would round people up for the tuberculosis screening visits by ship, and in the western Arctic, the Air Force would use their ski-equipped aircraft.[61] Condescending accounts that people hid from the ships simply because no one thought to explain their actual purpose highlight the assumption of implicit benevolence of Canadian healthcare that remains rooted in our national mythology. Communities were probably all too aware the purpose was to take them away from their families! Directed as they might be to physicians as an audience, twentieth-century narratives in settler medicine sometimes shone the spotlight on providers who cared for the Inuit, rather than on the Inuit themselves, marvelling that the professionals were able to witness a "culture in transition, as the influence of the industrial revolution finally reached the High Arctic."[62] The shortwave radio broadcasts to the North from sanatoria in Hamilton and Toronto, with photographs and taped messages sent to families back home, were considered more noteworthy than the analysis of how people on the other end experienced those missives — if they received them at all.

The story in northern Canada unfolded in Alaska too. In 1931, healthcare services for Indigenous peoples in Alaska moved from the Bureau of Education to the Office of Indian Affairs. Two new hospitals in rural Alaska were built. With the militarization of the state during the Second World War, with new roads and airports, society transformed rapidly. In 1946, the first Division of Tuberculosis Control was established. In 1953, the Parran report demonstrated the differences in healthcare services that Indigenous peoples and settlers in Alaska received, promoting action on this front. The first major dedicated institution built by the state for Indigenous healthcare was the Alaska Native Medical Center, inaugurated as a tuberculosis hospital in 1953, though it eventually evolved.[63]

Prior to that period, in the 1940s and 1950s, smaller sanatoria in Alaska operated too.[64] The one in Sitka made headlines because 130 people died at the institution, and with no funds to return bodies to their families, the remains were placed in a temporary bunker. Except that bunker became much more than temporary, with the bodies essentially forgotten until the mausoleum was rediscovered in the work to expand the Sitka airport in the 1990s. The bodies were eventually repatriated.[65] Although there is no proof of deliberate malevolence on the part of any individual, the logic of the colonial state unfolded in this manner, with priorities far removed from the communities whose control it grasped.

Farther south along the Pacific coast, Dr James Douglas Galbraith worked in Bella Coola in 1939 serving about 1500 people, mainly Scandinavian settlers and their descendants but also the Nuxalk people. Old Cahoose was one of Galbraith's patients who had been denied admission to the Tranquille tuberculosis sanatorium near Kamloops, established in 1907.[66] That hospital opened after the BC Society for the Prevention and Treatment of Consumption and Other Forms of Tuberculosis, founded in 1904 in the frenzy of tuberculosis panic that gripped Canada, bought farmland from the Fortune family. The Fortunes had already been allowing people with tuberculosis to live in tents and cabins on their property to try to recover from the illness, essentially providing them de facto isolation. The Tranquille sanatorium would grow from 49 to 360 beds, with about half of the beds provincially supported at one point, the others for private paying patients.[67] The sanatorium followed the typical pattern of promising fresh air away from the cities to settlers as a treatment for the disease. Old Cahoose had probably been denied admission as the sanatorium tried resolutely to remain all white.[68]

Like in Ontario, in British Columbia this access to wilderness was predicated on the dispossession of Indigenous peoples, who soon too would have to confront the disease. Old Cahoose was banished into isolation in a tent in his own community due to the sanatorium's refusal to admit him, and since the local general hospital did not receive dedicated tuberculosis funds from the federal government, they too declined to care for him. He dutifully followed his instructions to isolate for three years from 1936–1939, but died with his grandson becoming infected as well. In response to this situation, Dr Galbraith participated in the advocacy that led to the federal government taking some responsibility for healthcare services to Indigenous people with the infection.[69] Although the tuberculosis societies across Canada initially rarely mentioned the undue burden placed on Indigenous peoples by the disease, speaking more of poor settler communities instead as the target for projects of charity, by 1935, one-third of tuberculosis deaths in British Columbia were among Indigenous peoples.[70]

The first "Indian hospital," with 180 beds, for tuberculosis in British Columbia was opened in 1941 by the federal government in the Chilliwack area. It was only after the Second World War, with the birth of a dedicated federal health department for Indigenous peoples, that the expansion of the tuberculosis hospitals for Indigenous patients accelerated, with two others opening in the province, at Prince Rupert and Nanaimo, before the end of the 1940s. At a site now used by the Sto:lo Nation, Coqualeetza Indian Hospital opened in Sardis in 1941.[71] It had a checkered history from the very beginning, having previously been one of the residential schools where the rates of tuberculosis were so high that it turned into a default hospital anyway, the church setting up beds for the sickest children so that they would not return ill and infectious to their home community. In 1938 the Methodist missionaries turned the school over to the government, which subsequently opened the hospital in 1941, though it was significantly damaged by a fire in 1948. British Columbia initially included care at "Indian hospitals" under its provincial insurance program, but by 1960 retracted, saying it would only pay for care at the federal institution if the Indigenous patient had been denied admission at a provincial hospital.[72]

Galbraith also worked in the northern territories on tuberculosis control between 1966 and 1973, seeing some encouraging results, by which time "Indian hospitals" were established across the country.[73] The federal government was keen to centralize care, no longer trusting the patchwork of church hospitals scattered through Indigenous territories to further the "civilizing" mission as Canada itself secularized but also to shave off costs. Manitoba's first "Indian sanatorium," near Selkirk in 1939, faced criticism initially for causing an oversupply of beds in an era of private competition from a white sanatorium in nearby St Vital, which had recently added beds for Indigenous patients as a means to have access to federal government revenue.[74] The "Indian hospital" was repossessed by the Anglican Church in 1957 as need declined and became a school that eventually closed in 1990. It is now part of an addictions treatment centre for Indigenous peoples.

Similarly in the 1920s in Saskatchewan, a separate institution for Indigenous peoples in Battleford was delayed by twenty years partly because the Anglican bishop objected to the Catholic missionaries running the hospital.[75] The Fort Qu'Appelle institution, built in 1936 across the lake from the provincial Fort San sanatorium, holds a particular place in history as well. Before the arrival of antibiotic treatment for tuberculosis, vaccination with the BCG inoculation seemed a promising intervention to limit child tuberculosis mortality. In Saskatchewan in the 1930s, during the days of the provincial control program, Dr Ferguson, as secretary of the Commission, was a huge proponent as he did not think separation of the sick to limit transmission was always feasible, given that early twentieth-century Canadian policy on Indigenous children mandated their institutionalization. He oversaw experiments of the vaccine at Fort Qu'Appelle, where it showed evidence (as it continues to do this day) of providing some protection against serious forms of tuberculosis in children. He was so convinced that it would prove to be a safe and effective intervention that he claimed to have vaccinated his own children first in the study. He was aware of the implications of consent, expressing reservations to federal authorities about experiments on children who were "wards of the state."[76] Whether the children were appropriately placed under the authority of the federal government, however, is another question. Either way, parents had little say over their child as research subject, and the study proceeded anyway. In seven years of follow-up of the Indigenous children enrolled in the experiment, almost one in five died of other causes, highlighting the precarious health status of Indigenous populations in that time. The Fort Qu'Appelle Indian Hospital would eventually become the All Nations' Healing Hospital, which the local Tribal Council has run since 1996, opening a new building in 2004 away from the remnants of the old institution.

But one of the most important "Indian hospitals" in the country lay across the Prairies in Alberta. In November 2020, the City of Edmonton approved a rezoning permit for the Charles Camsell Indian Hospital site, allowing developers to expand their plans for an overhaul into residential real estate.[77] The site, closed since 1996, has a long history behind it. The hospital was named for Charles Camsell, the son of a Hudson Bay factor born in the Northwest Territories in 1876. Caught up in the gold rush in the Yukon as a young adult, he became interested in geology. He eventually got a public service job with the government, for which he did not even apply, due to the knowledge he acquired of the mining landscape in the North. No doubt the entitlement that came with being a white settler man assisted in simply walking into secure employment. He became deputy minister, the most senior public servant, of mines in 1920, and continued as such for twenty-six years.[78] Since Indigenous affairs were managed by the Department of Mines and Natural Resources at the time — just in case the federal government's interests were not clear enough — this tuberculosis hospital that opened in 1946 in Edmonton as Camsell prepared to retire was named for him, in deference to the person running the relationship between the Canadian state and Indigenous peoples suffering devastating disease.

The site started off as a Jesuit college in 1913, and in 1942 it became a headquarters for the US Army, which added to the complex. The Canadian forces bought it in 1944, turning it over to Indian Health Services in 1945 for an "Indian hospital" for tuberculosis. Local protests were vociferous, claiming that the decommissioned military barracks were better suited to solve local housing issues or that the hospital should be used for veterans, not tuberculous Indigenous people. Three hundred people showed up to protest these plans at a meeting in 1945. To appease the clamour, the federal government reassured neighbours that the hospital would not be for tuberculosis alone but to treat general conditions too, thereby siphoning Indigenous people away from other hospitals in the city: the settler populace was mollified by the entrenchment of medical apartheid, relieved at not having to see Indigenous people in the institutions where they sought care themselves. The grounds at Charles Camsell would be fenced, and its patients confined within them. There would be jobs for local people too.[79] Racial hierarchy was apparent within staff at the hospital, as settler staff kept their distance from Indigenous workers, who were mainly relegated to the lower ranks, although there were some bonds of friendship that formed with more recent immigrant employees.[80]

The Charles Camsell thus became the general hospital for Indigenous peoples in the Edmonton area. In the hospital's rush to accommodate all their heath concerns in a setting better suited for military dormitories, cross-contamination led to the spread of tuberculosis within the institution.[81] Pneumonia was the single largest reason for admission in the late 1950s.[82] One research project done at the hospital looked at about a hundred cases of the illness in children to ask whether underlying tuberculosis complicated their condition.[83] In many ways, this study reminded me of my own experiences with paediatric pneumonia in low-resource contexts in West Africa, where it causes a huge amount of mortality to this day. It seems almost unthinkable in Canada today that any child would die of pneumonia, but they did so frequently not so long ago. Most of the children in this study were not shipped in from the Far North but lived on the reserves around Edmonton. It is uncertain whether the guardians of the children were aware that

they were enrolled in a research project where their clinical trajectory was being examined. Another study done around the same
time compared the efficacy of various antibiotics used to treat the
pneumonia, although it is unclear if guardians were told that this
comparison was happening and how they would have reacted if
so.[84] In the first study, many children who had been transferred
from other institutions for more advanced care were excluded
from the study as they were already under a treatment protocol,
suggesting the patients studied had milder diseases and so perhaps
were not entirely typical of admission to the hospital. Nevertheless,
for its time, the study makes for absorbing reading on purely medical grounds. By my interpretation of the study notes, the children
received decent medical care for the time, and the authors describe
the death of a one-month child in some detail. Although the language is cold, they seem to have been moved by the death "despite
extensive attempts at resuscitation." Some Indigenous families in
the region did see the hospital as a site of recourse, demonstrated
by the case report the doctors use to discuss a young child who
had multiple cases of pneumonia. The mother brought him back
whenever he was unwell. Perhaps she considered the risks of the
hospital system worth the benefits — or she had few other choices.
What is striking is that 81 percent of the children studied showed
signs of anaemia, presumably due to nutritional deficiency. The authors also note that poor living conditions probably contributed to
pneumonia presentations.[85]

Although some people might have established personal relationships with staff at the Indian hospitals, many people detained
in the institutions simply remember missing their families more
than finding surrogates there.[86] Patients classified as Protestant
who died at Charles Camsell were buried on the grounds of a
residential school 20 kilometres away in Saint Albert, a historically Métis community that was separated from Edmonton by
farmland, with children at the residential school caring for the
graves.[87] (This same Saint-Albert had one-third of its population
die of smallpox in the 1870 epidemic despite the attempts of the
Grey Nuns to control it through launching a Board of Health.)[88]
The cemetery was eventually transferred to the care of the City
of Edmonton, which generally neglected it, and a brush fire from

the overgrown weeds destroyed all the grave markers. The city ultimately placed a cairn with the names of the ninety-eight people buried there.

In the February 1955 issue of the *Canadian Medical Association Journal*, an innocuous short case report by Corrigan et al. from the Charles Camsell details the somewhat rare case of co-infection with tuberculosis and brucellosis.[89] In about seven hundred words, the report coolly describes the course of a patient with the curious potential diagnosis of the two diseases. The patient, although initially showing some signs of improvement, died eighteen days after admission. She was only forty-nine.

Brucellosis is a common infection in the wild, usually associated with camels these days but can be found in other hoofed creatures. It can spread to humans, causing high fevers, fatigue, and joint pain. There were ten cases reported in Nunavut between 2007 and 2014.[90] In its clinical concision, the 1955 report does not talk about the story that predates the woman's death. Other than noting that she had lived her entire life in Bathurst Inlet (Qingaut) and somehow found herself in May 1954 in the Edmonton institution, there is little to suggest that this mid-twentieth-century case study is actually a story that stretches back decades. The medical journal reports drily on the pathology that led to her sickness, but we are left to imagine how someone who had spent almost fifty years of their life in the tundra should suddenly find themselves in the urban press of the boreal forest, perhaps aware that they were dying, this far away from home.

Similar stories that have occurred in the past reverberate through the practice of medicine in Canada today. In the account of a nurse working at the Charles Camsell from 1947 to 1971, she notes how foreign the institution was from anyone displaced from even the northern parts of the province to Edmonton, let alone farther afield.[91] Many of my colleagues consider such experiences, entrenched in the history of displacement that Indigenous peoples have confronted in the Canadian healthcare system, when making decisions on sending people away from their families for care, removing people from their homes purportedly for their own good.

We might try to manage with the resources at our disposal to have them stay home. For many older people in particular, that option is often a preference they express.

On the other hand, I wonder whether we as a result do not limit the care that people might get by focusing on this history. People's individual relationships to contemporary medicine may have changed. In the context of poorer health outcomes for Indigenous peoples, patients may want to assert their right to go away from home to seek treatment in better-resourced centres for their illnesses, illnesses often caused by colonialism. This redress to centuries of poorer health outcomes could be essential, rather than condemning people to a static belief of pristine attachment to land, with no dynamism or adaptation to the world around them. Of course, ideally, centres of care would be better resourced on territory itself! In the meantime, physicians in remote communities are often trained to make safe, effective treatment decisions with the tools at their disposal. I have had to develop skills of sound clinical judgement to know how to take care of problems without a CT-scanner down the hallway. But winning that trust takes work, not only in a world that now sees answers only in scans and tests, but also when the system has an indelible legacy of devaluing Indigenous life. As much as I believe that medicine nowadays is hyperinvasive, that we overdiagnose and medicalize all sorts of diversity in the human body, I am wary of my appearance as a gatekeeper to resources available to settler society. Generally, I opt for a clinical philosophy more focused on functioning rather than fixing. But still, transfer to technology — even though not medically necessary in the strictest terms — may be part of the relationship repair necessary to build trust over the longer term, so that, for better or for worse as representatives of colonial authority, doctors are not going to be complicit with dispossession and denial again.

Tuberculosis removals have slowly made their way into settler consciousness in Canada, even appearing as central themes in the 2008 film *Ce qu'il faut pour vivre*, which highly romanticizes them. Contemporary settler angst runs through the film in its retelling of the dislocation wreaked on the Inuit, where a patient finds his way back home cured, assisted by a white saviour figure in the form of a nurse. For inexplicable reasons, she alone is helpful in a kind, unthreatening way — the character an apparition of present-day white guilt, pandering to settler sensitivities.[92] The recognition of tuberculosis hospitals as another historical sin, convenient for contemporary Canadians to package colonialism away as a relic of the past, resulted in the apology offered by Prime Minister Trudeau in 2019 to the Inuit for the displacement that occurred, marking funds specifically not only for the elimination of tuberculosis in Inuit lands by 2030, but also to support families in finding and honouring their members who went missing in the medical abductions.[93]

The sanatoria largely closed down in the 1970s as tuberculosis rates decreased (although remaining higher in Indigenous peoples than the settler population) with some suggesting that this success was directly linked to the expansion of the federal government's Indian hospital system.[94] But in reality, tuberculosis treatment was transformed by the discovery of antibiotics, and as the pharmaceuticals were refined to allow oral instead of injectable treatment, inpatient care became less necessary.

How did the settler epidemic of tuberculosis become so entrenched in Indigenous communities despite policies of segregation that the Canadian state attempted to pursue? The loss of livelihood and nutrition, as seen in the example of the Inuit, played out in various scales across Canada. The first indication of what was to come on the Prairies occurred in the 1880s, when the bison population collapsed and Indigenous peoples were forced onto reserves. With the loss of this nutritional safety net and the crowding that began in settled life, coupled with deliberate government neglect of this problem, tuberculosis began to take hold, slowly but surely. It is possible that turning to tuberculosis-infected imported cattle for food to replace the lost bison contributed to tuberculosis outbreaks.[95]

But these unhappy circumstances are not all. Slower to emerge as a clinical syndrome in people than smallpox, a contemporary concern though stymied somewhat by vaccination, the government policy of institutionalizing every single Indigenous child in residential school seeded immense spread in the months or years it took to demonstrate active infection with tuberculosis. Inspections in 1907, 1908, and 1909 at the Tsuut'ina school run by the Anglican Church found every single child afflicted with tuberculosis. That school eventually became a hospital for the reserve, where the doctor was also the Indian agent — the federal government's representative — and the pass system was enforced on federal authority to limit Indigenous mobility on their own traditional territories, compounding malnutrition and overcrowding.[96] In Siksika territory, as another example, an x-ray survey in 1934 of the residential schools found that the health condition of 7 percent of the children warranted immediate hospitalization.[97] A survey in British Columbia in 1927 demonstrated that the use of raw cow's milk at residential schools contributed to the burden of tuberculosis in children.[98] In 1940, 70 percent of the residential school children in British Columbia were positive for carrying tuberculosis. At least one in ten students at Alert Bay school were transferred annually for sanatorium care in the 1940s.[99] The residential school, at least in British Columbia, continued to serve as a stand-in for medical care when sanatoria were not accessible to Indigenous peoples — children being admitted to them under the belief that some care was better than none, conflating all colonial institutions into one massive remote one.[100] So although fresh open air in the bush was touted as the cure for tuberculosis, Indigenous children were removed from it.

The link between residential school and death was clear to many Indigenous families, who nursed sick children released from the institutions sometimes to their deaths. The residential school at Kuper (Penelakut) Island had rates of tuberculosis that were notably high in the 1940s, but even prior to that, about a third of the children who had attended the school by 1919 had died a premature death. The Catholic Church ran this school, which was acknowledged to be in abysmal condition by its own managers, a school inspector noting in 1922 that Indigenous parents were inclined to boycott it on account of the deaths (though attendance was compulsory in Canada from 1920 to 1948 for Indigenous children). The Kuper Island school was notorious for its abuse, and the implications, both physiological and psychological, lasted well beyond the time it ceased operations.[101]

Through the course of this history, there were some from within the machinery of the colonial state who tried to resist too. Dr Bryce, as the first chief medical officer in the Department of Indian Affairs in 1904, alienated his bosses by highlighting the deaths caused by tuberculosis at the residential schools — although he had initially thought the institutions were underfunded to the point of being too anaemic an assimilative effort.[102] He however eventually became appalled at government inaction and got forced out of his position for his complaints, going on to publish a book in 1922 in which he lists the litany of recommendations for the health of Indigenous children he had made that were ignored by the department.[103]

His recommendations were not exactly liberatory as they never questioned the essence of the residential school as a colonial tool, but he did describe their outcome as "a national crime." Dr Bryce highlighted that Indigenous peoples were otherwise healthy in usually sanitary conditions, dismissing racialized arguments about inherent weakness. He proposed that Indigenous peoples were already contributing significantly to the Canadian labour force, citing statistics on agricultural productivity that showed Indigenous peoples outproducing Nova Scotia as a whole but that their death rate seemed extraordinarily high. He saw the clear and present danger of the schools as sites of incubation of an epidemic and questioned the general neglect of the federal government. He was thwarted in trying to get more than the basic statistical data in terse responses from the secretaries of the public service. He suggested to the government that the number of schools needed to grow in order to diminish crowding and bring children closer to their home territories and families. His anger in his book at the cover-ups and silencing of his reports and recommendations is palpable a century after its publication. For his role in pointing out the harm caused by residential schools, some contemporary advocates for Indigenous children, such as Cindy Blackstock, commemorate his grave in Ottawa in honour of his memory.[104]

The 1930s were a particularly important time in the racialization of medicine in Canada. The threat of tuberculosis as a disease of

Indigenous peoples began to supersede that of poor people with tuberculosis, communities who challenged the notion of the country the Canadian establishment wanted to fashion. Though menacing, the disease also provided an opportunity for intervention. Medical bureaucracies' role in the extension of colonial control is exemplified in the words of such people as Dr David Stewart, the superintendent of the Ninette sanatorium in Manitoba, who said Indigenous people "soaked in tuberculosis" were characterized by a "racial carelessness and ignorance."[105]

The social reformation efforts launched by the Canadian Tuberculosis Association (CTA) began in 1901, a project of the charitable elite, who had clear ideas of norms by which society should be shaped. The general sentiment among the health officials charged with running tuberculosis prevention efforts in Canada in the early twentieth century involved not just medicine or surgery, but as Saskatchewan's Dr Ferguson once said, "the development of faithful endeavour, helpfulness, earnestness, good humour, kindliness and forbearance." The idea that the cure for tuberculosis lay in forming model citizens persisted into the 1940s, when Dr Wherrett, executive secretary of the CTA, told a Department of Labour radio show that the sanatorium experience improved health, yes, but also improved workers.[106]

It was not until the 1930s that the CTA seriously began to confront the issue of tuberculosis in Indigenous communities, pointing it out as an "uncontrolled nuisance" which was a "menace" to "ordinary citizens." By this point tuberculosis rates had decreased in white Canada, largely due to improved access to housing and food, and the seeming reality that tuberculosis rates were higher in communities next to Indigenous reserves set off a racialized panic of epidemic threat. In 1937, the CTA met with government health officials to confront the issue of "Indian tuberculosis," coming to some decisions that were appalling, perhaps even for their context. In this meeting, with the blessing of the CTA, officials decided to prioritize intervention among the estimated two-thirds of Indigenous people who had regular contact with settlers, where they were a "menace," with Indigenous domestic workers highlighted as a feared source of contagion. Many others were children in residential schools, where it was already

easy to institutionalize people — though it was this very institutionalization that was enabling the spread of the disease. In
the end, the four western provinces received $35,000 to establish
preventative wards (preventoria) for children with early tuberculosis within the residential schools, with the churches tasked
to provide better nutrition only to the sickliest. The goal was to
make sure that the disease did not spread back to the reserves,
a perverse acknowledgement of the role the institutions played.
With that sum, the administrators of the program agreed to treat
at least 3500 children, at no more than $10/day. The preventoria
were explicitly slated to encourage young Indigenous people displaced from their home communities to assimilate into Canadian
standards through the care they received, similar to the goals of
residential schools. "Hopeless" cases — it is unclear whether the
CTA meant those most unlikely to recover or those most unlikely
to assimilate — were deemed to remain on their reserve and not
contaminate the white population. But young, "hopeful" cases,
whose intelligence and education would help in "raising the standards of the Indian generally," were to be offered places in these
institutions.[107]

At the Indian hospitals, nurses at the Charles Camsell, for example, provided information on "clean living," and distributed book-
lets such as *Good Health for Canada's Indians* and *The Book of
Wisdom*.[108] The hospitals became recruiting grounds for workers
in the hospital system itself, though even into the 1960s, the federal bureaucracy believed that, although useful for basic labour in
the institutions and thus giving them "meaningful" integration into
settler society, Indigenous peoples were not fit for high-paying jobs
in "modern" societies. Eventually, many Indigenous nurses came
through the ranks of the hospitals and served in many roles for
care, comfort, and connection for patients in the sanatoria, beyond
clinical duties alone.[109]

But despite this reforming zeal on the part of Canada, Indigenous
communities had to actively resist the substandard care that the
Canadian state provided them. In British Columbia, an Indian
Anti-Tuberculosis League was founded. In 1928 a delegation
from Pasqua First Nation in Saskatchewan travelled to Ottawa
to seek recourse for their exclusion from community hospitals.

Substandard service contributed to why many Indigenous people refused to engage with care. Colonial health authorities interpreted this resistance as wilful ignorance and sought ways to deal with this threat, the institution of the Indian hospital being one further way to disrupt Indigenous relationships with each other and their communities. Indigenous peoples also pushed back against efforts by the federal government to survey the rates of tuberculosis in their communities prior to the Second World War as the government offered little recourse to treat the problem, which by ethical principles is shoddy medical practice — you do not diagnose conditions if you have nothing to offer the person to treat it. But the federal government eventually found coercive ways to collect data, for instance withholding payment of annuities in 1949 for treaty parties in Manitoba unless they submitted to an x-ray.[110]

At stake was essentially penny-pinching, selective public austerity, Indigenous communities confronting this dynamic long before today's settler activists discovered it in the age of neoliberalism. There was never enough public money, according to federal bureaucrats, to pay for the care of Indigenous peoples. Delivery of healthcare has been considered implicit in the treaty relationship — although the reliability of the written text, a medium in which colonizers place so much faith, was imperfect at best. As late as 1969, Harold Cardinal had to point out that the promises related to healthcare delivery implicit in the treaties were actually not written down in Treaty 8, for example, leaving Indigenous peoples on shaky ground in a white legal system.[111] Only Treaty 6, signed in 1876, explicitly makes provisions for a medicine chest, but the fact that vaccinations were offered during payments of treaty annuities elsewhere too and that often the Indian agent would be the provider of healthcare on reserve made the link between colonial power and healthcare apparent.[112]

The standards imposed on Indigenous communities were modelled on those that Canadian public health had tried to impose on others unable to defend themselves from its "courtesy." Supporting good nutrition and ventilation prior to the antibiotic era were the key intervention, public health officials decided, but as Dr Dobbie,

Toronto sanatorium's chief, pointed out in 1935, the home would need to be improved in the control of tuberculosis among the urban poor, which was "the duty of welfare agencies."[113] Even in Toronto, the state began to encroach into private spaces through the paternalism of wanting what is "best" for people's health, though settlers did not face its full coercive wrath as Indigenous people did.

I struggle with this approach in my own practice. People's health outcomes would of course be better if their living environment were more conducive to protecting their health. Would I advocate for government welfare agencies to intervene in people's homes in a widespread manner to ensure it? And what would that stance mean for someone like me who believes in undoing the damage of colonialism's perpetual interference? Questions of medicine as an arm of the state continue to have relevance today when we consider why people might resist public health orders. While some people balk at an infringement of their centuries-old entitlement to individual bodily autonomy, for many others who have confronted repression and oppression in the past, public health's close association with the authoritarian powers of the state compromises its position: once compulsorily confined, twice shy. After all, the Indian Health Act was amended in 1953 to include the Indian Health Regulations. Within living memory of someone in their mid-seventies in Canada today, these rules compelled Indigenous people who thought they might have an infectious disease to seek the care of a doctor. They could be subject to arrest for mandatory treatment. There were many complaints of Indigenous people "hiding in the bush" to evade apprehension as a result.[114] In contrast, settlers could leave against medical advice with little consequence from the state.

This question of intervention would be more easily answered if communities had more control over the institutions that were meant to serve them. But often they do not. Indigenous peoples experienced sanatoria not unlike residential school and prison.[115] Standard treatment for tuberculosis even into the antibiotic era involved surveillance for protocols for bedrest, with only graduated layers of activity allowed, with talking also discouraged. Children in particular could find these routines difficult, with no sense of why they were being confined. One nurse recalled that

Indigenous children found the institution and the separation from familiar arms extremely traumatic, noting that children on other paediatric wards where she worked "did not cry like those at the Camsell."[116] Coercion within the hospital involved body casts for Indigenous children who were deemed too hyperactive or unable to adhere to the strict bedrest enforced. Adults had their clothing removed so that they were forced to stay in bed or risk being nude if they left, although people developed ways to resist such as climbing out of windows or wandering from ward to ward in the relative anonymity of street clothes in the larger institutions. Indigenous health practices also continued to survive within the hospitals. Practices such as traditional teachings to sick patients, rites for cleansing spaces, and the bringing in of herbal medicines and healing foods to the hospitalized were all documented in at least one institution in Coast Salish territory and were no doubt replicated elsewhere. While many health authorities either were oblivious to their presence or actively tried to suppress them, a few workers supported the continuation of such treatments alongside Western practices.[117]

To this day, active infection with tuberculosis is very strictly regulated, and Indigenous people bear the brunt of this scrutiny. I myself have had to care for at least two Indigenous people in Ontario who had been institutionalized and treated under court order, eventually transferred to the tuberculosis unit at West Park in Toronto. One of them, confined by law to the hospital for months on end, was actively being treated when I was their hospital physician for a week. The patient had been unable or unwilling to complete treatment at home on two previous occasions. During my rotation, I made tentative inquiries with public health whether we could consider releasing him from the hospital to find an alternate way of monitoring his treatment, but I was met with polite but firm refusal. I still wonder what I might have done differently during those seven days I was on the ward. Institutionalizing for care has always sat uneasily with me. While clinically it may make sense in the outbreak of infectious disease, the context in which it is done — who controls the institution, who invites the sick into them, who bears the costs of the resultant disruption to the community — reveal critical nuances with which we as care providers need to grapple before simply committing people to prison-like hospitals because we believe it has public health benefit.

The control of tuberculosis before the advent of antibiotics was one of the few times in the history of biomedicine that prevention overtook the impulse of cure.[118] The development of profitable pharmaceuticals rather than advocacy for cheaper, less commodifiable social shifts has often driven medicine's interventions. For immigrants and Indigenous peoples, the goal of eliminating tuberculosis is still a long way off, but as the disease became less common in settler Canada in the early part of the twentieth century, it became more feasible to attempt to beat it back to non-existence. One of the best ways to release the mycobacterium's stranglehold on communities is to limit the damage to people's immune systems through supportive nutrition and housing. Isolation of cases is important too, but given the very slow rate of growth and cure of tuberculosis, this process could take months. While tuberculosis was rampant, the benefits of quarantining active cases were minimal if everyone was walking around with tuberculosis (as an extreme rhetorical point). But as it became more sporadic, with cases cropping up only here and there, the idea of isolating people for their months of treatment became more tenable for the public at large. If it also fit neatly into anxieties fuelled by entrenched racism, it had further benefit. Removing someone with a transmissible illness from contact with others makes sense, but if there are no mechanisms put in place to address the loss of livelihood or caregiving that may result in their absence, communities are less able to participate in such preventative actions, especially if the demands come from agencies that are reminders of historical trauma.

In 1948, the Calgary Hospitals Board adopted a policy to refuse admission to Indigenous patients since the federal government, as provider of funds for care for Indigenous peoples even before the widespread institution of public health insurance in Canada, paid less than a non-Indigenous patient would pay for their care.[119] Versions of this jurisdictional squabble continue to this day, resulting in the institution of Jordan's Principle, for example. Named for

Jordan River Anderson of Norway House, who died in a Winnipeg hospital never having been home as the federal and provincial governments argued over who was to pay for the home care services he needed, the Principle allows for an Indigenous child in Canada to receive services first, with levels of government deciding who foots the bill only afterwards.[120] In the 1940s, even when the Tsuut'ina Nation used funds they derived from extractive projects on their territory to subsidize the care their community members received from Calgary hospitals, they were still relegated to the indigent ward as a way to enforce the colour line in Canadian hospitals.[121] Across much of western Canada in the early twentieth century, a separate "Indian" ward was common in hospitals run by businesses and charitable institutions alike, as well those run through some form of public financing. This practice persisted in many places well beyond the Second World War.

As healthcare systems became more established in Canada in the twentieth century, falling increasingly under the administrative purview of the state, the constitutional arrangement that made healthcare services provincial began to override the relationship between the Crown and Indigenous peoples. I am often in favour of the decentralization of decisions to places closest to the communities where they will be implemented, and so provincial oversight over healthcare makes sense. And indeed, decentralization as a means to restoring Indigenous sovereignty may be necessary to address the impact of colonialism in healthcare. But as the welfare state boomed in Canada during the twentieth century, the provinces — who were not parties to the initial treaties with Indigenous nations — often went ahead with developing services with little regard for the impact on Indigenous communities, which in their minds had always been a federal responsibility: funding streams for Indigenous people's healthcare — like other populations such as veterans and refugees — remained channelled through Ottawa. But the federal government in turn tried to offload the treaty obligation for healthcare through the burgeoning development of the "universal" system in the provinces. Ever intent on saving money off the backs of Indigenous peoples, the federal government saw the institution of "universal" health insurance in the provinces as the removal of financial barriers to care, and thus believed it unnecessary to continue investment in addressing the particular healthcare needs of Indigenous peoples.

As a result, the federal government tried to move towards an insurance model of healthcare, which had already won the battle for provision of services in Canada. It is not the only way, Canada's self-absorption with its healthcare system obscuring other ways to finance a public system. Rather than a healthcare service, such as that of the United Kingdom, where the state manages institutions and all employees of the service, in Canada, governments pay providers (hospitals and clinics, physicians) for furnishing the services. Although Tommy Douglas's initial goal in Canada was to establish a healthcare service similar to the UK model, the interests of the professional medical elite prevented it, leading to the compromise of the insurance system we have in effect in the provinces today.

The federal government adopted this model too and wanted to pay providers — the provinces in this instance — for services offered to Indigenous peoples. The trial of this approach in the 1960s, in lieu of offering a healthcare service as is implied in the treaties, galvanized a resistance that pushed Indigenous peoples, particularly in Treaty 6 territory, to reclaim the Indian hospital, especially as their focus shifted from tuberculosis to general medical care, as one of the institutions where clear indication of their ongoing treaty relationship with the federal government persisted. For example, the Indian Association of Alberta advised its members in 1969 to provide their treaty card, not their provincial Medicare number, when seeking healthcare.[122]

Our assumption as Canadian healthcare workers that the services we provide and the universality we represent are uncontroversial in their magnanimity requires some recasting. First of all, it is not universal, given significant chunks of largely migrant populations in Canada who remain uncovered. Second, the supposed universality arose in the context of deliberate obfuscation of the founding relationships of our society — agreements between settlers and Indigenous peoples. And last, the well-publicized events of outright racism that Indigenous peoples experience within this system well into the twenty-first century, three hundred years after some of these first agreements, demand some introspection at the very least for those of us who work within and support these institutions.

While undermining the treaty relationship through financing arrangements designed to assimilate, the federal government also actively repressed Indigenous attempts to manage their own healthcare. As late as 1940, the Siksika nation near Calgary had an independent fund from land sales that gave them a generous annuity. These monies were managed by the Department of Indian Affairs to run all reserve operations rather than using the federal dollars that would otherwise pay for treaty obligations. The Siksika had established their own hospital through this autonomous wealth, which the Department then operated through this budget. Yet, federal mismanagement of the health funds led to poor capacity for care at the hospital, resulting in the nation having to pay for six patients at the Central Alberta sanatorium in Bowness, west of Calgary, which did not generally accept Indigenous patients, even though the province had instituted free tuberculosis treatment in 1936.[123]

The Siksika hospital's autonomy was not only an affront to the government but to professional authority too. Doctors disapproved that so many people resident in the hospital in the 1920s were not actually sick, but rather the extended family of patients, as befit local traditions of comfort and care. About a quarter of the reserve's annual expenditure by 1940 was going to healthcare, and the federal government objected to the Siksika's continued assertion that they would use their hospital as they see fit.[124] Around this time of the Siksika claims of autonomy, federally managed Indian hospitals were being built on the premise that their operating costs would be half of that of general hospitals, that is, only half as much would be spent on Indigenous peoples as would be on settlers.

Hospital costs skyrocketed in Canada after the Second World War. For settlers, the government poured in funds to grant programs for operating costs, increasingly transforming the private, often charitable church-based, institutions into public organizations. But Percy Moore, the Indian Health Service director from 1946–1955, notorious for overseeing experiments that withheld adequate treatment in malnourished Indigenous children,[125] said that he wanted to see more and more Indigenous nations pay for their healthcare, as the Siksika struggled to do with their depleted funds and increasing costs.[126] This perverse devolution — decision-making power without the resources to implement those decisions — is a continued threat to this day, most notably in austerity measures where government offloads social costs onto communities, giving them "autonomy" but with few avenues for revenue to enact it.[127] A common feature in today's political context of global neoliberalism, I noticed it most cruelly at the height of the HIV epidemic in South Africa in 2003. All the while denying people access to treatment, the government at the time also expected strapped community groups, on the most meagre of volunteer stipends, to provide home care to the sick, support food security for those unable to work, and do prevention work. In particular, my friends Anicia and Daniel strove to care for over a dozen children orphaned by the epidemic on these funds, with little power to influence the social development department's policies or distribution of resources. At around this time, South Africa's income inequality — already egregious due to apartheid — actually worsened.[128] The richest in South Africa accumulated even more wealth while my friends struggled to address needs in their community that only the resources a government possessed could truly meet. The fact that they persevered despite this unjust arrangement makes Anicia and Daniel two of the most remarkable people I have ever met.

Within a few years of his original statement insisting the Siksika pay for their healthcare, even while the federal government was increasingly funding provincial hospitals through grants, Dr Moore had changed his mind, professional pride insulted by the fact the Siksika still used the hospital as they wished with little deference to medical authority. A cost-sharing agreement had been instituted, but as with land, the federal government encroached on Indigenous autonomy, and the increasingly underfunded hospital could no longer meet community needs by the late 1950s. Patients ended up in the Charles Camsell Indian Hospital in Edmonton. This institution, the largest of its kind in the country, drew on the vast area it served and provided much fodder for medical education at the University of Alberta, Indigenous bodies the subject of professional scrutiny.[129] Historians recognize that the persistence of surgical tu-berculosis treatment in Canada, particularly on Indigenous bodies, even after other countries abandoned it with the advent of antibi-otics, promoted the development of thoracic surgery as a specialty in this country.[130] As a clinician, I am highly aware that I still learn from the bodies of many people, who are often in distress. What I learn from one person, although perhaps of no immediate benefit to them, will possibly be useful to the person I encounter next. Honouring this knowledge patients offer becomes difficult when there are vast oceans of power separating us, waves of which reach practices of "global health" to this day, where medical trainees de-velop skills during overseas trips on bodies that may not have easy options to go elsewhere for care.

The expansion of the government social programs throughout the twentieth century reverberates through how we in Canada may perceive the care and support we provide collectively. For those of us who are invested in protecting the welfare state, we need to be honest about its history. Many people have fought for a reliable social safety net in Canada, to ensure that redistribution of wealth is not left to the charitable whims of a few rich people in comforta-ble households. Contemporary austerity has eroded the wins: from 2009–2018, a smaller proportion of all spending in the Canadian economy was devoted to the social sector than even in the United States.[131] But far from benign, our prized social programs recy-cle wealth extracted without consent from Indigenous nations: we have only been able to fund our health and welfare systems by exploiting resources, be they fur, forests, or fuel, from land that we have occupied. As governments became more involved in redistrib-uting that wealth, in regulating the lives, relationships, and trans-actions that underpin our communal life, it also meant that the ap-paratus and arms of government, the most efficient instruments of colonial oppression, were also growing. The technocratic twentieth century, privileging the role of science and public administration, where all problems could have a technical "fix," obscured the core reality that systemic poverty, rather than individual behaviours, in settler society was contributing to ill health in children. This absence of analysis would be extended in Indigenous communities, where the loss of livelihoods and dispossession from land drove huge declines in well-being. It was easier to soothe the symptom than cure the cause.

This transition is apparent even in the way doctors wrote about their patients, with clinical notes in the early part of the twentieth century more narrative and descriptive, rather than analytical and technical. As practice moved towards a more technocratic medicine, the shift to biomedical antibiotic therapy coincided with a depersonalization of the medical chart, with less about social context and more about biochemical measures and markers.[132] Within the constraints of the form of the contemporary medical note, I know that I squeeze in a largely narrative style that sometimes annoys my colleagues, as they have to dig through my text to find key points, but it reassures me to know that there have been traditions of storytelling in the medical field before. It is not reassuring however that this style of descriptive, narrative medicine that more thoroughly sketched out a person's history, personal and social as well as clinical, did not make it immune from repressive practice.

Colonial states the world over have long drawn populations on their periphery into their snare by enlacing them in webs of social and economic relationships that are hard to untangle, making dependency so extreme, such as the British did in India, that the dependency itself becomes one of the arguments for continued domination. Even there, medicine became part of the logic with which the British imposed colonial rule.[133] It is no different in North America. Into twentieth-century Canada, this policy of "bureaucratic colonialism" has worked to serve the agenda of resource extraction, including in regions where I am now part of its infrastructure as a practising physician.[134] The persistence of tuberculosis bares the myth of the Canadian healthcare system as universal and as somehow free from colonial repercussions.[135] Healthcare, with its technical and scientific rigour, was used as an alternate article of faith in a secularized society to impose colonial will on Indigenous peoples. Through the machinations of doctors and drugs, medicine injected empire into the bodies of the colony, just as churches, schools, business and governments did. Through residential schools and tuberculosis sanatoria, the expansion of healthcare became a continuation of the civilizing motif that was used by missionaries in their quest to deal with the "Indian problem" in Canada. To assume that the institution was somehow aloof and detached from the essence of the society that produced it is naive. We as healthcare workers need to understand that history in our own work in our daily lives in Canada today. Tuberculosis was a key part of that narrative.

Indigenous nations have had to navigate the institutions of healthcare as one of the resources available to them to address the disease and distress caused by colonization when so many other options have been taken away.[136] Some may have chosen not to engage with healthcare services offered from the outside, a less-resourced autonomy more valuable than a better-resourced dependence. Others, though disappointed by deliberate underfunding of services to them, recognized the utility of colonizing medicine to treat colonizing diseases, a nuanced take on the mediaeval European view that the cure for a disease was found where it occurred, with many people actively seeking out care, knowing that their loved ones were sick and needed help, especially as colonizers undermine other healing systems. Indigenous peoples have also used syncretism as a tool, melding knowledges and traditions, to be able to better respond to problems — an open dynamism of learning that those of us who work within the constraints of medicine determined by Euro-American social and economic processes may benefit from mimicking.

The same year that the first tuberculosis sanatorium in Canada opened in Muskoka, 1897, the federal government built Parc Savard Hospital in Quebec City to house immigrants with infectious diseases, rebuilt in 1905 after a fire destroyed it. It housed veterans, often with contagious diseases, during the world wars. In 1937, it also turned into a quarantine facility for immigrants as Grosse-Île had closed in 1932, where many migrants had died, contracting typhoid fever there itself. In the 1940s, Parc Savard began to serve as a tuberculosis hospital for Indigenous patients. The fact that the federal government used this one institution for all these purposes tells a rich tapestry of the way healthcare has been used in the country. The building no longer stands in Quebec City, though the site is still active. A general hospital by the name of Christ-Roi was built there after Parc Savard's demolition once it fell into disuse by the 1950s. That hospital eventually incorporated into the provincial regime through the expansion of health insurance and has become a long-term care and community health centre. It is an uninspiring, practical-looking building, apart from its somewhat alarming yellow colour, on a busy avenue through a Quebec City suburb, its role in history obscured.

Perhaps fitting in the context of history of places like Parc Savard, tuberculosis in Canada remains a disease that immigrants and Indigenous peoples share. High rates of tuberculosis in Indigenous populations persist to this day. In the 1980s, Inuit living in Canada confronted a rate twenty-four times that of settler Canadians, even though there had been a sustained, coordinated program to bring down the rates. At one point, they had the highest rate of tuberculosis in the world. For registered Indians, the rate was sixteens times higher, although there has not been the same government-coordinated effort to sharply reduce the rate of infection in First Nations communities.[137]

We have come some way from 1829, when the last surviving Beothuk person, Shanawdithit, died of tuberculosis in Newfoundland.[138] For example, in the 1980s, 341 Inuit people in Igloolik participated in a study looking at the way an intervening decade had changed the lung function, given increased settlement, exposure to snowmobiles with concomitant reduction in activity, and increased smoking rates. But there had been no real change in the lung function over the ten years, perhaps because it was a relatively small time period but because other factors such as improved control of tuberculosis might have offset potential declines. However, the people of Arctic Bay (Ikpiarjuk) had a substantial decline in lung function, although the authors were reluctant to ascribe the discrepancy to the exposure to mining in that region at Nanisivik (a town that has now been closed.)[139]

But issues remain. Even until the late 1990s, a molecular sampling study showed that transmission of tuberculosis in Vancouver was particularly active among young Indigenous people, the disease still dynamically growing in that group.[140] In 2003, genetically similar tuberculosis strains were more likely to be found in clusters of infection among Indigenous peoples in western Canada, suggesting active transmission. While a potential genetic susceptibility to the development of active tuberculosis is sometimes bandied about as an explanation, people living in homelessness or with HIV infection — known risk factors — also showed clustering, suggesting that these factors may be more important than genetic susceptibility to disease. Non-Indigenous people born in Canada showed some evidence of strains of tuberculosis clustering, with foreign-born patients having the least, reflecting the variety of lineages of tuberculosis circulating around the world.[141]

Between 1996 and 2007 in Montreal, a city where Indigenous people were overrepresented in the unhoused population, displaced from their own lands, homelessness was a clear risk factor of ongoing tuberculosis transmission.[142] Similar findings persisted in 2013 in the Northwest Territories, where unsurprisingly, unemployment and homelessness were found to be factors having a significant impact on transmission.[143] On average, every three days in 2006–2010, one Indigenous person was diagnosed with tuberculosis in the three Prairie Provinces alone. Contrary to the white plague fears of the 1930s, the majority of transmission events eighty years later happened locally within communities of the same type, rather than across communities, such as reserve to city.[144]

In 1998–2008, the Children's Hospital of Eastern Ontario showed that children from Baffin Island bore a disproportionate burden in tuberculosis in Canada well into the twenty-first century. Even though the population of Baffin Island (Qikiqtaaluk) only made up 1 percent of the population in the hospital's catchment area, it accounted for 35 percent of the cases of tuberculosis in that period. A further 45 percent were foreign-born children residing in the much larger catchment area around the hospital. A remaining 15 percent were Canadian-born outside of Qikiqtaaluk.[145]

Many of the dynamics of colonial healthcare that played out through tuberculosis are not unique to Canada. In 2005, forty-five states in the United States declared at least one tuberculosis case in an Indigenous person between 1993 and 2002 — the east being the most spared. In Alaska, Montana, and South Dakota the majority of reported tuberculosis cases in that period were among Indigenous peoples.[146]

Tuberculosis has been an issue across the peripolar world. Comparing Alaska, Greenland, Eeyou Istchee, Nunavik, Nunavut, and Indigenous people living in Alberta, a study demonstrated that BCG vaccination and a regular screening program were significant contributors to keeping tuberculosis rates down in Indigenous communities. While the exact nature of programs was not studied in depth, which might have been revealing in how they achieved their successes, it was also apparent that underlying health disparities contributed to poorer tuberculosis outcomes in some regions over others.[147] Eeyou Istchee, for instance, in light of its renegotiated relationship with colonial governments, has seen some relative success. Nunavut in particular has seen a plateau in its ability to bring down tuberculosis rates, while Alaska in comparison showed improvement. One suggestion has been that the Alaskan model for tuberculosis programs relied heavily on community-based workers, while Nunavut programs relied more on southern healthcare professionals reaching out to patients from within their institutions, identifying cases when they showed up in a clinic, rather than seeking them out in the community.[148] The disparity in outcomes between the two jurisdictions reveals how self-government does not automatically mean the healthcare system is decolonized overnight: a concerted, deliberate effort within its institutions is required. The hospital-centric approach used in Nunavut limits active case-finding, a method of control in infectious diseases where infections are identified before people complain of symptoms. Nunavut's more passive methodology excludes the identification of all carriers who might have no other reason to visit a health centre or who might even be actively avoiding the institution. Additionally, those of us who work within healthcare institutions often get swallowed up by the demands of acute medical care. Long-term preventative work often gets pushed aside, which I recognize within my own practice: the instinct to act on the problems immediately in front of me can bias interventions in favour of the most dramatic, visible issues, thus neglecting longer-term conditions that remain a droning hum in the background. Structures have to be put into place in medicine to correct for this impulse, and these structures need to be maintained.

Outbreaks of tuberculosis in the James Bay area eventually came under relative control through aggressive screening and the advent of antibiotic therapy. Many people exposed through the residential school system and carrying latent infection underwent prophylactic treatment well into the 1980s, the detail an oft-overlooked part of their medical history scribbled into the chart. At least on the Quebec side of the region, where Eeyou Istchee is covered by the James Bay Northern Quebec Agreement, with considerable autonomy over healthcare and social services and a marked improvement in living standards in the wake of that agreement, it is relatively uncommon (though not unknown) in my experience to find someone nowadays who tests positive as a latent carrier of tuberculosis.

George Wherrett, mentioned earlier as the one-time executive secretary of the Canadian Tuberculosis Association, highlighted in his 1977 account of the fight against tuberculosis how it underpinned much of the expansion of healthcare in the country.[149] Successes in the North even led to rosy predictions that Canada would be approaching the elimination of tuberculosis. But the massive disengagement and disinvestment in healthcare services by the federal government in the late twentieth century scuttled that possibility. Major resources from the national level, as was seen in the early twentieth century, would be required to see the end of endemic tuberculosis in Canada.[150] The large scale, coordinated public health program, like Dr Grzybowski's mass treatment of latent tuberculosis in the North in the 1970s, had a huge impact on rates, and this investment, had it been continued, would still make an impact.[151]

It is not merely a question of spending money but also who decides how the money is spent. The reorientation of colonial relationships is a central question of how we engage with problems of health, certainly in the context of Canadian colonialism but anywhere issues are riddled with questions of historically unjust and imbalanced power relations. The external imposition of priorities for healthcare systems can distort locally driven responses, as has been seen with the extensive global HIV response, which, at least initially, with its parallel systems, ended up sucking resources away from other equally worthy battles against malaria, pneumonias, and diarrhoea.[152] Health ministries that receive funding from global aid agencies only have so much clout within pre-existing relationships of power that have been set up over the centuries, and international priorities can often override local ones.[153] The recognition that healthcare systems respond better to specific illnesses if they are more robust as a whole is now abundantly clear, especially given developments such as the massive Ebola outbreak in 2014–2016 in West Africa, where it was evident how the systematic decimation of healthcare systems contributed to the death toll.[154]

At the bottom of a 1986 article in the *Canadian Medical Association Journal* advocating for the elimination of tuberculosis as a fatal disease for Indigenous peoples in Canada is the following rather bizarre quote from Arthur M Walker,[155] who was in charge of the Veterans Administration anti-tuberculosis medications research wing in the United States in the early 1950s: "I would like to remind those responsible for the treatment of tuberculosis that Keats wrote his best poems while dying of this disease. In my opinion he would never have done so under the influence of modern chemotherapy."[156] While it is unclear in what context Dr Walker made the statement, it is even more unclear why the CMAJ would place such a quote under a paper arguing for better treatment of this disease for a population made vulnerable to its attack. Were they suggesting poetry workshops as a public health measure? As I was working on this chapter in early 2022, I corresponded over text with a paediatrician friend working in a remote, rural part of a sub-Saharan country in Africa. We discussed some diagnostic quandaries she was having because, as I have described, she simply had to assume that some children had tuberculosis because she had no reliable way to test for it in the severe constraints of her context. A four-year-old child seemed to have another bacterial infection in the lung, which she treated, her text to me upbeat and hopeful. But I woke one morning to a sorrowful message informing me that the child had died. There was no way to know exactly what happened, but the question of underlying tuberculosis causing complications remained. We exchanged a few sad notes on this loss, one of too many to count. The World Health Organization estimated that on average, over 4000 people died of tuberculosis worldwide each and every single day in 2020.[157] After a slow trend in improvement over decades, this statistic may be slightly worse than the previous year.[158] The pandemic that is tuberculosis continues unabated, the gash left on human history profound, and yet to be healed. Poetry has so far proven to be a paltry balm.

5

Fevers Future

How We Respond to Infections to Come

A small village of less than a thousand people in the mountains of northern England seems like an implausible place from which to draw lessons, especially from 350 years ago. But Eyam is celebrated for its actions in 1665 in the face of a devastating outbreak, even though many accounts of it are now fictionalized. The tales suggest that an outbreak of plague started in Eyam through a bundle of damp cloth arriving from London at the shop of Alexander Hadfield, the tailor in the village. It is unclear now why this bundle would transmit *Yersinia pestis*, unless it was infested with fleas that had recently fed off of an infected human or rodent. Infectious droplets or direct contact with infected tissues or fluids were also possibilities. But Hadfield's assistant, Mr Viccars, died soon after, and the disease started to spread. One winter wave was bad enough, but the second wave in the spring was devastating. Under the guidance of the local minister, Reverend Mompesson, the community instituted a number of measures to stop the spread, including most famously, isolating itself from the world so as not to infect neighbours. Merchants from nearby villages would bring supplies to boundary stones, where people would place vinegar-soaked coins in repayment. While the epidemic killed many people in the village over the course of fourteen months — estimates vary from a third to three-quarters of the population — their actions prevented spread to close communities. The quarantine was seemingly in place for about the latter half of the outbreak's duration. Church services were moved to an outdoor space, and families were asked to bury their own dead on their own grounds to prevent gatherings at funerals, all of which is eerily familiar today.

There are of course questions about whether this account is really how it all played out. Certainly, there must have been those who exploited the situation. Some say Reverend Mompesson himself made sure his children were safely out of the village before imposing the quarantine, and it is possible that other wealthy residents made similar arrangements. But nonetheless, the story is inspiring. Rather than keeping the disease out, the community — without any real enforcement authority that can be easily identified — made a collective pact to keep the disease within itself, enduring incredible loss without seeking to escape it. The Reverend himself lost his wife to the outbreak.[1]

I think often about Eyam, about how this will to protect others must have arisen. Perhaps they already knew that escape would mean little if the disease were already among them, and so it was better to endure at home without inflicting misery on others. But this sort of solidarity with distant others is not easy. Pepys wrote of the quarantine in London around the same time, noting how it made people cruel to each other. But Eyam's citizens managed to counter this unravelling and in fact, managed to bind together even further.

Is there anything to learn from Eyam? Perhaps it is impossible to ask people in today's world to undergo that self-sacrifice. Perhaps it was the desire not to contravene theological authority or spiritual discipline in the pronouncements of a priest. Perhaps it was the nature of small villages, in that people knew and trusted each other enough to embark on a collective project together in a way would not have been possible in London. But I wonder what this experience tells us about our ability to to contextualize our own concerns within the relationships we hold in the wider community to which we belong.

When I first started to put together material for this book in the summer of 2019, I had considered proposing a thought experiment on what would occur if a mysterious disease emerged among us, to contemplate how we might try to control such an epidemic in the light of all that we have learned historically but also how this new disease might offer us transformative, liberatory possibilities.

I did not have to propose this flight of fancy. As I drew my research together and started to write in earnest early in 2020, I was soon writing with a background of the pandemic of the century. What struck me most, poring over archives and articles, is how the themes were timeless. Obsessions over origins of no clinical utility whatsoever dominated by global politics. Squabbles over who is responsible for quarantine expenses. The aching chaos of scrambling to care for those sick with an unknown entity where traditional means of treatment do not work. The desperate, confusing claims and counterclaims in understanding transmission. The calculated, cold imperative of who gets protected by medications and vaccines first. The cost of harried mechanisms enforced by authorities to stem the outbreak borne by those who have borne so much before. All these themes, obvious in confrontations with cycles of pestilence previously, are intensely familiar to people today.

I made a deliberate choice not to discuss COVID-19 by name through the course of this writing — although the subtext appears in several places — partly because I felt the connections would be obvious to any contemporary reader and partly because I wanted the story of the three diseases explored in this book to be told on their own terms, with their own contexts, and their own consequences. Seeing everything in the light of our contemporary woes is unfair to what people lived in their own times.

But we always project our own realities onto the past, and no doubt, I have done the same on multiple occasions. My frustration with the cocoon of hubris with which we live in North America has also influenced my perspective. Infectious disease, as the preceding chapters discuss, has indelibly altered people's lives in concrete ways: they have fashioned relationships of power, built institutions, distorted livelihoods. Not all lessons from the past are immediately useful, but we have to consider, in the light of all that has gone before, how we are not anywhere very different from what many people already confront. And alas, although I had hoped in my original proposal of an imagined outbreak to uplift opportunities for healing, perhaps the cruel reality of COVID-19 simply demonstrates how we are apt to make the same mistakes.

My father recalls getting smallpox booster shots regularly as a child, the municipal vaccinators in our neighbourhood summoned to their home by the family patriarch regularly in post-independence India. How odd, I think, to consider all the factors that must have converged to make such a program possible. A technology known in places like India and China brought to England, transformed, and then returned through the dizzying integration of even small, obscure villages outside of Calcutta into a global paradigm, sustained even after the British withdrew. Contemporary medicine as an institution has been greatly shaped by systems of oppression such as patriarchy and racism, but do we then abandon it completely because of this association? Some would go so far as to argue that colonialism cannot have been so bad if it can have brought the clear benefit to quality of life as medicine has.

Not only does this conviction overlook that it has not done so for everyone, but I increasingly believe that this equation is contorted in its logic. In the societies in which it has flourished, the form of medicine derived from Euro-American practices has managed to monopolize resources, political power, and knowledge in ways that have buttressed its competencies. Interprofessional battles undermined folk medicine practitioners, such as midwives, as healing work was professionalized and elite interests took over the work of care. It is not because Euro-American medicine is effective that it is powerful. Rather, the inverse is true: because it has been powerful, it has become effective. Systems of healing that we dismiss as superstitious or unscientific are not all that different from the bloodletting and the purging that dominated in Europe not all that long ago. What Euro-American medicine has had in its favour is an entire infrastructure devoted to extracting knowledge, resources, and labour to be able to enhance its practices, with plenty of time and capacity for research and reflection. Its institutions have been protected by law, the language of its knowledge globalized, its workers valorized. Many other healing systems that were not so closely tied to European colonial power received none of those considerations — and in fact were actively displaced by the sharp elbows of doctors of Western medicine — although post-independence India and contemporary China, among other countries, have shown some investment in other medical traditions.

The diseases discussed in this volume reflect on these global dynamics: treponematoses have circled the planet with humans, popping up with variants and variations in innumerable ways, their most fearsome incarnation yet erupting in the clash of colonialism. Tuberculosis has reared its head under every deep wound in societies around the world, whether it be in the slums of industrializing Europe or in the wake of HIV tearing through sub-Saharan Africa. Smallpox was eradicated at the end only through a concerted, co-ordinated international effort to stamp out residual outbreaks flaring up worldwide. But in their local expression in North America, these epidemics throw into stark relief how Canada's lust for land overrode everything — that at its heart, this country of poxes rendered even the experience of illness and the process of recovery dependent on its logic of dispossession.

How do we soothe the wounds left behind? In the context of my work of over a decade in medicine in Canada, I consider three factors, in no way the only ones nor necessarily the most important, but there are parallels in other societies where the impact of historical domination and dispossession also play out within settings of healthcare and medicine.

The first, the most immediate, is to address how Indigenous peoples receive care when sick. In Canada, the federal government continues to take the medicine chest clause in treaty relationships almost literally, often maintaining nothing more than the bare bones of a dispensary — a chest of medicines — in Indigenous communities. Nursing staff present are stretched to the maximum. Although there has been change, with attempts to keep larger numbers of human resources in communities, the model that marked the launch of Canada, with healthcare as moralizing missions for uncivilized savages, roaming agents for smallpox vaccination to facilitate trade, and wandering physicians in the Prairies to protect white people from tuberculosis, has continued to mark the way healthcare is delivered in Indigenous communities. As much as these diseases were part of the colonial experience, the response to them was driven by the need to prolong colonial control.

The amount of investment that has gone into healthcare in Indigenous jurisdictions is nowhere near the amount needed to repair the harm done by colonial policy — not only residential school, but also the loss of land and livelihood, the isolation imposed by forced settlement onto remote territories, and the demographic decimation caused by policies of assimilation and genocide. Guidance on how to repair the damage done over the centuries already exists. The Truth and Reconciliation Commission lists seven specific calls to action for the healthcare sector.[2] The Viens Commission in Quebec, studying the relationship between Indigenous communities and the public service in the province in the wake of evidence of police abuse of Indigenous women in Val d'Or, also looks at the implications for healthcare.[3] In late 2020, Joyce's Principle emerged to demand specific action in the realm of healthcare, after the death of Joyce Echaquan in a Quebec hospital, not unlike the death of Brian Sinclair in Winnipeg a few years earlier.[4]

The three documents echo each other in their simple demands. While the Truth and Reconciliation Commission provides general principles by which governments should act, the Viens Commission's thirty-four recommendations for health and social services in Quebec are detailed — and have resonance across the country. They both specifically push the federal government to expand access to appropriate healthcare services for underserved Indigenous populations. The incorporation of Indigenous healing traditions is also a theme in the documents.

The significance of appropriate training for healthcare professionals is addressed in all three documents. On my first day of medical school in 2007, we reviewed the Krebs cycle — the intricate processes within the cell to unlock energy from glucose that your digestive system has broken down, delivered to your cells by the blood system. In the intervening fifteen years, I have not once used the Krebs cycle to make any decision in my medical career. But within ten years after that class, I returned to the school as a faculty member to guide medical students on their first day. No more Krebs cycle, but instead a case study on health concerns in an Indigenous community, through which students worked to understand how health status was determined by things other than biology alone. I could assure them that they would use those ideas within fifteen years of medical practice at least once more than they would use the Krebs cycle, no matter their discipline.

This small sign of change is demonstrative of the way medical practice in Canada is finally responding to the work of the many scholars and activists who have pushed all of Canada's institutions to a reckoning with colonialism. I noticed this shift truly start to come to academic medicine in the rise of Idle No More in 2014. The College of Family Physicians of Canada and the Royal College of Physicians and Surgeons of Canada have since put together guidelines on how to work effectively in Indigenous healthcare, with committees led by Indigenous physicians, such as Darlene Kitty and Marcia Anderson.[5] Other healthcare professions are also going through transformative work in addressing the roles they have played in the establishment of healthcare services in Indigenous territories.

A second consideration in navigating how we respond to the way epidemics have been used to dispossess asks about the larger nature of the relationship between settlers and Indigenous peoples. The relationship between, say India and the UK, though fraught with nuance, is made clearer by a definitive break-up. But it is harder for wounds to heal when they are continuously inflicted, as they are in settler states.

The federal office responsible for Indigenous healthcare has had an ever-changing identity. In 2012, it was known as First Nations and Inuit Health, and it developed a program to eliminate tuberculosis on-reserve by identifying outbreaks and working in partnership with communities to suppress them. Scholars have asked if this orientation could be seen to operate under the terms of treaties already negotiated, like Kaswentha, represented by the Two Row Wampum.[6] Kaswentha was agreed upon between Dutch traders and the Haudenosaunee in the seventeenth century and is considered the first agreement between an Indigenous nation and a European country. The Haudenosaunee captured the meaning of the treaty in a wampum (shell bead) belt as a visual representation, which denotes two parallel lines suggestive of two vessels travelling the same waterway, not interfering with each other but ready to help if necessary. This spirit imbued Indigenous perspectives on the new arrivals, with many nations believing this first agreement of mutual non-interference and support would be the basis of future relations, before that trust was shattered.[7]

Imagining this spirit infusing healthcare systems could serve as a model on how we work to restore the intent of Kaswentha in Canada, with emerging examples such as the Cree Board of Health and Social Services of James Bay in Quebec and the First Nations Health Authority in British Columbia. We could dream of this work as underpinned by principles of non-interference, two boats navigating waters side by side, prepared to lend a hand if necessary but not getting in the other's way.[8] This framework helps me reorient the spirit in which I approach my own work in clinical settings as duty-bound by the relationships we have with fellow travellers, on parallel paths but on the same waterway as depicted on Kaswentha.

There are practical implications for such an approach as well. Contact tracing, for example, is essential for limiting the propagation of infectious disease but needs to be done with careful consideration with how intrusive this process might seem when cast in historical light.[9] Mass testing of people to identify infection better has its drawbacks if not done properly — subjecting bodies to interventions they have not necessarily sought can alienate people if coming from external, hostile authorities. Indigenous nations retaking control of these aspects of care could be one practical step in undoing the damage of colonialism, though it would be naive to think that it would resolve all issues of coercion in public health. Our assumption in the healthcare system that the goals we have are the goals everyone has is not necessarily true. People may be fighting other wars that make the battles we see secondary. Simply identifying illness is necessary but not sufficient for a person to want to pursue treatment.[10]

The importance of self-government over healthcare services, including public health, has been a longstanding call in Indigenous communities and not only to control infectious disease such as the tuberculosis epidemic.[11] But structural impediments in self-governance also need to be addressed: Indigenous communities still struggle to get access to their own health data. The changing nature of the relations of research and policy administration is shifting this balance, but it is very slow.[12]

A two-row wampum approach to clinical practice also means that the way we currently practise medicine in Canada must fundamentally transform, aiming for truly syncretic healing systems. Traditional practices that were driven underground or lost need to be restored to their rightful place, honouring those who have kept their knowledge safe. Healthcare professionals in Canada increasingly need to learn to work with healers from different traditions as partners, with mechanisms of redress put in place for how devastatingly under-resourced traditional knowledges have been for decades in their capacity to flourish as disciplines of practice.[13]

This approach could also help transform the idea of preventative care. Currently, it has a narrow scope of protecting individuals from specific pathologies, as I wheedle people to take medications to stave off heart attacks and strokes. Partly, I act on behalf of the government in order to avoid the burden these consequences would be on the public purse. But people may not see the same logic as I do: they may say that since they do not feel unwell, why should they be inconvenienced to act on something that may or may not happen in the future? This reasoning has my sympathies. After all, I used it myself to decide not to take treatment for potential latent tuberculosis infection. Much of what transpires in this calculation we all make internally is how much we trust that the authority in front of us has our best interests at heart and represents our aspirations too. If as a physician I am making pleas to you to behave in a way to protect a community, do you see yourself as embraced by that same community? Many people may not identify with the state or its needs but may be more willing to engage in preventing illness when it seems a direct threat to a community to whom they do feel a sense of duty. This consideration does not just come down to ideas of national belonging but are related to one's social position in many ways. Some men I see in my practice are not proactive about their own health, as they have been made oblivious to the cost their future ill health will have on those assigned to be their caregivers, often women.

But if people have more trusting relationships with health authorities, this concern may be less pressing. And there is the possibility that other modes of clinical thinking, where prevention is not just about limiting damage to individual bodies but about protecting the balance of relationship within the ecosystem in which we find ourselves, the meaning of preventative medicine may change for us. For settler medicine, this paradigm shift to repairing relationship not just with self but with land too would be revolutionary, but many Indigenous communities are already striving to restore health — in concrete ways to treat diabetes and addiction, for example — by reconnecting with land from which they have been displaced.[14]

Kaswentha provides this guidance for how to work within the healthcare system, but the same principles could transform the legacy of colonialism in other fields too. It also compels us to ask questions about how we can recast the cause of disease and despair in our societies. Previous colonizers bemoaned the dangers of tuberculosis spilling out of hospitals and reserves and into the (white) community through innocuous transactions, such as the sale of berries and handicrafts by Indigenous households in order make money to access goods through the cash economy.[15] When we speak of health in contemporary times, we must beware how intent we become on perpetuating the identification of Indigenous communities with illness. Rather than speaking about the way settler society is sick in its quest for control, we focus on the pathology of the colonized. A response to the focus on damage is to think about how people have survived, how people have desired other, better things for their lives.[16] The focus on aspiration troubles a distorted image of communities as simply broken. I have had to learn that the well-meaning, progressive concern for health outcomes for Indigenous peoples still marks the Indigenous as ill, as diseased communities that need to be healed through my ministrations, upholding a saviour complex, a messianic quest not unlike the one embodied by the Duchess of Aiguillon in seventeenth-century France.

This founding document of Kaswentha also needs to be part of the way more recent immigrants to North America understand their relationship to where they settle. Many years ago, I was visiting a wise friend on the Pacific coast who was entertaining guests from Australia at the same time. Conversations around similarities and differences between the two countries dominated the dinner table. I was mildly suspicious of the visitors' perspectives on politics, hostile to what I imagined white Australia to be. One evening after I had gone to bed, apparently a question came up that had not been asked in front of me. But my friend over a quiet breakfast together said, "You know, they asked an interesting question last night. Should the Australian government accept immigrants while the question of whose land it is remains unresolved?"

Almost apoplectic, I snorted in derision over my fresh bread and homemade jam. I did not trust the Australian guests to be such allies of Indigenous peoples to believe their question was coming from a place of genuine solidarity, rather than established anti-migrant sentiment. But over two decades, I have internalized that question — and while I would not put it in the same exclusionary terms, I do wonder what it means to be coming to this country from abroad. As I grapple with the role I play in Canada's history of furthering control of land through settlement, I — as well as many others — need to think about the country's responsibility in its amassed wealth to welcome people displaced from elsewhere but also to consider how those resources are accumulated through forced displacement here. Telling the story of these diseases to the communities who come here, who may also have intense historical familiarity with colonial devastation in their homes of origin, is a way of revealing what Canada is to those who might otherwise have had that history obscured to them.

And third, in thinking about the lessons of these diseases, we need to consider fevers of the future. COVID-19 is not the beginning nor the end of pandemics.

When the first wave of COVID-19 hit, I was in the midst of a long stretch of work. Even though we were relatively protected in the North at that time with strict travel restrictions, we were working hours on end in preparation for the virus's inevitable arrival in our context of austerity. I had a day off every ten or eleven days. One night on call, my patience already fragile after a litany of irritants during the day, the crescent moon was hanging low above the horizon when I left the clinic the first time. When I returned, jerked crankily out of a shallow sleep, it was gone. The northern horizon never quite darkened at that time of year — a grey glow lingered where the sun skimmed along just beneath it.

I surprised myself by sounding kinder than I felt. Fatigue had made me brittle, but rote training stepped in. I did not say any of the angry things I rehearsed to myself as I drove furiously back. Automatically as I entered, I quietened my voice, I asked everyone else to leave. I sat lower than her. Managing her emotions meant having to manage mine. I answered her questions directly, I made sure she had what she needed, someone instructed to get the power cord for her phone. The entire air ambulance team I had summoned from far away earlier in the evening for thousands of public dollars waited outside to transfer her to the hospital where I determined she needed more intensive treatment. Her balking tantrum at 1:30 a.m., her attempt to leave as she ripped off the cords of the beeping monitor, was part of a pattern she and I had. But I knew where it would end. Through tears, fifteen minutes later, "But does it have to be Montreal?" she whispered. "What if I get COVID-19? What if I bring it back to my sick daughter?"

COVID-19 has been revelatory as I have written, the stories I am reading from five hundred years ago becoming startlingly contemporary. For many, the pandemic's vagaries are not a surprise: they have not needed to be reminded, the threat of disease overwhelming their communities still within grasp of communal memory. But as I studied this endless cycle of repetition, I may have been more conciliatory about the way the COVID-19 pandemic has unfolded, maybe even more resigned, than many other settler friends in North America, particularly those who are white, who may not have had infectious outbreaks engraved into their collective psyches. Later in the colonial period, epidemics became marked in the imagination of Europe as always something that happened elsewhere, a threat from abroad, a necessary evil to pay for the glory of empire. But for many of us who have lived in those places, we still tell the tales of our body's vulnerabilities to onslaughts from others: none of it is new.

That acceptance does not mean I am immune to rage at the injustice in the way we choose to respond. Maldistribution of vaccines, the blithe oblivion to the costs of isolation, inadequate protection for workers exposed to high risk. We may know the answers to these questions, but we fail when put to the test. The final toll of COVID-19 for Indigenous communities across Canada remains to be seen, even though initial assessments were quite optimistic, given how quickly communities asserted their authority to protect themselves, having learned from the lessons of the brutal H1N1 pandemic about a decade earlier, where almost 25 percent of intensive care admissions in Canada during its first wave were Indigenous people.[17] This process of reclaiming control over the territories, putting in place quarantine mechanisms and entry control procedures, was unsettling to many settler healthcare-worker colleagues, who grumbled about the strict isolation measures imposed on them. But Indigenous nations were well within their sovereignty to exert this authority. We could learn from these efforts to choose what determines our own communities' health.

We live too closely with our fellow creatures not to have quarrelsome relations with some of them. And even then, we live in a world that binds us closer and closer together as a planet, through the rigours of an economy bent on mining every last drop of value from resources, no matter how far away. This integration brings us many benefits, but it also drives transport and transmission of any variety of germs: pandemics are by definition global, and they occur because our societies are global in their extractivist greed. The more we advance avariciously into the depths of creation grasping for more material, the more we will come into conflict with nature's defences. But this way of being is not the only way to be connected with others across the planet. Can we, those of us who have been alienated from our relationship with land for so long, relearn what it means to live in a way that is not predicated on extraction, but on exchange with our environment? Indigenous communities the world over have preserved this knowledge over centuries, and their guidance, with appropriate compensation for it, will be critical for us

Illnesses are woven through our lives as individuals and the societies in which we live. I struggle with the desire to eliminate disease as though it did not exist, coupled with a doctor's pragmatism that it always will, striking the best of us with absurdity. I want to resist how stupidly we might respond to sudden widespread sickness but also accept that it takes years, decades, before we know enough not to make mistakes, often forced into decisions with incomplete information. How do we prepare ourselves for how these new intruders in our relationships with each other will inevitably warp us? How do we know that we will respond to these epidemics, not with mercenary goals of continuing to draw profit and prestige from it, but in ways that respond to people's needs — in ways that care and cure?

Smallpox was easy to eradicate as it lived in no other host except humans. There was no asymptomatic transmission, so contacts were relatively easy to identify. The only other viral disease that has been effectively eradicated has been rinderpest, a disease specific to cattle. We are perhaps on the verge of eradicating polio, which has circulated since time immemorial but where a concerted effort to eradicate it began in 1988 — an effort which is taking around thirty years. Afghanistan and Pakistan are the only countries in the world where there are still cases of intermittent wild polio, the control of which has been complicated by the vaccine-derived version of the disease that causes rare outbreaks.[18] The polio virus too has humans as their only reservoir species: it does not flourish in other animals, so finely tuned is it to the human environment, so eradication may be tantalizingly possible.

Every year, ten million across the world fall sick with tuberculosis. The United Nations nonetheless does have a plan to reduce the disease by a significant amount by 2030. No easy feat, given its ubiquity, the possibility of asymptomatic infection, and its slow-growing nature, when people can become quite sick after a long period of imperceptible decline. Treating it takes long periods of therapy as well, which is not always possible for people to pursue consistently. Effective treatment is now also threatened by the germ's evolving resistance to many medications. The possibility that it may infect us from species that live very closely with us also complicates our future with this organism. In Canada, we continue to struggle with eliminating the disease, but it probably will not improve until there is much better access not only to care but to housing and nutrition in the populations that are most affected: immigrants and Indigenous peoples.

Syphilis continues to roam the world practically with impunity. It probably has more cases than tuberculosis every year, and its impact on newborns and young children is great. While we have the tendency to dismiss the disease as a minor inconvenience, it still causes about a million deaths every year. Some estimates say anywhere from a fifth to a third of neonatal deaths in poorer parts of the world may be due to syphilis infection in the uterus. It only lives in humans, but there is no easy vaccine, and treatment requires being able to diagnose it consistently and broadly. Syphilis control programs worldwide focus on screening pregnant women in order to limit transmission to children and to any subsequent sexual partners. Even though there were plans to eliminate syphilis within the borders of countries like Canada and the United States, recent climb in rates has made that goal seem unlikely or has at least delayed it.[19] As is obvious, it is the most marginalized populations that have the highest rates of infection.

These sobering realities demonstrate that infectious disease riddles our society still, infesting every crack in our togetherness. Texts from earlier this century that trumpeted the end of infectious disease are the epitome of human hubris. Triumphalist approaches to health which assume there is a steady progression in disease control as technology advances have evidently been false. Within medicine, we are coming to a revolution in the way we understand infectious disease as part of our relationship with our environment and with each other in a collective healthcare approach. In comparison, the term public health can seem reductive to this more holistic stance. Doctors are latecomers to this understanding as this knowledge has been part of Indigenous healthcare systems worldwide for centuries, aware that disruptions to carefully negotiated balances with the ecosystem can unleash havoc. The forced displacement from land that is the defining feature of colonialism in settled North America has reinforced these teachings in Indigenous communities here; at its core, the question of health returns to our relationship with the land. This conversation can be unsettling for many people because it asks us to do just that, as Paulette Regan, who served as research director of the Truth and Reconciliation Commission has written: to unsettle.[20] There is of course no returning to a pristine precolonial past. But just as diseases have been used in the taking of territory, they open opportunities to build healing responses. Across the world, epidemics leave detritus in their wakes, families in mourning, communities scrambling to recover. The resources available to a community to respond can determine how they move on from devastation. One community where I worked in West Africa had not been badly hit by the 2014–2016 Ebola epidemic, but an isolation ward was built with foreign money as donations eventually trickled down to remote areas of the country. Even if we were not confronting outbreaks of haemorrhagic fevers, the isolation ward was useful for other contagious diseases, such as pertussis and diphtheria, allowing us a modicum of control over the way diseases were spread among the children admitted to the paediatric ward. It also served as a step-down ward during peak malaria season for children recovering from serious infection when the regular ward was overflowing with patients. We took what the devastation of previous epidemics had left us and tried to find ways forward.

We can do the same elsewhere. The blueprint of what we have to do as a society already exists. Indigenous nations in Canada have made tremendous progress in restoring autonomy in healthcare services, with examples like the Cree Board of Health and Social Services of James Bay and the First Nations Health Authority in British Columbia. In recent years, the Canadian government has signed agreements with many Indigenous governing agencies to establish autonomy in healthcare administration and delivery, such as the 2020 memorandum of understanding with the Southern Chiefs' Organization exploring new care delivery models in Anishinaabeg and Dakota communities in southern Manitoba, similar to the Keewatinohk Inniniw Minoayawin, which is reviewing healthcare services in twenty-three Indigenous communities in the north of the province.[21] In 2021, the Nishnawbe Aski Nation signed an agreement with Canada and Ontario to fund an Indigenous healthcare system across their territory, similar to what First Nations in Quebec outside of Cree and Inuit territories also did with federal and provincial governments in 2019.[22]

But beyond that step alone, deeper work is necessary. Many Indigenous views of balance with the ecosystem may guide us in rectifying the way we have approached preventative health, which I have been learning a lot about in my work with anti-extractive organizers across the Americas who look at health as something shared with all living things.[23] Now, attention returns to Indigenous systems of knowledge in medicine.[24] The same appears to be happening in fields as disparate as botany[25] and history.[26] These frameworks of understanding the world might also benefit from the support Western scientific systems have monopolized for centuries and guide our frameworks of how to be in this world. All of it means not only healing humans but healing our relationship with the land that hosts us.

In the journey I have taken to explore these diseases, I think about how my own clinical work has changed in learning more about this history. People in Canada have fought hard to have healthcare services that are of high quality and widespread access. But we cannot stop here with all that we know they still fail to do. The conversations around this book have helped shape how I imagine the future. We cannot move forward if we do not question the well-meaning belief that access to systems of biomedical care as currently developed is necessarily benign. Whether I work in a village in Guinea or on the streets of Montreal, the theme is the same: trust needs to be continually rebuilt with a system that has emerged from a history of imposition and control. Those of us within the system need to take the responsibility of extending ourselves to demonstrate that we deserve such faith. And while I am someone who tends to focus on the structural rather than the individual, I also recognize that this means that we as practitioners also have to work hard to change the way we practise as workers. People may choose not to engage with us until we prove ourselves worthy.

For surely the times we live in show us that we cannot simply continue down the path we have pursued for this long. A collective reimagining of our relationship to land, to water, to air must arise to diminish the risk of the next pandemic unleashing itself among us. And when it comes — for it will — we can be prepared, our relationship with all creation reimagined. We can move for forward to nurture each other, widening the circle of whom we include in the embrace of our support. It may be inevitable that we transmit disease from one to another in our togetherness, but so it will also be how we heal.

Notes

Chapter 1: Pandemics Past

1. W.H. Man, W.A.A. de Steenhuijsen Piters, and D. Bogaert, "The Microbiota of the Respiratory Tract: Gatekeeper to Respiratory Health," *Nature Reviews Microbiology* 15 (2017): 259–270.
2. C. Férec and V. Scotet, "Genetics of Cystic Fibrosis: Basics," *Archives De Pédiatrie: Supplement* 1, 27 (2020): 7, https://doi.org/10.1016/S0929-693X(20)30043-9.
3. M. Kempner, "The Genetic Mutation Behind the Only Apparent Cure for HIV" (2019), thebodypro.com/article/genetic-mutation-behind-hiv-cure.
4. K.J. Pittman, L.C. Glover, L. Wang, et al., "The Legacy of Past Pandemics: Common Human Infections That Protect Against Infectious Disease," *PLOS Pathogens* 12, 7, (2016): e1005680. https://doi.org/10.1371/journal.ppat.1005680.
5. B. Banerjee, "Blood Types Around the World" (2021), https://www.visualcapitalist.com/wp-content/uploads/2021/11/Most-Common-Blood-Types-by-Country.html.
6. G. Dewan, "Comparative Frequency and Allelic Distribution of ABO and Rh (D) Blood Groups of Major Tribal Communities of Southern Bangladesh with General Population and Their Determinants," *Egyptian Journal of Medical Human Genetics* 16, 2 (2015).
7. S. Shaheen-Hussain, *Fighting for a Hand to Hold: Confronting Medical Colonialism Against Indigenous Children in Canada* (Montreal: McGill-Queen's University Press, 2021).
8. J. Daschuk, *Clearing the Plains: Disease, the Politics of Starvation, and the Loss of Aboriginal Life* (Regina: University of Regina Press, 2019).
9. M.-E. Kelm, *Colonizing Bodies: Aboriginal Health and Healing in British Columbia 1900–50* (Vancouver: UBC Press, 1998).
10. G. Geddes, *Medicine Unbundled* (Victoria: Heritage House Publishers, 2017).
11. There is significant debate about the most appropriate name to describe this empire, given the complexities of language, ethnicity, geography, and politics involved, but Aztec remains the most commonly understood descriptor.
12. P. Shaffer, *The Royal Hunt of the Sun* (London: Samuel French, 1964).
13. Royal College of Physicians, *History of the Royal College of Physicians* (n.d.), rcplondon.ac.uk/about-us/who-we-are/history-royal-college-physicians.
14. I.M. Moriyama, R.M. Loy, and A.H.T. Robb-Smith, "History of the Statistical Classification of Diseases and Causes of Death," Hyattsville: National

Center for Health Statistics (2011), cdc.gov/nchs/data/misc/classification_diseases2011.pdf.

15. A.M. Shkilnyk, *A Poison Stronger Than Love: The Destruction of an Ojibway Community* (New Haven: Yale University Press, 1985).

16. Free Grassy Narrows, Support Grassy Narrows First Nation (n.d.), freegrassy.net.

17. I. McCleery, "What Is 'Colonial' About *Medieval* Colonial Medicine? Iberian Health in Global Context," *Journal of Medieval Iberian Studies* 7, 2 (2015): 151–175. https://doi.org/10.1080/17546559.2015.1077390.

18. P.E. Bickler, J.R. Feiner, and J.W. Severinghaus, "Effects of Skin Pigmentation on Pulse Oximeter Accuracy at Low Saturation," *Anesthesiology* 102, 4 (2005): 715–719.

19. S. Ahmed, C.T. Nutt, N.D. Eneanya, et al., "Examining the Potential Impact of Race Multiplier Utilization in Estimated Glomerular Filtration Rate Calculation on African-American Care Outcomes," *Journal of General Internal Medicine* 36, 2 (2021): 464–471, https://doi.org/10.1007/s11606-020-06280-5.

20. M. Mukwende, *Black and Brown Skin* (2020), blackandbrownskin.co.uk/.

21. S. Lowes and E. Montero, "Historical Experiences and Foreign Aid Efficacy: The Unintended Consequences of Colonial Medical Campaigns in Central Africa," *VoxEU* (2018), voxeu.org/article/historical-experiences-and-foreign-aid-efficacy.

22. P. Farmer, *Fevers, Feuds, and Diamonds* (New York: Farrar, Straus and Giroux, 2020).

23. V. Sriram, V.R. Keshri, and K. Kumbhar, "The Impact of Colonial-Era Policies on Health Workforce Regulation in India: Lessons for Contemporary Reform," *Human Resources for Health* 19 (2021): 100, https://doi.org/10.1186/s12960-021-00640-w.

24. B. Mukhopadhyay, "Care as Colonialism: Immigrant Health Workers at Canada's Frontiers," *Upping the Anti* 19 (2017), uppingtheanti.org/journal/article/19-care-as-colonialism.

25. C. Bartlett, M. Marshall, and A. Marshall, "Two-Eyed Seeing and Other Lessons Learned Within a Co-Learning Journey of Bringing Together Indigenous and Mainstream Knowledges and Ways of Knowing," *Journal of Environmental Studies and Sciences* 2, 4 (2012): 331–340.

Chapter 2: Syphilis

1. D.J. Ortner, "Identification of Pathological Conditions in Human Skeletal Remains" (Amsterdam: Academic Press, 2003): 273.

2. P.F. Hall, "Letters: Diabetes in Aboriginal populations," *Canadian Medical Association Journal* 162,1. (2000): 11-12.

3. O.T. Beall and R.H. Shryock, *Cotton Mather: First Significant Figure in American Medicine* (Baltimore: Johns Hopkins Press, 1954): 129, https://www.americanantiquarian.org/proceedings/44817435.pdf.

4. L.V. Stamm, "Pinta: Latin America's Forgotten Disease?" *The American Journal of Tropical Medicine and Hygiene* 93, 5 (2015): 901–903.

5. P.K. Wilson, "Bad Habits and Bad Genes: Early 20th-Century Eugenic Attempts to Eliminate Syphilis and Associated 'Defects' from the United States,"

Canadian Bulletin of Medical History 20, 1 (2003): 11–41.

6. M. Marks, D. Lebari, A. W. Solomon, et al., "Yaws," *International Journal of STD & AIDS* 26, 10 (2015): 696–703, https://doi.org/10.1177/0956462414549036.

7. H. Wilson, "Sarsaparilla in Syphilis," *Provincial Medical Journal and Retrospect of the Medical Sciences* 6, 134 (1843): 71, https://doi.org/10.1136/bmj.s1-6.134.71.

8. B. Baker, G. Crane-Kramer, M. Dee, et al., "Advancing the Understanding of Treponemal Disease in the Past and Present," *American Journal of Physical Anthropology* 171, 70 (2020): 5–41.

9. R.S. Morton, "The Sibbens of Scotland," *Medical History* 11, 4 (1967): 374–380.

10. Rénald Lessard, "'Direction pour la Guérison du Mal de la Baie St Paul': La Première Publication Médicale Canadienne," *Canadian Bulletin of Medical History* 12, 2 (1995): 369–372.

11. W.R. Riddell, "La Maladie de la Baie de St Paul," *The Public Health Journal* 15, 4 (1924): 145–157, http://www.jstor.org/stable/41973143.

12. K. Majander, S. Pfrengle, A. Kocher, et al., "Ancient Bacterial Genomes Reveal a High Diversity of Treponema Pallidum Strains in Early Modern Europe," *Current Biology* 30, 19 (2020): 3788–3803.e3710.

13. J. Leckie, "Missing or Misdiagnosed? General Paralysis of the Insane, Yaws, and Syphilis in Fiji, 1884–1940," *Journal of Pacific History* 55, 1 (2020): 37–57.

14. G. Fracastoro, *Syphilis, ou, Le Mal Vénérien, Poeme Latine avec la Traduction en français et des notes*, translated by P. Macuer and J. Lacombe (Paris: Jean-Claude Lucet, 1796): 8–12.

15. S. Watts, *Epidemics and History: Disease, Power and Imperialism* (New Haven: Yale University Press, 1999): 128–129, 136.

16. J.M. Zeserson, "How Japanese Women Talk about Hot Flushes: Implications for Menopause Research," *Medical Anthropology Quarterly* 15, 2 (2001): 189–205.

17. E.H. Hudson, "Christopher Columbus and the History of Syphilis," *Acta Tropica* 25 (1968): 1–16, p. 5.

18. J. Frith, "Syphilis — Its Early History and Treatment Until Penicillin and the Debate on Its Origins," *Journal of Military and Veterans' Health* (2012): 49–58, p. 55.

19. S. Boumediene, *La colonisation du savoir: Une histoire des plantes médicinales du "Nouveau Monde" (1492–1750)* (Vaulx-en-Velin: Éditions des Mondes à Faire, 2016): 63–66.

20. S. Watts, *Epidemics and History*: 130.

21. G. Riccomi and V. Giuffra, "First Portrait of a Syphilitic Patient: Ulrich Von Hutten," *The American Journal of Medicine* 131 (2018).

22. J. Parascandola, "From Mercury to Miracle Drugs: Syphilis Therapy over the Centuries," *Pharmacy in History* 51, 1 (2009): 14–23, p. 15, https://www.jstor.org/stable/41112412.

23. W B Konkle, "Voltaire on Syphilis," *Medical Library and Historical Journal*, 3 117–27 (1905).

24. S. Watts, *Epidemics and History*: 94–98.

25. E.H. Hudson, "Christopher Columbus": 4.

26. S. Watts, *Epidemics and History*: 97–98.

27. M.G. Ucay, *Nouveau traité de la maladie venerienne. Ou après avoir demontré que la methode ordinaire de la guerir est tres dangereuse, douteuse & difficile; on en propose une autre fort facile & fort asseurée. Avec quelques problèmes curieux sur cette matiere*, Paris: Laurent d'Houry (1693): 148–157.

28. Ibid., 158–163.

29. E.H. Hudson, "Christopher Columbus": 13.

30. D. Turner, *Syphilis. A Practical Dissertation on the Venereal Disease … in Two Parts* (Gale Ecco, Print Editions, 2010 [1717]): 6.

31. C. Wymant, D. Bezemer, F. Blanquart, et al., 2022. "A Highly Virulent Variant of HIV-1 Circulating in the Netherlands," *Science* 375 (6580): 540–45. https://doi.org/10.1126/science.abk1688.

32. R. Barnett, "Syphilis," *The Lancet* 391, 10129 (April 2018): 1471.

33. M.G. Ucay, *Nouveau traité de la maladie venerienne*: 10–11.

34. D. Turner, *Syphilis, A Practical Dissertation*: 4.

35. W. Klein, "Plant of the Month: Sarsaparilla," *JSTOR Daily* (June 2021), https://daily.jstor.org/plant-of-the-month-sarsaparilla/.

36. S. Drapeau, "Hôtel-Dieu de Québec," *Histoire des institutions de charité de bienfaisance et d'éducation du Canada depuir leur fondation jusqu'à nos jours, 1er volume — Hôpitaux* (Ottawa, Foyer domestique, 1877): 2.

37. S. Drapeau, "Hôtel-Dieu de Québec": 7.

38. R.G. Thwaites, *The Jesuit Relations and Allied Documents* (Cleveland, Ohio, Burrows Brothers Company, 1896–1901), Vol. XX: p. 232–252; Vol. XXVI: p. 203, 305.

39. P.-F.-X. De Charlevoix, *Histoire et description générale de la Nouvelle France: avec le journal historique d'un voyage fait par ordre du roi dans l'Amérique septentrionale* (Paris: Chez Rolin fils, 1744): 203.

40. J.S. Marr and J.T. Cathey, "New Hypothesis for Cause of Epidemic among Native Americans, New England, 1616–1619." *Emerging Infectious Diseases* 16, 2 (2010): 281–286, https://doi.org/10.3201/eid1602.090276.

41. M. Cadotte, "Epidemics of Canada," *The Canadian Encyclopaedia* (2020), https://www.thecanadianencyclopedia.ca/en/article/epidemic.

42. J. Murphy, *An American Plague: The True and Terrifying Story of the Yellow Fever Epidemic of 1793*, (Boston: Clarion Books, 2003).

43. S. Slater, "'Nought but Women': Constructions of Masculinities and Modes of Emasculation in the New World," in *Gender and Sexuality in Indigenous North America, 1400–1850*, edited by S Slater and F.A. Yarbrough (Columbia, SC: University of South Carolina Press, 2012): 30–53, p. 47.

44. K. Faull, "Contact and Negotiation: Masculinity in the Eighteenth-Century Moravian Mission Field." *Journal of Moravian History* 13, 1 (2013): 29–30.

45. B. De las Casas, "A Brief Account of the Destruction of the Indies Or, a faithful NARRATIVE OF THE Horrid and Unexampled Massacres, Butcheries, and all manner of Cruelties, that Hell and Malice could invent, committed by the Popish *Spanish* Party on the inhabitants of *West-India*, TOGETHER With the Devastations of several Kingdoms in *America* by Fire and Sword, for the space of Forty and Two Years, from the time of its first Discovery by them" (Translation of Brevisima relacion de la destruccíon de las Indias, first published 1552 in Seville). London: R. Hewson, accessed at the Gutenberg Project (1689), https://www.gutenberg.org/cache/epub/20321/pg20321-images.html.

46. A. McClintock, "The Lay of the Land," in *Imperial Leather: Race, Gender and Sexuality in the Colonial Contest* (New York: Routledge, 1995): 21–74.

47. D. Tanck de Estrada, "Who Was Salvadora de los Santoz Ramirez, Otomi Indian?" in *Gender and Sexuality in Indigenous North America, 1400–1850*, edited by S Slater and F.A. Yarbrough (Columbia, SC, University of South Carolina Press, 2012): 80.

48. J.E. Chaplin, "Natural Philosophy and an Early Racial Idiom in North America: Comparing English and Indian Bodies," *The William and Mary Quarterly* 54, 1 (1997): 229–252, p. 245.

49. J. Parascondola, *Sex, Sin, and Science: A History of Syphilis in America* (Westport, CT: Greenwood Publishing Group, 2008), p.24, The Colonial Period in Chapter 2, "A Secret Disease."

50. P.C. Newman, *Company of Adventurers, Volume I* (Markham, ON: Penguin Canada, 1985): 159, 202–204.

51. E. Coues, *New light on the early history of the greater Northwest: The manuscript journals of Alexander Henry, fur trader of the Northwest Company, and of David Thompson, official geographer of the same company 1799–1814 ....* (New York: Francis P. Harper, 1897): 835–836.

52. J. Parascondola, *Sex, Sin, and Science,* p. 26, The Colonial Period in Chapter 2, "A Secret Disease."

53. W. Preston, "Serpent in Eden: Dispersal of Foreign Diseases Into Pre-Mission California," *Journal of California and Great Basin Anthropology* 18, 1 (1996): 2–37, pp. 23-25.

54. T.P. Lowry, *Venereal Disease and the Lewis and Clark Expedition* (Lincoln: University of Nebraska Press, 2004): 29.

55. Ibid., 43–45.

56. J. Parascondola, *Sex, Sin, and Science,* p. 25, The Colonial Period in Chapter 2, "A Secret Disease."

57. M. Nagy, "Le désir de l'Autre chez le missionnaire Émile Petitot," in *Éros et tabou. Sexualité et genre chez les Amérindiens et les Inuit*, edited by Frédéric Laugrand and Gilles Havard (Quebec City: Septentrion, 2014): 408–430.

58. M. Walls, "The Disposition of the Ladies: Mi'kmaw Women and the Removal of the King's Road Reserve, Sydney, Nova Scotia," *Journal of Canadian Studies* 50, 3 (2017): 538–565.

59. G.D. Smithers, "The 'Pursuits of the Civilized Man': Race and the Meaning of Civilization in the United States and Australia, 1790s–1850s," *Journal of World History* 20, 2 (2009): 245-272, pp. 251-256.

60. P. Edmonds, "Unpacking Settler Colonialism's Urban Strategies: Indigenous Peoples in Victoria, British Columbia, and the Transition to a Settler-Colonial City," *Urban History Review* 38, 2 (2010): 4–20, p. 12–14.

61. J. Wingrove, "Alberta's Rate of Syphilis Infection Still Rising." *Globe and Mail* (2010), theglobeandmail.com/life/health-and-fitness/health/conditions/albertas-rate-of-syphilis-infection-still-rising/article572646/.

62. M. Walls, "The Disposition of the Ladies": 538–565, p. 549.

63. E.S. Wyness, "A Social Work Approach to the Venereal Disease Problem in British Columbia: An Analysis of the Social Problems Involved in Controlling the Infected Individual, with Particular Reference to Recidivism at the Vancouver Clinic, Division of Venereal Disease Control, British Columbia" (Thesis: Department of Social Work, University of British Columbia, Vancou-

ver 1950): 23.

64. R. Fox, "Bigger Issues than VD, Native Peoples Official Protests," *Globe and Mail (1936–2017)*, (May 12, 1976): 7. Retrieved from https://proxy.library.mcgill.ca/login?url=https://www.proquest.com/historical-newspapers/bigger-issues-than-vd-native-peoples-official/docview/1239366911/se-2?accountid=12339.

65. T. Ornstein, "Indian College," *Globe and Mail (1936–2017)*, (May 17, 1976): 6. Retrieved from https://proxy.library.mcgill.ca/login?url=https://www.proquest.com/historical-newspapers/letters-editor/docview/1239373213/se-2?accountid=12339.

66. J. MacDonald, "Tourist Season," in *Bridge Out of Town* (Ottawa: Oberon Press, 1986): 53–71.

67. P. Levine, *Prostitution, Race and Politics: Policing Venereal Disease in the British Empire* (New York: Routledge, 2003): 42.

68. P. Levine, *Prostitution, Race and Politics*: 38.

69. J.B. Hamilton, "Closure of Lock Hospitals in India," *Lancet*, 128, 3284 (1886): 270–271, https://doi.org/10.1016/S0140-6736(02)10390-4.

70. P. Levine, *Prostitution, Race and Politics*: 121–122.

71. C. Kindell, "'Brothel of the Pacific': Syphilis and the Urban Regulation of Laikini Wahine in Honolulu, 1855–75," *Journal of Pacific History* 55, 1 (2020): 18–36.

72. S. Watts, *Epidemics and History:*165.

73. Ibid.:163

74. S. Weale, "Structural Racism at London School of Hygiene & Tropical Medicine, Finds Report," *The Guardian* (2021), theguardian.com/education/2021/dec/13/structural-racism-at-london-school-of-hygiene-tropical-medicine-finds-report.

75. F. Proschan, "'Syphilis, Opiomania, and Pederasty': Colonial Constructions of Vietnamese (and French) Social Diseases," *Journal of the History of Sexuality* 11, 4 (2002): 610–636.

76. H.-L. Clark, "Civilization and Syphilization: A Doctor and His Disease in Colonial Morocco." *Bulletin of the History of Medicine* 87, 1 (2013): 86–114.

77. S. Watts, *Epidemics and History:* 132–133.

78. J.E. Chaplin, "Natural Philosophy and an Early Racial Idiom: 229–252.

79. H.M.J. Desruelles, *Memoir on the treatment of venereal diseases without mercury: employed at the military hospital of the Val-de-Grace / translated from the French of H.M.J. Desruelles; to which is added Observations on the treatment of the venereal disease without mercury by G.J. Guthrie and various documents showing the results of this mode of treatment in Great Britain, France, Germany, and America* (Philadelphia: Carey and Lea, 1830): 47–49.

80. J.E. Chaplin, "Natural Philosophy and an Early Racial Idiom: 229–252, pp. 242–244.

81. S. Watts, *Epidemics and History*: pp. 147–161.

82. J. Parascondola, *Sex, Sin, and Science*, pp. 7-14, Sex and Women in Chapter 1 "The Great Pox."

83. S. Watts, *Epidemics and History:* p. 148.

84. J. Parascondola, *Sex, Sin, and Science*, p. 37, A New Century Dawns in Chap-

ter 2 "A Secret Disease."
85. A.M. Brandt, *No Magic Bullet: A Social History of Venereal Disease in the United States Since 1880* (New York: Oxford University Press, 1985): 43–44.
86. F.E. Hodgins, *Report on Venereal Diseases, Royal Commission on The Care and Control of the Mentally Defective and Feeble-minded in Ontario (and the Prevalence of Venereal Disease)*, Second Interim Report (Toronto: A.T. Wilgress (King's Printer), 1919): 4–6.
87. A.M. Brandt, *No Magic Bullet:* 157–158.
88. Ibid.: 15–16.
89. Ibid.: 66, 71–80.
90. K. Bogaert, "Patient Experience and the Treatment of Venereal Disease in Toronto's Military Base Hospital during the First World War," *Canadian Military History* 26, 2 (2017).
91. P. Levine, *Prostitution, Race and Politics*: 163.
92. D.G. Jeffreys (editor), *Views of Ancient Egypt since Napoleon Bonaparte: Imperialism, Colonialism and Modern Appropriations* (Routledge, 2016), https://www.taylorfrancis.com/books/e/9781315416014.
93. A. Christie, *Murder in Mesopotamia* (Glasgow: Collins' Crime Club, 1936).
94. J.S. Johnson, "Consolidation of Archeological Bone: A Conservation Perspective," *Journal of Field Archeology* 21 (1994): 22–233, https://repository.si.edu/bitstream/handle/10088/56522/529866.pdf?isAllowed=y&sequence=1.
95. T.E. von Hunnius, D. Yang, B. Eng, et al., "Digging Deeper into the Limits of Ancient DNA Research on Syphilis." *Journal of Archaeological Science* 34, 12 (2007): 2091–2100, pp. 2097–2098.
96. S.E. Baires, "White Settlers Buried the Truth About the Midwest's Mysterious Mound Cities," *Smithsonian Magazine* (2018), smithsonianmag.com/history/white-settlers-buried-truth-about-midwests-mysterious-mound-cities-180968246/.
97. J.E. Buikstra, "Introduction," in J.E. Buikstra and L.A. Beck (eds.), *Bioarcheology: The Contextual Analysis of Human Remains* (New York: Routledge, 2006): 9–13.
98. M.L. Powell, Georgieann Bogdan, Jane E. Buikstra, et al., "Invisible Hands: Women in Bioaechaeology," in *Bioarchaeology*, edited by Jane E. Buikstra (New York, Routledge, 2006): 158–159.
99. D.C. Cook, "The Old Physical Anthropology and the New World: A Look at the Accomplishments of an Antiquated Paradigm," in J.E. Buikstra and L.A. Beck (eds.), *Bioarcheology: The Contextual Analysis of Human Remains* (New York: Routledge, 2006): 27–72.
100. "Race Prejudice and World Peace," *Nature* 129 (1932): 572, https://doi.org/10.1038/129572c0.
101. T.J. Ferguson, "Native Americans and the Practice of Archaeology," *Annual Review of Anthropology* 25, 1 (1996): 63–79, p. 65.
102. E. Pilkington, "Bones of Black Children Killed in Police Bombing Used in Ivy League Anthropology Course," *Guardian* (23 April 2021), theguardian.com/us-news/2021/apr/2022/move-bombing-black-children-bones-philadelphia-princeton-pennsylvania.
103. D.P. Ball, "How Indigenous Researchers Are Reclaiming Archeology and Anthropology," *Globe and Mail* (29 June 2021), theglobeandmail.com/canada/british-columbia/article-how-indigenous-researchers-are-reclaiming-archeol-

ogy-and-anthropology/.
104. G. McMaster, "U of A Archeologist Helps Indigenous Communities Uncover Their Own Stories," *University of Alberta* (27 April 2021), www.ualberta.ca/folio/2021/04/u-of-a-archeologist-helps-indigenous-communities-uncover-their-own-stories.html.
105. S. Adams, R. Martin, S. Phillips, et al., "Truth-Telling in the Wake of European Contact: Historical Investigation of Aboriginal Skeletal Remains from Normanton," *Archaeologies-Journal of the World Archaeological Congress* 14, 3 (2018): 412–442.
106. K. Burnett, *Taking Medicine: Women's Healing Work and Colonial Contact in Southern Alberta, 1880–1930* (Vancouver: University of British Columbia Press, 2010): 154.
107. E. Dyck and M.K. Lux, *Challenging Choices: Canada's Population Control in the 1970s* (Montreal: McGill-Queen's University Press, 2020): 16–18, and Chapter 3 "Indigenous Women in the Provincial South," pp. 73–88.
108. A. Stubblefield, "'Beyond the Pale': Tainted Whiteness, Cognitive Disability, and Eugenic Sterilization," *Hypatia* 22, 2 (2007): 162–181, pp. 173–174, doi.org/10.1111/j.1527-2001.2007.tb00987.x.
109. J. Grekul, A. Krahn, and D. Odynak, "Sterilizing the 'Feeble-minded': Eugenics in Alberta, Canada, 1929–1972," *Journal of Historical Sociology* 17, 4 (2004): 358–384, pp. 371–375, doi.org/10.1111/j.1467-6443.2004.00237.x.
110. Public Health Agency of Canada, *Syphilis in Canada: Technical Report on Epidemiological Trends, Determinants and Interventions* (2020), p. 61, canada.ca/en/services/health/publications/diseases-conditions/syphilis-epidemiological-report.html.
111. A.E. Singh and B.Romanowski, "The Return of Syphilis in Canada: A Failed Plan to Eliminate This Infection," *Official Journal of the Association of Medical Microbiology and Infectious Disease Canada* 4, 4 (2019): 215–217, doi.org/10.3138/jammi.2019-08-22.
112. Canadian Press, "Quebec Doctors Urged to Look Out for Signs of Syphilis in Pregnant Women," *CTV News* (2 February 2019), www.ctvnews.ca/health/quebec-doctors-urged-to-look-out-for-signs-of-syphilis-in-pregnant-women-1.4280473.
113. T. Grennan, E. Griesbrecht, G. Ogilvie, et al., "Syphilis Outbreak in BC: Changes to Syphilis Screening in Pregnancy," *BC Medical Journal* 61, 8 (2019): 328.
114. I. Froese, "Manitoba Shatters Grim Record with Sharp Rise in Newborns with Syphilis," *CBC News* (27 October 2020), cbc.ca/news/canada/manitoba/manitoba-syphilis-grim-record-newborns-sharp-rise-congenital-1.5779397.
115. Government of Canada, "Infection Syphilis and Congenital Syphilis in Canada, 2020" (2021), www.canada.ca/en/public-health/services/publications/diseases-conditions/infectious-syphilis-congenital-syphilis-canada-2020.html.
116. Ibid.
117. N. Yousif, "Alberta Declares Provincewide Syphilis Outbreak as Reported Cases Reach All-Time High," *Star Edmonton* (16 July 2019), www.thestar.com/edmonton/2019/07/16/alberta-declares-provincewide-syphilis-outbreak-as-reported-cases-reach-all-time-high.html.
118. Centers for Disease Control and Prevention, "Syphilis Outbreak among American Indians — Arizona, 2007–2009," *Morbidity and Mortality Weekly*

Report 59, 6 (2010): 158–161.

119. K.E. Toomey, A.G. Oberschelp and J.R. Greenspan, "Sexually Transmitted Diseases and Native Americans: Trends in Reported Gonorrhea and Syphilis Morbidity, 1984–88," *Public Health Rep* 104, 6 (1989): 566–572, p. 571.

120. E.C. Bartlett, C. Zavaleta, C. Fernandez, et al., "Expansion of HIV and Syphilis into the Peruvian Amazon: A Survey of Four Communities of an Indigenous Amazonian Ethnic Group," *International Journal of Infectious Diseases* 12, 6 (2008): E89–E94.

121. B. Stime, N. Laliberte, and S. Waters, "Surveillance and the Settler State: Monitoring structures That Impede Well-Being," Indigenous Health Conference (Mississauga, ON, 2016).

122. T.W. van Heiningen, "Jean-Baptiste Sarlandière's Mechanical Leeches (1817–1825): An Early Response in the Netherlands to a Shortage of Leeches," *Medical History* 53, 2 (2009): 253–270.

123. D.R. Varma, *Medicine, Healthcare and the Raj* (Gurgaon: Three Essays Collective, 2015): 28.

124. J. Downs, *Maladies of Empire: How Colonialism, Slavery, and War Transformed Medicine* (Cambridge: Harvard University Press, 2021).

125. M.A. Rodriguez and R. García, "First, Do No Harm: The US Sexually Transmitted Disease Experiments in Guatemala," *American Journal of Public Health* 103, 12 (2013): 2122–2126, p. 2123.

126. E. Lesley, "Cultural Impairment and the Genocidal Potential of Intoxicants: Alcohol Use in Colonial North America," *Genocide Studies and Prevention: An International Journal* 13, 1 (2019): 88-97, pp. 91-95.

127. S. Biswas, "How Britain's Opium Trade Impoverished Indians." BBC News (2019), https://www.bbc.com/news/world-asia-india-49404024.

128. J.N. Wilford, "Genetic Study Bolsters Columbus Link to Syphilis," *New York Times* (2008), https://nytimes.com/2008/01/15/science/15syph.html.

129. D.C. Cook and M.L. Powell, "Piecing the Puzzle Together: North American Treponematosis in Overview," in *The Myth of Syphilis: The Natural History of Treponematosis in North America*, edited by M.L. Powell and D.C. Cook (Ser. Ripley p. bullen series) (University Press of Florida, 2005), p. 477.

130. B. Baker, G. Crane-Kramer, M. Dee, et al., "Advancing the Understanding": 5–41, p. 6.

Chapter 3: Smallpox

1. S. Davey, "Smallpox Vaccination in Early Colonial India: Diversity in Resistance," *South Asia Research* 38, 2 (2018): 130–139.

2. A. Alluri, "The Indian Queens Who Modelled for the World's First Vaccine," BBC News (19 September 2020), bbc.com/news/world-asia-india-53944723.

3. C. Lahariya, "A Brief History of Vaccines & Vaccination in India," *The Indian Journal of Medical Research* 139, 4 (2014): 491-511, p. 493.

4. Centers for Disease Control and Prevention, "History of Smallpox" (2021), https://www.cdc.gov/smallpox/history/history.html.

5. P. Foster, "A Massive Public Health Effort Eradicated Smallpox but Scientists Are Still Studying the Deadly Virus," *The Conversation* (2020) theconversation.com/a-massive-public-health-effort-eradicated-smallpox-but-scientists-are-still-studying-the-deadly-virus-139468.

6. P. Berche, "Life and Death of Smallpox," *La Presse Médicale* 51, 3 (2022): 3, https://doi.org/10.1016/j.lpm.2022.104117.
7. Centers for Disease Control and Prevention, "History of Smallpox."
8. Nigeria Centre for Disease Control, "Update on Monkeypox Outbreak in Nigeria: Situation Report" (November 2021), https://reliefweb.int/report/nigeria/monthly-update-monkeypox-mpx-nigeria-epi-week-47-november-30-2021.
9. S.N. Isaacs, "Monkeypox," *UpToDate* (2022) https://www.uptodate.com/contents/monkeypox.
10. H.M. Friedman and S.N. Isaacs, "Variola Virus (Smallpox)," UpToDate (2022), https://www.uptodate.com/contents/variola-virus-smallpox.
11. Ibid.
12. A. Boylston, *Defying Providence: Smallpox and the Forgotten 18th Century Medical Revolution* (Charleston: CreateSpace, Chapter 2, 2012).
13. O. Krylova and D.J.D. Earn. "Patterns of Smallpox Mortality in London, England, over Three Centuries," *PLoS Biology* 18, 12 (2020): e3000506, p. 5.
14. R. McCaa, "Spanish and Nahuatl Views on Smallpox and Demographic Catastrophe in Mexico," *The Journal of Interdisciplinary History* 25, 3 (1995): 397–431, pp. 408–409, 423–429.
15. A.T. Duggan, M.F. Perdomo, D. Piombino-Mascali, et al., "17(th) Century Variola Virus Reveals the Recent History of Smallpox," *Current Biology* 26, 24 (2016): 3407–3412, p. 3411.
16. J.O. Wertheim, "Viral Evolution: Mummy Virus Challenges Presumed History of Smallpox," *Current Biology* 27, 3 (2017): R119–R120.
17. A. Campsie, "The Tiny Scottish Island Wiped Out by Disease," *The Scotsman* (2019), scotsman.com/heritage-and-retro/heritage/tiny-scottish-island-wiped-out-disease-1404837.
18. P. Berche, "Life and Death of Smallpox": 3.
19. D. Arnold, *Colonizing the Body: State Medicine and Epidemic Disease in Nineteenth-Century India* (Berkeley: University of California Press, 1993): 121–133.
20. R. Huntley, A.L.S. to an unidentified correspondent concerning 3 patients who have recovered from smallpox: manuscript, Catalogue key 6805108 (Montréal, QB, Thomas Fisher Rare Book Library, 1773).
21. D. MacPherson, *Notes on Nursing: How to Treat Smallpox -Guaranteed to Prevent Disfiguration and Lessen Suffering: Cure for Cholera, Cancer, Sprains, &c., &c.* (Montreal: John Lovell & Son, 1890): 3–4.
22. Ibid., p. 3–4.
23. P. Hackett, "Averting Disaster: The Hudson's Bay Company and Smallpox in Western Canada during the Late Eighteenth and Early Nineteenth Centuries," *Bulletin of the History of Medicine* 78 (2004): 575–609, pp. 584-585.
24. U.L. Ogbogu, "Vaccination and the Law in Ontario and Nova Scotia (1800–1924)," thesis: Doctor of Juridicial Science, Toronto: Faculty of Law, University of Toronto, 2014: 227–229.
25. G.D. Gibb, "Epidemic of Small-Pox in Quebec, Supposed to Depend upon the Opening of an Intramural Small-Pox Cemetery, 214 Years Old," *Journal of Public Health, and Sanitary Review* 1, 2 (1855): 113–117, pp. 114–116.
26. *Siberian Times,* "Experts Warn of Threat of Born-Again Smallpox from Old

Siberian Graveyards" (August 2016), siberiantimes.com/science/opinion/features/f0249-experts-warn-of-threat-of-born-again-smallpox-from-old-siberian-graveyards/.

27. H. Julien, *Montreal's Night-Mayor on His Ghostly Rounds (Dedicated to the Board of Health)*, Photolithograph, McCord Museum collections (1875), http://collections.musee-mccord.qc.ca/en/collection/artifacts/M992X.5.82.

28. R. Harris, "An Incident of the Small-Pox Epidemic in Montreal," New York: *Harper's Weekly* (1885), https://ville.montreal.qc.ca/memoiresdesmontrealais/files/variole-incident-en-1885.

29. J. Geddes, "When the Plague Won: A History of Vaccine Hesitancy," *Macleans* (7 April 2021), macleans.ca/society/health/when-the-plague-won-a-history-of-vaccine-hesitancy/.

30. Conseil d'hygiène de Montréal, "Rapport du Sous-comité du Conseil d'hygiène de Montréal sur l'origine de l'épidémie de la variole: reçue et adopté unanimement à l'assemblée du dit Conseil tenue samedi le 9 janvier 1886 et imprimé par ordre du dit Conseil," Montréal (1886), https://www.canadiana.ca/view/oocihm.04727/1.

31. J. Bemrose, "Tragedy of Errors," *Macleans* (28 October 1991), https://archive.macleans.ca/article/1991/10/28/tragedy-of-errors.

32. J.H. Marsh, "The 1885 Montreal Smallpox Epidemic," *The Canadian Encyclopedia* (2015), https://www.thecanadianencyclopedia.ca/en/article/plague-the-red-death-strikes-montreal-feature.

33. T. Nichol, *Smallpox and Its Prevention* (Montréal, W. Drysdale & Co., 1885): 32, 57-58.

34. J. Bemrose, "Tragedy of Errors."

35. J.M. Berman, "When Antivaccine Sentiment Turned Violent: The Montréal Vaccine Riot of 1885," *Canadian Medical Association Journal* 193, 14 (2021): E490-E492, p. E491, https://doi.org/10.1503/cmaj.202820.

36. J.W. McIntyre and C.S. Houston, "Smallpox and Its Eradication in Canada," CMAJ 161, 12 (1999): 1543-1547, p. 1546.

37. Centers for Disease Control and Prevention, "History of Smallpox."

38. S. Watts, *Epidemics and History*: 89.

39. Ibid., p. 90.

40. R. McCaa, "Spanish and Nahuatl Views on Smallpox": 408.

41. Å.J. Vågene, A. Herbig, M.G. Campana, et al., "Salmonella Enterica Genomes from Victims of a Major Sixteenth-Century Epidemic in Mexico," *Nature Ecology & Evolution* 2, 3 (2018): 520–528.

42. C.J. Rutty, "A Pox on Our Nation," *Canada's History* 95, 1 (2015): 28–35, p. 29.

43. G. Warrick, "European Infectious Disease and Depopulation of the Wendat-Tionontate (Huron-Petun)," *World Archaeology* 35, 2 (2003): 258–275, p. 263, https://doi.org/10.1080/0043824032000111416.

44. J. Duffy, "Smallpox and the Indians in the American Colonies," *Bulletin of the History of Medicine* 25, 4 (1951): 324–341, p. 326.

45. S. Watts, *Epidemics and History*: 98–99

46. P. Kelton, "Introduction," in *Cherokee Medicine, Colonial Germs: An Indigenous Nation's Fight Against Smallpox,1518–1824* (Norman: University of Oklahoma Press, 2015): pp. 3–20.

47. J. Duffy, "Smallpox and the Indians in the American Colonies": 327–340.

478.E.C. Tandy, "Local Quarantine and Inoculation for Smallpox in the American Colonies (1620–1775)," *American Journal of Public Health* 13, 3 (1923): 203–207, p. 204.

49. T. Worcester, "A Defensive Discourse: Jesuits on Disease in Seventeenth-Century New France." *French Colonial History* 6 (2005): 1–15, p. 5.

50. Ibid.: 2–3.

51. R.G. Thwaites, *Jesuit Relations Volume XIX* (Cleveland: Burrows Brothers Company, 1896–1901): 123.

52. M.K. Lux, "'We Demand 'Unconditional Surrender': Making and Unmaking the Blackfoot Hospital, 1890s to 1950s," *Social History of Medicine* 25, 3 (2011): 665–684, pp. 669–670, https://doi.org/10.1093/shm/hkr152.

53. R.G. Thwaites, *Jesuit Relations: Volume XIII* (Cleveland: Burrows Brothers Company, 1896–1901): 165.

54. Ibid, p. 171.

55. R.G. Thwaites, *Jesuit Relations Volume XIX* (Cleveland: Burrows Brothers Company, 1896–1901): 93-95.

56. P. Kelton, *Cherokee Medicine, Colonial Germs: An Indigenous Nation's Fight Against Smallpox,1518–1824* (Norman: University of Oklahoma Press, 2015): 87, 91–96.

57. R.G. Thwaites, *Jesuit Relations Volume XIX* (Cleveland: Burrows Brothers Company, 1896–1901): 89.

58. H. Markel and A.M. Stern, "The Foreignness of Germs: The Persistent Association of Immigrants and Disease in American Society," *The Milbank Quarterly* 80, 4 (2002): 757–788.

59. S. Reitmanova, D.L. Gustafson, and R. Ahmed, "'Immigrants can be deadly': Critical Discourse Analysis of Racialization of Immigrant Health in the Canadian Press and Public Health Policies," *Canadian Journal of Communication* 40, 3 (2015): 471–487.

60. S.L. Gilman, "AIDS and Syphilis: The Iconography of Disease," *October* 43 (1987): 87–107.

61. T. Worcester, "A Defensive Discourse": 1–15, p. 9.

62. J. Duffy, "Smallpox and the Indians in the American Colonies": 324–341, p. 331.

63. D.P. MacLeod, "Microbes and Muskets: Smallpox and the Participation of the Amerindian Allies of New France in the Seven Years' War," *Ethnohistory* 39, 1 (1992): 42–64, p. 56.

64. B.A. Mann, *The Tainted Gift: The Disease Method of Frontier Expansion* (Praeger, 2009).

65. P. Kelton, *Cherokee Medicine, Colonial Germs*: 108.

66. D.P. MacLeod, "Microbes and Muskets: 42–64, p. 50.

67. R.G. Thwaites, *Jesuit Relations: Volume XV* (Cleveland: Burrows Brothers Company, 1896–1901): p. 237.

68. S. Watts, *Epidemics and History*: 101.

69. P. Hackett, "Averting Disaster": 575–609, p. 577.

70. C. Harris, "Voices of Disaster: Smallpox around the Strait of Georgia in 1782," *Ethnohistory* 41, 4 (1994): 591–626, p. 604.

71. D. Meyer and D. Russell, "'So Fine and Pleasant, Beyond Description': The Lands and Lives of the Pegogamaw Crees," *Plains Anthropologist* 49, 191 (2004): 217–252, p. 223.

72. P. Hackett, "Averting Disaster": 575–609, see reference 14, p. 581.
73. A.M. Carlos and F.D. Lewis, "Smallpox and Native American Mortality: The 1780s Epidemic in the Hudson Bay Region," *Explorations in Economic History* 49, 3 (2012): 277–290, p. 285.
74. A.R. Hodge, "'In Want of Nourishment for to Keep Them Alive': Climate Fluctuations, Bison Scarcity, and the Smallpox Epidemic of 1780–82 on the Northern Great Plains," *Environmental History* 17, 2 (2012): 365–403, p. 366.
75. J.W. McIntyre and C.S. Houston, "Smallpox and Its Control in Canada": 1543–1547, p. 1545.
76. P. Hackett, "Averting Disaster": 575–609, p. 585–588.
77. C. Harris, "Voices of Disaster": 591–626, p. 596–600.
78. P. Hackett, "Averting Disaster": 575–609, p. 589.
79. R.C. Harris and E Leinberger with R Galois, "A Population Geography of British Columbia in 1881," in *The Resettlement of British Columbia: Essays on Colonialism and Geographical Change* (UBC Press, 1997): p. 147.
80. G. Geddes, *Medicine Unbundled*: pp. 71–73.
81. W. Butler, *Report by Lieutenant William Butler, (69th Regiment) of His Journey from Fort Garry to Rocky Mountain House and Back, under Instructions from the Lieutenant-Governor of Manitoba, During the Winter of 1870–71* (Ottawa: The Times Printing and Publishing Company, 1871): p. 5.
82. J.W. McIntyre and C.S. Houston, "Smallpox and Its Control in Canada": 1543–1547, p. 1546.
83. W. Butler, *Report by Lieutenant William Butler*, p.11.
84. Ibid., p.12–13.
85. Ibid., p. 15.
86. J.W. McIntyre and C.S. Houston, "Smallpox and Its Control in Canada": 1543–1547, p. 1546.
87. T. Hopper, "Here Is What Sir John A. Macdonald did to Indigenous People," *National Post* (28 August 2018), https://nationalpost.com/news/canada/here-is-what-sir-john-a-macdonald-did-to-indigenous-people.
88. J. Daschuk, *Clearing the Plains*: 115–117.
89. A. Sen, *Democracy as Freedom* (New York: Alfred A. Knopf, 1999): pp. 160–188.
90. J. Daschuk, *Clearing the Plains*: 118.
91. Library and Archives of Canada, Clandeboye Agency — Correspondence Regarding an Outbreak of Smallpox among the Indians of Lake Winnipeg and the Subsequent Vaccination Campaign, RG10, Volume/box number: 3638, File number: 7213, Ottawa, Ontario (1876): p. 3–12.
92. R.C. Eyford, "Quarantined Within a New Colonial Order: The 1876–1877 Lake Winnipeg Smallpox Epidemic," *Journal of the Canadian Historical Association* 17, 1 (2006): 55–78, p. 65.
93. Ibid., p. 77.
94. D. Mackenzie, "Icelanders Argue Over Their Ancestors," *New Scientist* (1996), newscientist.com/article/mg15020321-100-icelanders-argue-over-their-ancestors.
95. R.C. Eyford, "Quarantined Within a New Colonial Order": 55–78, p. 66–68.
96. Ibid., p. 60.
97. Ibid., p. 76.

98. Ibid., p. 74.

99. Ibid., pp. 70–72.

100. L. Bisaillon, "The Politics of Practice and the Contradictions for People, Policy, and Providing Care: Investigations into the Implications of Health Work Organized Within State Interests," *Public Health Ethics* 7, 3 (2014): 225–228.

101. M.K. Wynia, "Civic Obligations in Medicine: Does 'Professional' Civil Disobedience Tear, or Repair, the Basic Fabric of Society?" *Virtual Mentor* 6, 1 (2004): 30–32, https://doi.org/10.1001/virtualmentor.2004.6.1.pfor1-0401.

102. G. Kinsman, "Gary Kinsman on Troubling Public Health as part of 'We Can't Police Our Way Out of the Pandemic'," *Radical Noise* (30 April 2020), radicalnoise.ca/2020/04/30/gary-kinsman-on-troubling-public-health-as-part-of-we-cant-police-our-way-out-of-the-pandemic.

103. S.M. Weaver, "Smallpox or Chickenpox: An Iroquoian Community's Reaction to Crisis, 1901–1902," *Ethnohistory* 18, 4 (1971): 361–377, p. 365.

104. Ibid., p. 365.

105. Ibid., p. 366–368.

106. Ibid., pp. 367, 374-375.

107. Northern Ontario School of Medicine, "Remote First Nations Stream," *NOSM University* (2021), https://www.nosm.ca/familymedicine/our-streams-at-a-glance/remotefirstnations/.

108. B. Mukhopadhyay, "Care as Colonialism."

109. S.M. Weaver, "Smallpox or Chickenpox": 361–377, 370–374.

110. H. Dobyns, *Their Number Become Thinned: Native American Populations Dynamics in Eastern North America* (Knoxville: University of Tennessee Press, 1983).

111. A.F. Ramenofsky, A.K. Wilbur, and A.C. Stone, "Native American Disease History: Past, Present and Future Directions," *World Archaeology* 35, 2 (2003): 241–257.

112. A.M. Carlos and F.D. Lewis, "Smallpox and Native American Mortality": 277–290, p. 285–286.

113. P. Kelton, *Cherokee Medicine, Colonial Germs*: 97.

114. College of Physicians of Philadelphia, "17th Century Smallpox Treatment," The History of Vaccines (2021), https://historyofvaccines.org/history/smallpox/timeline.

115. D. Arnold, *Colonizing the Body*: 128–129.

116. P. Kelton, *Cherokee Medicine, Colonial Germs*: 94–95.

117. P. Hackett, *A Very Remarkable Sickness: Epidemics in the Petit Nord, 1670 to 1846* (Winnipeg: University of Manitoba Press, 2002), p. 17.

118. R.V. Santos, C.E.A Coimbra, and J. Radin, "'Why Did They Die?' Biomedical Narratives of Epidemics and Mortality among Amazonian Indigenous Populations in Sociohistorical and Anthropological Contexts," *Current Anthropology* 61, 4 (2020): 441–70, p. 448, https://doi.org/10.1086/710079.

119. J.D. Grabenstein and W. Winkenwerder, "US Military Smallpox Vaccination Program Experience," *JAMA* 289, 24 (2003): 32783282.

120. M. May, "Inoculating the Urban Poor in the Late 18th Century," *British Journal for the History of Science* 30, 3 (1997): 291–305, p. 292–293.

121. A. Flemming, "The Origins of Vaccination," *Nature Portfolio* (20 September 2020), nature.com/articles/d42859-020-00006-7.

122.A. Boylston, *Defying Providence.*
123.*Boston Magazine*, "The 100 Best Bostonians of All Time," *Boston Magazine* (2016), https://www.bostonmagazine.com/news/2016/01/05/100-best-bostonians/.
124.A. Boylston, "A Lunatic Physician," in *Defying Providence.*
125.A. Boylston, "An Illiterate Cutter for the Stone," in *Defying Providence.*
126.A. Boylston, "Disaster," in *Defying Providence*; "Prisoners and Orphans," in *Defying Providence.*
127.S.J. Weinreich, "Unaccountable Subjects: Contracting Legal and Medical Authority in the Newgate Smallpox Experiment (1721)," *History Workshop Journal* 89 (2019): 22–44, p. 30.
128.Ibid., pp. 32, 36.
129.A. Boylston, "Prisoners and Orphans," in *Defying Providence.*
130.I. Massey, *A Short and Plain Account of Inoculation with Some Remarks on the Main Arguments Made Use of to Recommend That Practice, by Mr Maitland and Others* (London: W. Meadows, 1722), p. 15.
131.J. Arbuthnot, *Mr Maitland's Account of Inoculating the Smallpox Vindicated, from Dr Wagstaffe's Misrepresentations of the Practice; with some Remarks on Mr Massey's Sermon. The Second Edition. To which is added, His First Account of Inoculating the Small pox* (London: J. Peele, 1722): p. 4.
132.A. Boylston, "Boylston's Book," in *Defying Providence.*
133.A. Boylston, "Slaves, Peasants, and the Sons of Rich Men" in *Defying Providence.*
134.W.L. Langer, "Immunization against Smallpox before Jenner," *Scientific American* 234, 1 (1976): 112–117, p. 115.
135.D. Alden and J.C. Miller, "Out of Africa: The Slave Trade and the Transmission of Smallpox to Brazil, 1560–1831," *The Journal of Interdisciplinary History* 18, 2 (1987), MIT Press: 195–224, p. 210–211.
136.J.W. McIntyre and C.S. Houston, "Smallpox and Its Control in Canada": 1543–1547, p. 1544–1545.
137.E.P. Hamilton, "General John Thomas," *Proceedings of the Massachusetts Historical Society* 84 (1972): 44–52, p. 52, http://www.jstor.org/stable/25080728.
138.P. Hackett, "Averting Disaster": 575–609, p. 583–584.
139.A.J. Ray, "Smallpox: The Epidemic of 1837–38," *Beaver* 306, 2 (1975): 8–13, p. 9.
140.J.W. McIntyre and C.S. Houston, "Smallpox and Its Control in Canada": 1543–1547, p. 1545.
141.A.M. Behbehani, "The Smallpox Story: Life and Death of an Old Disease," *Microbiological Reviews* 47, 4 (1983): 455–509, p. 467.
142.L. Thurston, "Jenner, Fewster and Jesty," *British Society for the History of Medicine* (8 May 2018), https://bshm.org.uk/jenner-fewster-and-jesty/.
143.A.M. Behbehani, "The Smallpox Story": 455–509, p. 468.
144.J.W. McIntyre and C.S. Houston, "Smallpox and Its Control in Canada": 1543–1547, p. 1543.
145.S. Watts, *Epidemics and History:* 118–119.
146.J.W. McIntyre and C.S. Houston, "Smallpox and Its Control in Canada": 1543–1547, p. 1545.
147.Royal Jennerian Society for the Extermination of the Smallpox by the Exten-

sion of Vaccination, *Annual Report 1817* (London: James Swan, 1817): 26.

148.Ibid., p. 27–28.

149.M.D. Walters "'Your Sovereign and Our Father': The Imperial Crown and the Idea of Legal-Ethnohistory," in *Law and Politics in British Colonial Thought: Transpositions of Empire*, edited by S. Dorsett and I. Hunter (New York: Palgrave Macmillan US, 2010), pp. 91–108.

150.P. Hackett, "Averting Disaster": 575–609, p. 593.

151.*An Act to encourage and diffuse the practice of Vaccine Inoculation [A provincial statute of Lower Canada, enacted by the King's Most Excellent Majesty …: passed in the thirty-first year of the reign of George the Third* (25 March 1815), Quebec, printed under the authority and by command of His Excellency the Governor in Chief; as the act of the provincial Parliament directs, by P.E. Desbarats, law printer to the King's Most Excellent Majesty.

152.Bureau du Sécretaire provincial, *Bureau de vaccine établi en vertu de l'acte de la législature provinciale pour empêcher la petite vérole de se répandre, et encourager dans toute la province l'inoculation de la vaccine* (Québec: T. Cary, Jun. & Co., 24 March 1821).

153.P. Hackett, "Averting Disaster": 575–609, p. 598.

154.Ibid, p. 605, footnote 100.

155.A.J. Ray, "Smallpox: The Epidemic of 1837–38": 8–13, pp. 9–12.

156.J. Daschuk, *Clearing the Plains*: p. 68.

157.A.J. Ray, "Smallpox: The Epidemic of 1837-38": 8-13, pp. 9-12.

158.P. Hackett, "Averting Disaster": 575–609, p. 601–607.

159.World Health Organization, "Circulating Vaccine-Derived Poliovirus Type 2 — Global Update" (2021), who.int/emergencies/disease-outbreak-news/item/circulating-vaccine-derived-poliovirus-type-2-global-update.

160 A. von Peteghem, *Small Pox and Vaccination*, The Fisher Rare Book Library OCLC: 978217810 (Quebec City, Quebec, 1847).

161.P. Hackett, "Averting Disaster": 575–609, p. 608–609.

162.J.M. Howell, "Edmonton Board of Health Celebrates 100 Years — or More," *Canadian Journal of Public Health* 83, 4 (1992): 306307, p. 306.

163.J. Daschuk, *Clearing the Plains*: 105.

164.P. Malissard, "Pharming' à l'ancienne: les fermes vaccinales canadiennes," *Canadian Historical Review* 85, 1 (2004): 35–62, p. 41.

165.J. Keelan, "Risk, Efficacy and Viral Attenuation in Debates over Smallpox Vaccination in Montreal, 1870–1877," in *Crafting Immunity: Working Histories of Clinical Immunology*, edited by J. Keelan and K. Kroker (New York: Routledge, 2016 [2008]): 44–45.

166.C. Rutty and S.C. Sullivan, *This Is Public Health: A Canadian History* (Ottawa: Canadian Public Health Association, 2010) 1.11.

167.P. Malissard, "Pharming' à l'ancienne": 35–62, p. 41–43.

168.Ontario Heritage Trust, "The Ontario Vaccine Farm," Date unknown, heritagetrust.on.ca/en/plaques/ontario-vaccine-farm.

169.W.B. Spaulding, "The Ontario Vaccine Farm, 1885–1916," *Canadian Bulletin of Medical History* 6 (1989): 45–56, p. 54.

170.C.J. Rutty, "Precision Innovations: Rabies Vaccines, Tuberculin PPD & Sulphated Insulin at Connaught Labs, 1958–1970," Connaught Fund, undated, https://connaught.research.utoronto.ca/history/article11/.

171.S. Palmer, G. Hochman, and D. Arbex, "Smallpox Eradication, Laboratory

Visits, and a Touch of Tourism: Travel Notes of a Canadian Scientist in Brazil," *Historia, Ciencias, Saude—Manguinhos* 17, 3 (2010): 777–790, p. 778.
172. E.A. Fenn, *Pox Americana: The Great Smallpox Epidemic of 1775–82* (1st ed.) (Hill and Wang 2001).

Chapter 4: Tuberculosis

1. World Health Organization, "BCG Vaccine," Undated, https://www.who.int/teams/health-product-policy-and-standards/standards-and-specifications/vaccines-quality/bcg.
2. Nunatsiaq News, "Nunavut announces changes to newborns' immunization schedule" (September 9 2020), https://nunatsiaq.com/stories/article/nunavut-announces-change-to-newborns-immunization-schedule/; Public Health Agency of Canada, "Bacille Calmette-Guérin (BCG) Vaccine: Canadian Immunization Guide," Government of Canada (2014), https://www.canada.ca/en/public-health/services/publications/healthy-living/canadian-immunization-guide-part-4-active-vaccines/page-2-bacille-calmette-guerin-vaccine.html.
3. World Health Organization, "Tuberculosis — Overview" (2021), https://www.who.int/health-topics/tuberculosis.
4. G.B. Migliori, Edward Nardell, Askar Yedilbayev, et al., "Reducing Tuberculosis Transmission: A Consensus Document from the World Health Organization Regional Office for Europe," *European Respiratory Journal* 53, 6 (June 1, 2019): 1900391, pp. 3–4, https://doi.org/10.1183/13993003.00391-2019.
5. N.G. Reed, "The History of Ultraviolet Germicidal Irradiation for Air Disinfection," *Public Health Reports* (Washington, DC, 1974), 125, 1 (2010): 15–27, p. 16–17, https://doi.org/10.1177/003335491012500105.
6. World Health Organization, "Tuberculosis — Key Facts" (2021), https://www.who.int/news-room/fact-sheets/detail/tuberculosis.
7. S. Law, D. Menzies, M. Pai, et al., "The Online TST/IGRA Interpreter v3.0," Undated, http://www.tstin3d.com/en/calc.html.
8. S. Grzybowski and E,A, Allen, "Tuberculosis: 2. History of the disease in Canada," Canadian Medical Association Journal 160, 7 (1999): 1025–1028, p. 1026.
9. Public Health Agency of Canada, "Recommendations on Interferon Gamma Release Assays for the Diagnosis of Latent Tuberculosis Infection—2010 Update," Canada Communicable Disease Report 36 ACS-5 (2010), https://www.canada.ca/en/public-health/services/reports-publications/canada-communicable-disease-report-ccdr/monthly-issue/2010-36/canada-communicable-disease-report-10.html.
10. G. Warrick, "European Infectious Disease": 258–275, pp. 268–269.
11. C.V. Mulholland, A.C. Shockey, H.L. Aung, et al., "Dispersal of Mycobacterium Tuberculosis Driven by Historical European Trade in the South Pacific," *Frontiers in Microbiology* 10 (2019), https://doi.org/10.3389/fmicb.2019.02778.
12. J. Daschuk, *Clearing the Plains*: 124-126.
13. V. Chernick and R.B. Mellins, "Pediatric Pulmonology: A Developmental History in North America," *Pediatric Research* 55, 3 (2004): 514–520, p.

516, https://doi.org/10.1203/01.Pdr.0000112035.77683.91.

14. M.C. Guthrie, "The Health of the American Indian," *Public Health Reports (1896–1970)* 44, 16 (1929): 945–957, p. 949–950, https://doi.org/10.2307/4579216.

15. C. Pepperell, A.H. Chang, W. Wobeser, et al., "Local Epidemic History as a Predictor of Tuberculosis Incidence in Saskatchewan Aboriginal Communities," *International Journal of Tuberculosis and Lung Disease* 15, 7 (2011): 899–905, p. 5, https://doi.org/10.5588/ijtld.10.0556.

16. R. Long, M. Zielinski, D. Kunimoto, et al., "The Emergency Department Is a Determinant Point of Contact of Tuberculosis Patients Prior to Diagnosis," *International Journal of Tuberculosis and Lung Disease* 6, 4 (2002): 332–339.

17. G. Wobeser, "Bovine Tuberculosis in Canadian Wildlife: An Updated History," *Canadian Veterinary Journal-Revue Veterinaire Canadienne* 50, 11 (2009): 1169–1176, p. 1171, ncbi.nlm.nih.gov/pmc/articles/PMC2764465/pdf/cvj_11_1169.pdf.

18. P.N. Nation, E.A. Fanning, H.B. Hopf, et al., "Observations on Animal and Human Health During the Outbreak of Mycobacterium Bovis in Game Farm Wapiti in Alberta," *Canadian Veterinary Journal-Revue Veterinaire Canadienne* 40, 2 (1999): 113–117, p. 115, ncbi.nlm.nih.gov/pmc/articles/PMC1539558/pdf/canvetj00135-0035.pdf.

19. S. Grzybowski and E.A. Allen, "Tuberculosis: 2. History of the Disease in Canada," *Canadian Medical Association Journal* 160, 7 (1999): 1025–1028, p. 1026.

20. F.C. Middleton, "Evolution of Tuberculosis Control in Saskatchewan," *Canadian Public Health Journal* 24, 11 (1933): 505–513, p. 506.

21. M.K. Lux, "Perfect Subjects: Race, Tuberculosis, and the Qu'Appelle BCG Vaccine Trial," *Canadian Bulletin of Medical History* 15, 2 (1998): 277–295, p. 280, https://doi.org/10.3138/cbmh.15.2.277.

22. A. Bamford, "Former Patient Alleges Physical, Sexual Abuse at Sask. Tuberculosis Hospital," cTV News (March 2022), https://regina.ctvnews.ca/former-patient-alleges-physical-sexual-abuse-at-sask-tuberculosis-hospital-1.5818644.

23. F.C. Middleton, "Evolution of Tuberculosis Control in Saskatchewan": 505–513, pp. 506–507.

24. Ibid., p. 507.

25. Ibid., p. 507.

26. Ibid., p. 509–510.

27. Ibid., p. 511.

28. Ibid., pp. 512–513.

29. S. Niessen, *Shattering the Silence: The Hidden History of Indian Residential Schools in Saskatchewan* (Regina: Faculty of Education, University of Regina, 2017): 36.

30. M.K. Lux, "We Demand 'Unconditional Surrender'": 665–684, p. 666.

31. S. Niessen, *Shattering the Silence:*, p. 36.

32. Ibid., p. 37.

33. Ibid.: p. 37.

34. Innisfill Library, "The Reserves," *First Nations of Simcoe County* (2021), firstnations.innisfillibrary.ca/15-the-reserves/.

35. A. Wilson, "Colborne, John, 1st Baron Seaton," in *Dictionary of Canadian Biography* 9, University of Toronto/Université Laval, 2003–, 1976, http://www.biographi.ca/en/bio/colborne_john_9E.html.
36. P. Wilton, "The Toronto Free Hospital for Consumptive Poor," *Canadian Medical Association Journal* 146, 10 (1992): 1812–1814, p. 1813.
37. S. Burke, *Building Resistance:* 21–24.
38. S. Grzybowski and E.A. Allen, "Tuberculosis: 2": 1025–1028, pp. 1026–1027.
39. S. Burke, *Building Resistance:* pp. 7–8.
40. J.F. Murray, D.E. Schraufnagel, and P.C. Hopewell, "Treatment of Tuberculosis: A Historical Perspective," *Annals of the American Thoracic Society* 12, 12 (2015): 1749–1759, p. 1750, https://doi.org/10.1513/AnnalsATS.201509-632PS.
41. S. Grzybowski and E.A. Allen, "Tuberculosis: 2": 1025–1028, p. 1026.
42. Ibid., p. 1027.
43. M.K. Lux, "Care for the 'Racially Careless': Indian Hospitals in the Canadian West, 1920–1950s," *Canadian Historical Review* 91, 3 (2010): 407–434, p. 420, https://doi.org/10.3138/chr.91.3.407.
44. S. Burke, *Building Resistance: Children, Tuberculosis, and the Toronto Sanatorium* (Montréal: McGill-Queen's University Press, 2018): 67–68.
45. H. Turcotte, "Hospitals for Chinese in Canada: Montreal (1918) and Vancouver (1921)," *Historical Studies* 70 (2004): 131–142.
46. E. Olofsson, T.L. Holton, and I.J. Partridge, "Negotiating Identities: Inuit Tuberculosis Evacuees in the 1940s–1950s," *Études Inuit Studies* 32, 2 (2008), 127–149. p. 128, https://doi.org/10.7202/038219ar.
47. L. Meijer Drees, *Healing Histories: Stories from Canada's Indian Hospitals* (Edmonton: University of Alberta Press, 2013): 45.
48. P.W. Lackenbauer and M. Farish, "The Cold War on Canadian Soil: Militarizing a Northern Environment," *Environmental History* 12, 4 (October 2007): 920–950, p. 923.
49. E. Debicka and A. Friedman, "From Policies to Building: Public Housing in Canada's Eastern Arctic 1950s to 1980s," *Canadian Journal of Urban Research* 18, 2 (2009): 25–39, p. 29.
50. E. Olofsson, T.L. Holton, and I.J. Partridge, "Negotiating Identities": 127–149, p. 134.
51. H. Moore and B. Guyot, "'It Was Censorship': Letters from Inuit TB Patients Reveal Loneliness and Government Surveillance," *APTN News* (15 May 2020), aptnnews.ca/investigates/it-was-censorship-letters-from-inuit-tb-patients-reveal-loneliness-and-government-surveillance/.
52. E. Olofsson, T.L. Holton, and I.J. Partridge, "Negotiating Identities": 127–149, p. 140–143.
53. Ibid., p. 137.
54. M. Wiseman, "Unlocking the 'Eskimo Secret': Defence Science in the Cold War Canadian Arctic, 1947–1954," *Journal of the Canadian Historical Association / Revue de la Société historique du Canada* 26, 1 (2015): 191–223, https://doi.org/10.7202/1037202ar.
55. T. Kovesi, "Respiratory Medicine in Nunavut and Northern Canada," *Canadian Journal of Respiratory Critical Care and Sleep Medicine* 3, 3 (2019): 166–171, p. 166, https://doi.org/10.1080/24745332.2018.1483784.

56. P. Wilton, "'TB Voyages' into High Arctic Gave MDs a Look at a Culture in Transition," *Canadian Medical Association Journal* 148, 9 (1993): 1608–1609.
57. T. Kovesi, "Respiratory Medicine in Nunavut and Northern Canada": 166–171, p. 166.
58. Ibid., p. 168.
59. M. Blackburn, "Canada Says Sorry for Inuit Relocation," *APTN News* (14 September 2010), https://www.aptnnews.ca/national-news/canada-says-sorry-for-inuit-relocation/.
60. Qikiqtani Truth Commission, "Key Findings (May 2021), https://www.qt-commission.ca/en/key-findings.
61. T. Kovesi, "Respiratory Medicine in Nunavut and Northern Canada": 166–171, p. 167.
62. P. Wilton, "'TB Voyages' into High Arctic": 1608–1609, p. 1609.
63. K. Murray, "Health Aspects of Arctic Exploration—Alaska's Medical History Based on the Research Files of Dr Robert Fortuine," *International Journal of Circumpolar Health* 72 (2013), https://doi.org/10.3402/ijch.v72i0.21264.
64. S. Haugland, "Sitka Nurses Recall War Against Killer Disease," *Juneau Empire* (10 October 2016), juneauempire.com/news/sitka-nurses-recall-war-against-killer-disease/.
65. K. Murray, "Health Aspects of Arctic Exploration."
66. N. Schmitt, "Douglas Galbraith Fights TB among Indians and Inuit," *Canadian Medical Association Journal* 134, 10 (1986): 1184–1185, p. 1184, ncbi.nlm.nih.gov/pmc/articles/PMC1491041/pdf/cmaj00118-0090.pdf.
67. J. Wheeler, "The Deep, Dark and Mysterious History of Tranquille Sanatorium and Psychiatric Institution," *Kamloops News* (03 October 2020), infotel.ca/newsitem/the-deep-dark-and-mysterious-history-of-tranquille-sanatorium-and-psychiatric-hospital/it64157.
68. M.-E. Kelm, *Colonizing Bodies*: p. 122.
69. N. Schmitt, "Douglas Galbraith Fights TB among Indians and Inuit": 1184–1185.
70 J. Wheeler, "The Deep, Dark and Mysterious History."
71. Stó:lō Nation, "Stó:lō Service Agency: Our History," 2018, stolonation.bc.ca/history.
72. M.K. Lux, *Separate Beds: A History of Indian Hospitals in Canada, 1920s–1980s* (Toronto: University of Toronto Press, 2016): 38, 150.
73. N. Schmitt, "Douglas Galbraith Fights TB among Indians and Inuit": 1184–1185, p. 1185.
74. M.K. Lux, *Separate Beds: A History of Indian Hospitals in Canada*: 36–37.
75. Ibid., p. 25.
76. S. Niessen, *Shattering the Silence*:37.
77. N. Riebe, "Camsell Housing Plan Moves Ahead after Edmonton City Council Agrees to Rezoning," *CBC News* (17 November 2020), cbc.ca/news/canada/edmonton/charles-camsell-hospital-city-council-1.5806016.
78. Natural Resources Canada, Government of Canada, "Trailblazer: Charles Camsell, 1876–1958" (30 December 2008), web.archive.org/web/20100203041213/http://www.nrcan.gc.ca/com/deptmini/traipion/charlescamsell-eng.php.
79. M.K. Lux, "Care for the 'Racially Careless'": 407–434, p. 430.

80. Meijer Drees, *Healing Histories:* pp. 65–66, 160–161.
81. M.K. Lux, "Care for the 'Racially Careless'": 407–434, pp. 432–433.
82. M.K. Lux, *Separate Beds: A History of Indian Hospitals in Canada*: 58.
83. F.A. Herbert, W.A. Mahon, D. Wilkinson, et al., "Pneumonia in Indian and Eskimo Infants and Children. I. A Clinical Study," *Canadian Medical Association Journal* 96, 5 (1967): 257–265, ncbi.nlm.nih.gov/pmc/articles/PMC1936921/pdf/canmedaj01201-0014.pdf.
84. W.A. Mahon, F.A. Herbert, D. Wilkinson, et al., "Pneumonia in Indian and Eskimo Infants and Children. II. A Controlled Clinical Trial of Antibiotics," *Canadian Medical Association Journal* 96, 5 (1967): 265–268. pubmed.ncbi.nlm.nih.gov/4959789.
85. F.A. Herbert, W.A. Mahon, D. Wilkinson, et al., "Pneumonia in Indian and Eskimo Infants and Children": 257–265, p. 263.
86. Meijer Drees, *Healing Histories:* pp. 78–80.
87. B. Morin, "Former Edmonton Hospital Still Haunts Families Searching for Lost Loved Ones," APTN (9 July 2015), https://www.aptnnews.ca/national-news/former-edmonton-hospital-still-haunts-families-searching-lost-loved-ones/.
88. J. Daschuk, *Clearing the Plains*: p. 88.
89. C. Corrigan and S. Hanson, "Brucellosis and Miliary Tuberculosis in an Eskimo Woman," *Canadian Medical Association Journal* 72, 3 (1955): 217–218, ncbi.nlm.nih.gov/pmc/articles/PMC1825587/pdf/canmedaj00702-0054.pdf.
90. J. George, "Brucellosis Is Affecting Western Nunavut's Caribou, Muskox: Researcher," *Nunatsiaq News* (1 October 2019), nunatsiaq.com/stories/article/brucellosis-is-affecting-western-nunavuts-caribou-muskox-researcher/.
91. Meijer Drees, *Healing Histories:* pp. 34.
92. B. Pilon, "Ce qu'il faut pour vivre" (Montréal: Association coopérative de productions audiovisuelles, 2008).
93. J. Trudeau. "Statement of Apology on Behalf of the Government of Canada to Inuit for the Management of the Tuberculosis Epidemic from the 1940s–1960s," *Prime Minister of Canada Justin Trudeau* (08 March 2019), pm.gc.ca/en/news/speeches/2019/03/08/statement-apology-behalf-government-canada-inuit-management-tuberculosis.
94. N. Schmitt, "Douglas Galbraith Fights TB among Indians and Inuit": 1184–1185, p. 1185.
95. James Daschuk, *Clearing the Plains*: pp. 102–103.
96. Ibid., p. 162.
97. M. Lux, "We Demand 'Unconditional Surrender'": 665–684, p. 674.
98. M.K. Lux, "Care for the 'Racially Careless'": 407-434, p. 413.
99. Mary-Ellen Kelm, *Colonizing Bodies:* p. 66.
100. Ibid., p. 68.
101. T. Hopper, "The Names of All 202 Children Known to Have Died in Vancouver Island Residential Schools," *Capital Daily* (2 October 2019), https://www.capitaldaily.ca/news/here-are-all-202-children-known-to-have-died-in-vancouver-island-residential-schools.
102. M. Sproule-Jones, "Crusading for the Forgotten: Dr Peter Bryce, Public Health, and Prairie Native Residential Schools," *Canadian Bulletin of Medical History / Bulletin Canadien D'histoire de la Medecine* 13, 2 (1996): 199–224, p. 206, 211.

103. P.H. Bryce, *The Story of a National Crime* (Ottawa: James Hope & Sons, 1922).

104. Z. Tennant, "Pushed Out and Silenced: How One Doctor Was Punished for Speaking Out about Residential Schools," CBC News (17 April 2020), https://www.cbc.ca/radio/unreserved/exploring-the-past-finding-connections-in-little-known-indigenous-history-1.5531914/pushed-out-and-silenced-how-one-doctor-was-punished-for-speaking-out-about-residential-schools-1.5534953.

105. M.K. Lux, "Care for the 'Racially Careless'": 407–434, p. 409.

106. M.K. Lux, *Separate Beds: A History of Indian Hospitals in Canada*: 10–12.

107. Ibid., 33–35.

108. Meijer Drees, *Healing Histories:* pp. 53–54.

109. Meijer Drees, *Healing Histories:* pp. 143–167.

110. M.K. Lux, "Care for the 'Racially Careless'": 407–434, p. 416, 422.

111. H. Cardinal, *The Unjust Society: The Tragedy of Canada's Indians* (Vancouver: Douglas & McIntyre, 1999): 19, p. 35–36.

112. S. Burke, *Building Resistance:* 46.

113. M.K. Lux, *Medicine that Walks: Disease, Medicine and Canadian Plains Native People, 1880-1940* (Toronto: University of Toronto Press, 2001): pp. 34, 184.

114. M.K. Lux, "Care for the 'Racially Careless'": 407-434, p. 433.

115. M.K. Lux, "Care for the 'Racially Careless'": 407–434, p. 411, 434.

116. L. Meijer Drees, "Marjorie Warke in 'Nursing at the Camsell'," in *Healing Histories: Stories from Canada's Indian Hospitals* (Edmonton: University of Alberta Press, 2013), p. 66.

117. L. Meijer Drees, "Snuwuyulth," in *Healing Histories: Stories from Canada's Indian Hospitals* (Edmonton: University of Alberta Press, 2013), pp. 121–132.

118. S. Burke, *Building Resistance:* 31.

119. M.K. Lux, "Care for the 'Racially Careless'": 407–434, p. 417–418.

120. First Nations Child and Family Caring Society, "Jordan's Principle," undated, https://fncaringsociety.com/jordans-principle.

121. M.K. Lux, "Care for the 'Racially Careless'": 407–434, p. 418–419.

122. M.K. Lux, *Separate Beds: A History of Indian Hospitals in Canada*: p. 157.

123. M. K. Lux, "We Demand 'Unconditional Surrender'": 665–684, p. 675.

124. Ibid., p. 676–677.

125. N.E. Macdonald, R. Stanwick, and A. Lynk, "Canada's Shameful History of Nutrition Research on Residential School Children: The Need for Strong Medical Ethics in Aboriginal Health Research," *Paediatrics & Child Health* 19, 2 (2014): 64, https://doi.org/10.1093/pch/19.2.64.

126. M.K. Lux, "We Demand 'Unconditional Surrender'": 665–684, p. 678.

127. F. MacDonald, "Indigenous Peoples and Neoliberal 'Privatization' in Canada: Opportunities, Cautions and Constraints," *Canadian Journal of Political Science / Revue Canadienne de Science Politique* 44, 2 (2011): 257–273.

128. International Monetary Fund, "Six Charts Explain South Africa's Inequality" (30 January 2020), https://www.imf.org/en/News/Articles/2020/01/29/na012820six-charts-on-south-africas-persistent-and-multi-faceted-inequality.

129. M.K. Lux, *Separate Beds: A History of Indian Hospitals in Canada*: pp. 61–67.

130. S.C. Grondin and C. Schieman, "Thoracic Surgery Education in Canada," *Journal of Thoracic and Cardiovascular Surgery* 153, 2 (2017): 493–497. https://doi.org/10.1016/j.jtcvs.2016.09.082.

131. Organization for Economic Cooperation and Development, "Social Spending," OECD *Data* (2021), https://data.oecd.org/socialexp/social-spending.htm.

132. S. Burke, *Building Resistance: 56–58.*

133. D. Arnold, *Colonizing the Body.*

134. T. Morantz, *The White Man's Gonna Getcha: The Colonial Challenge to the Crees in Quebec* (Montréal: McGill-Queen's University Press, 2002).

135. S. Hick, "The Enduring Plague: How Tuberculosis in Canadian Indigenous Communities Is Emblematic of a Greater Failure in Healthcare Equality," *Journal of Epidemiology and Global Health* 9, 2 (2019): 89–92, https://doi.org/10.2991/jegh.k.190314.002.

136. M.K. Lux, *Separate Beds: A History of Indian Hospitals in Canada.*

137. D.A. Enarson and S. Grzybowski, "Incidence of Active Tuberculosis in the Native Population of Canada," *Canadian Medical Association Journal* 134, 10 (1986): 1149–1152, ncbi.nlm.nih.gov/pmc/articles/PMC1491042/pdf/cmaj00118-0055.pdf.

138. R. Dearing, "Call for Statue in St John's to Remember Shanawdithit, Last of Her People," CBC News (9 June 2018), https://www.cbc.ca/news/canada/newfoundland-labrador/shanawdithit-beothuk-statue-1.4710707.

139. A. Rode and R.J. Shephard, "Lung Function in Canadian Inuit: A Follow-Up Study," *Canadian Medical Association Journal* 131, 7 (1984): 741–744, ncbi.nlm.nih.gov/pmc/articles/PMC1483593/pdf/canmedaj00369-0039.pdf.

140. E. Hernandez-Garduno, D. Kunimoto, L. Wang, et al., "Predictors of Clustering of Tuberculosis in Greater Vancouver: A Molecular Epidemiologic Study," *Canadian Medical Association Journal* 167, 4 (2002): 349–352, p. 350.

141. J.M. FitzGerald, A. Fanning, V. Hoepnner, et al., "The Molecular Epidemiology of Tuberculosis in Western Canada," *International Journal of Tuberculosis and Lung Disease* 7, 2 (2003): 132–138.

142. J.T. de Bibiana, C. Rossi, P. Rivest, et al., "Tuberculosis and Homelessness in Montreal: A Retrospective Cohort Study," BMC *Public Health* 11 (28 October 2011): 833, https://doi.org/10.1186/1471-2458-11-833.

143. C. Case, K. Kandola, L. Chui, et al., "Examining DNA Fingerprinting as an Epidemiology Tool in the Tuberculosis Program in the Northwest Territories, Canada," *International Journal of Circumpolar Health* 72, 1 (2013), https://doi.org/10.3402/ijch.v72i0.20067.

144. S. Patel, C. Paulsen, C. Heffernan, et al., "Tuberculosis Transmission in the Indigenous Peoples of the Canadian Prairies," *Plos One* 12, 11 (2017), https://doi.org/10.1371/journal.pone.0188189.

145. M. Clark and C. Hui, "Children from Baffin Island Have a Disproportionate Burden of Tuberculosis in Canada: Data from the Children's Hospital of Eastern Ontario (1998–2008)," BMC *Pediatrics* 10 (2010): 102, https://doi.org/10.1186/1471-2431-10-102.

146. E. Schneider, "Tuberculosis among American Indians and Alaska Natives in the United States, 1993–2002," *American Journal of Public Health* 95, 5 (2005): 873–880, https://doi.org/10.2105/ajph.2004.052456.

147. K. Dehghani, Z. Lan, P. Li, et al., "Determinants of Tuberculosis Trends in Six Indigenous Populations of the USA, Canada, and Greenland from 1960 to 2014: A Population-Based Study," *Lancet Public Health* 3, 3 (2018): e133–e142, https://doi.org/10.1016/s2468-2667(18)30002-1.

148. P. Orr, "Tuberculosis in Nunavut: Looking Back, Moving Forward," *Canadian Medical Association Journal* 185, 4 (2013): 287–288, https://doi.org/10.1503/cmaj.121536.

149. G.J. Wherrett, *The Miracle of Empty Beds: A History of Tuberculosis in Canada* (Toronto: University of Toronto Press, 1977).

150. C.A. Basham, B. Elias, and P. Orr, "Tuberculosis Elimination in Canada," *Lancet* 394, 10195 (2019): 300–301, https://doi.org/10.1016/s0140-6736(19)31122-5.

151. P. Orr, "Tuberculosis in Nunavut": 287–288.

152. R.G. Biesma, R. Brugha, A. Harmer, et al., "The Effects of Global Health Initiatives on Country Health Systems: A Review of the Evidence from HIV/AIDS Control," *Health Policy and Planning* 24, 4 (2009): 239–252, https://doi.org/10.1093/heapol/czp025.

153. E. Gómez, "The Politics of Receptivity and Resistance: How Brazil, India, China, and Russia Strategically Use the International Health Community in Response to HIV/AIDS: A Theory," *Governance: Global Health* 3, 1 (2009).

154. P. Farmer, *Fevers, Feuds, and Diamonds*.

155. J.A. Myers, "Arthur M. Walker 1896–1955," *Diseases of the Chest* 29, 5 (1956): 592–593, https://doi.org/10.1016/S0096-0217(15)32007-0.

156. D.A. Enarson and S. Grzybowski, "Incidence of Active Tuberculosis": 1149–1152, p. 1152.

157. World Health Organization," Tuberculosis" (14 October 2021), who.int/news-room/fact-sheets/detail/tuberculosis.

158. World Health Organization, "Tuberculosis Profiles" (2022), https://worldhealthorg.shinyapps.io/tb_profiles/.

Chapter 5: Fevers Future

1. G. Spitale, "COVID-19 and the Ethics of Quarantine: A Lesson from the Eyam Plague," *Medicine, Health Care and Philosophy* 23, 4 (2020): 603–609.

2. Truth and Reconciliation Commission of Canada, *Truth and Reconciliation Commission of Canada: Calls to Action* (Winnipeg: Truth and Reconciliation Commission of Canada 2012): 2–3, https://ehprnh2mwo3.exactdn.com/wp-content/uploads/2021/01/Calls_to_Action_English2.pdf.

3. Gouvernement du Québec, *Public Inquiry Commission on Relations between Indigenous Peoples and Certain Public Services in Québec: Listening, Reconciliation and Progress*, Final Report (Quebec City, 2019), pp. 480–482, https://www.cerp.gouv.qc.ca/fileadmin/Fichiers_clients/Rapport/Final_report.pdf.

4. Atikamekw Nehirowisiw, "Joyce's Principle," Brief presented by the Council of the Atikamekw of Manawan and the Conseil de la Nation" (2020), https://principedejoyce.com/sn_uploads/principe/Joyce_s_Principle_brief___Eng.pdf.

5. College of Family Physicians of Canada, "Indigenous Health Committee" (2022), https://www.cfpc.ca/en/member-services/committees/indigenous-health

-committee; Indigenous Health Writing Group, Royal College of Physicians and Surgeons of Canada, (2019), "Indigenous Health Primer," https://www.royalcollege.ca/rcsite/health-policy/indigenous-health-e.

6. R. Long, C. Heffernan, M. Cardinal-Grant, et al., "Two Row Wampum, Human Rights, and the Elimination of Tuberculosis from High-Incidence Indigenous Communities," *Health Hum Rights* 21, 1 (2019): 253–265, ncbi.nlm.nih.gov/pmc/articles/PMC6586970/pdf/hhr-21-01-253.pdf.

7. J. Parmenter, "The Meaning of Kaswentha and the Two Row Wampum Belt in Haudenosaunee (Iroquois) History: Can Indigenous Oral Tradition Be Reconciled with the Documentary Record?" *Journal of Early American History* 3, 1 (2013): 82–109, pp. 84–85, https://doi.org/10.1163/18770703-00301005 Web.

8. R. Hill, "Talking Points on History and Meaning of the Two Row Wampum Belt," *Honor the Two Row* (2013) honorthetworow.org/wp-content/uploads/2013/03/TwoRowTalkingPoints-Rick-Hill.pdf.

9. L. Eisenbeis, Z. Gao, C. Heffernan, et al., "Contact Investigation Outcomes of Canadian-Born Adults with Tuberculosis in Indigenous and Non-Indigenous Populations in Alberta," *Canadian Journal of Public Health* 107, 1 (2016): e106-e111, p. E110, https://doi.org/10.17269/cjph.107.5255.

10. P. Brassard, K.K. Anderson, K. Schwartzman, et al., "Challenges to Tuberculin Screening and Follow-Up in an Urban Aboriginal Sample in Montreal, Canada," *Journal Health Care Poor Underserved* 19, 2 (2008): 369–379, https://doi.org/10.1353/hpu.0.0029.

11. D.A. Enarson and S. Grzybowski, "Incidence of Active Tuberculosis": 1149–1152, p. 1152.

12. S.R. Carroll, I. Garba, O.L. Figueroa-Rodríguez, et al., "The CARE Principles for Indigenous Data Governance," *Data Science Journal* 19, 1 (2020): 43, http://doi.org/10.5334/dsj-2020-043.

13. K. Murray, "Health Aspects of Arctic Exploration."

14. R. Linklater, "Land-Based Healing in First Nations Communities," Centre for Addiction and Mental Health, Toronto: Centre for Addiction and Mental Health (2018), https://www.camh.ca/en/camh-news-and-stories/land-based-healing-in-first-nations-communities; R.T. Oster, A. Grier, R. Lightning, et al., "Cultural Continuity, Traditional Indigenous Language, and Diabetes in Alberta First Nations: A Mixed Methods Study," *International Journal for Equity in Health* 13, 92 (2014), https://doi.org/10.1186/s12939-014-0092-4.

15. M.K. Lux, *Separate Beds: A History of Indian Hospitals in Canada*: p. 9.

16. E. Tuck, "Suspending Damage: A Letter to Communities," *Harvard Educational Review* 79, 3 (2009): 409–427.

17. A. Kumar, R. Zarychanski, R. Pinto, et al., 2009. "Critically Ill Patients with 2009 Influenza A(HINI) Infection in Canada," *JAMA* 302, 17: 1872–1879, https://doi.org/10.1001/jama.2009.1496.

18. World Health Organization, "Poliomyelitis" (2022), https://www.who.int/health-topics/poliomyelitis#tab=tab_1.

19. E.S. Ameeta and B. Romanowski, "The Return of Syphilis in Canada": *JAMMI* 4, 4: 215–217, https://doi.org/10.3138/jammi.2019-08-22.

20. P. Regan, *Unsettling the Settler Within: Indian Residential Schools, Truth Telling, and Reconciliation in Canada* (Vancouver: UBC Press, 2010).

21. Southern Chiefs' Organization, "Health Transformation" (2022), https://sco-

inc.mb.ca/health-transformation/; Keewatinohk Inniniw Minoawayin Inc., "Governance" (2022), https://kiminoayawin.com/governance/.

22. Government of Canada, "Indigenous Health Care in Canada" (2021), https://www.sac-isc.gc.ca/eng/1626810177053/1626810219482.

23. E, Arteaga-Cruz, B. Mukhopadhyay, S. Shannon, et al., "Connecting the Right to Health and Anti-Extractivism Globally," *Saúde em Debate* 44 (Spe1) (2020): 100–108, https://doi.org/10.1590/0103-11042020s108.

24. D. McCue, "This Plant Medicine Teacher Is Reclaiming Anishinaabe Names for Species: Why That Could Be Good for the Planet," cbc *Radio* (2021), https://www.cbc.ca/radio/thecurrent/back-to-the-land-preserving-indigenous-language-1.6152854.

25. R.W. Kimmerer, *Braiding Sweetgrass,* first ed. (Minneapolis, MN: Milkweed Editions, 2013).

26. N. Mortillaro, "How Science and First Nations Oral Tradition Are Converging," cbc *News* (22November 2016), https://www.cbc.ca/news/science/science-first-nations-oral-tradition-converging-1.3853799.

Index